D1103853

THE CONCEPT OF DEVELOPMENT

The Minnesota Symposia
on Child Psychology
Volume 15

EDITED BY

W. ANDREW COLLINS
University of Minnesota

LAWRENCE ERLBAUM ASSOCIATES, PUBLISHERS
1982   Hillsdale, New Jersey

Lawrence Erlbaum Associates, Inc., Publishers
365 Broadway
Hillsdale, New Jersey 07642

Library of Congress Cataloging in Publication Data
Main entry under title:

The Concept of development.

    "The Minnesota Symposia on Child Psychology,
volume 15."
    Papers from the 15th annual Minnesota Symposium on
Child Psychology, Oct. 30–Nov. 1, 1980, University of
Minnesota, Minneapolis, sponsored by the Institute of
Child Development.
    Bibliography: p.
    Includes indexes.
    1. Child psychology—Congresses. 2. Developmental
psychology—Congresses. I. Collins, W. Andrew,
II. Minnesota Symposium on Child Psychology (15th : 1980 :
University of Minnesota, Minneapolis) III. University of
Minnesota (Minneapolis-St. Paul campus). Institute of
Child Development.
BF721.C588   155.4   81-17326
ISBN 0-89859-159-7   AACR2

Printed in the United States of America

Contents

iii

MAY 6 1992

Foreword

The specific occasion for the first conference on the Concept of Development, 25 years ago, was the celebration of 30 years of vigorous life in Minnesota's Institute, then the Institute of Child Welfare, under the leadership of John E. Anderson, who had just relinquished the Directorship. The selection of the theme for the conference requires a somewhat longer statement.

The dominant concern in psychology at that time was to create a rigorous science of experimental behavior change. In this effort, Clark Hull's positivistic approach to theory construction was still very influential. According to this approach, a formal theory with axioms and postulates is erected from which hypotheses may be deduced to be submitted to the test of crucial experiment. In the view of learning theory consequent to such a model, child psychology becomes an anomaly; behavior is behavior, wherever and whenever found. Development as a process of behavior change, particularly human development, is not very susceptible to crucial experiment. For one thing, time periods involved are too long for sustained control. For another, both intrinsic and extrinsic variables are too numerous and complexly interrelated, and, in many cases, ethical considerations are too formidable to permit the clean controls dictated by Hull's model. So that first conference sought to review with some care the *concept* of development and the general observational and longitudinal methods that had been so useful in establishing this approach to human behavior.

In this effort we were influenced by two considerations that were still operative in this Institute under the conditions of its founding by the Laura Spelman Rockefeller Fund. These two considerations were the interdisciplinary approach mandated in the Institute's structure and the model of the U. S. Department of Agriculture's Experimental Stations, research centers that sought also to turn back their findings directly to the agriculturalists of the nation. We sought to examine the idea of development, considered generally as change in form and function over time, as that concept is used in both scientific and in certain applied fields. Could an examination of the term development, as used in a variety of different fields, yield any common elements? Would such common themes, if found, be useful in advancing the study of human behavior as a process of *developmental* change? The then existing notions of the genetic or developmental in psychology were traditional, descriptive, and certainly not formulated to the satisfaction of rigorous behaviorism. We did not expect to arrive at rigorous formulations through a broadly conceived approach to the concept of development. We sought, rather, an heuristic effect on parochialism through exposing one another to our various uses of the term.

We recruited a philosopher of science and several biologists especially concerned with experimental embryology and with growth. We invited comparative, social, and experimental psychologists. We were bold enough to include representatives from the social sciences and from the humanities as well, for we believed that a science of child or human development had inescapable humanistic considerations. We sought to examine how the concept of development might be used in the fields of pediatrics, child psychiatry, social work, and education, important areas of application to human concerns.

We failed to get one seminal theorist—Ludwig von Bertalanffy—many of whose constructs are still with us in Systems Theory. We did not include sociology, although a few of its scholars were beginning to look at institutional change over time. Nor did we include economics, although its concerns with time series analysis even then had methodological potential for both learning psychologists and developmental psychologists.

A reconsideration of the concept of development is overdue. The setting of 1980 differs markedly from that of 1955. To mention just a few considerations: Then, a rigorous positivism enthralled psychology. Even those of us who were not enthusiastic Hullians or Skinnerians were reluctant to abandon the clean and spare language and structure advocated by Behaviorism. Although personally attracted by a dynamic/organismic view of behavioral development, I found myself, in introducing the papers of the conference, advocating a pluralistic theoretical approach.

The more doctrinaire experimentalists in psychology were then advocating a "mini-theory" approach to psychological research, convinced that a general viewpoint could only obscure, not illuminate. Although I concurred that a unified theory was not (and is not yet) possible in psychology, I was coming to believe that a particular viewpoint toward behavior is implicit in any theoretical stance, a kind of metatheory, as it were. I considered that the assumptions behind a developmental as contrasted with a strictly behavioristic approach to the study of the person was rather unique in psychology in its many presentations. It is with this particular and peculiar contribution of a *developmental* viewpoint to the study of human beings that I have continued to be concerned.

Psychologists today are much more cognizant of "philosophy of science" and much less sure that logical positivism is the road to all good science. Rigorous S-R behaviorism has been very considerably modified by the introduction of intervening variables and by the recognition of limitations on laboratory experimentation in the study of complex behaviors. Even those technologists of psychology, the behavior mod people, have grown more concerned with the person and somewhat less with specific habits *in vacuum,* as it were.

Certainly, graduate students are today much more wholistic and "humanistic" in their expectations of psychology than two decades ago. Although many of us, despite our doubts, still present formal classical models of behavior theory in our instruction, it remains to be seen whether such indoctrination can altogether knock this nonsense out of today's students. Whereas about the time of that first conference a distinguished child psychologist held that research in our field was seriously retarded by the lack of a Skinner box or its equivalent, there is now a noticeable return to the methodology of naturalistic observation. One seldom hears now, as we were beginning to then, of the contrast between developmental and "experimental child" psychologists, often drawn by the latter with a certain pride of distinction.

Today, I sense a certain widespread and growing skepticism; many more of us than in 1955 are disenchanted with the possibility of clean and complete objectivity in our work. This view is spreading among the social sciences. Psychologists have shown how implicit assumptions can color the experimenter's conclusions drawn from even the most carefully controlled observations. Anthropologists now suggest the impossibility of ever getting inside the heads of people of other cultures, even relativistically. Historians demonstrate that there is no such thing as a theoretically impartial observer. Yet, few of us are willing to go to the logical extreme of this trend—to assert a complete relativity of truth. Many of us are more likely to use that noun in the plural form and with a small "t" than we were in those possibly more dogmatic days. There is, if anything, less attention paid to the interdisciplinary; this emphasis has disappeared with the carefully designed longitudinal study projected over a span of years. Both concepts seemed to have succumbed to the pressing need to get many publications out rapidly in the interest of tenure and promotion.

Yet, certain issues persist. A year or two after the former conference, I attempted to set down issues that I thought developmental theories (note the plural) would have to reckon with as such theories took shape. Among the nine or ten issues that I identified were the problem of behavior patterning, the complex relationships in behavior implied by the term *organization,* and the definition and place of such related concepts as differentiation and integration, which had been rather widely used in the early child development movement. There were, in addition, the matters of the place and status of scientific reductionism in the study of complex and hierarchically organized behavior, and the necessity of a comparative approach if general principles of development were to be formulated. There was also the phenomenon of directionality exhibited in many features of development; how could we deal with this in an *ateleological* science? How could we treat the place and status of *potential* in the study of development?

And pervading all considerations of development were numerous persisting paradoxes in the phenomena we study. Paradox vexes a good scientist. It constantly confronts the developmentalist, for developmental processes over reaches of time reveal both continuities and differences in behavior characteristics; one can find continuous change by small increments, yet one sees also the fact of qualitative, quantum-like shifts in how the person relates to the demands of his environment. And so on; one could list many such anomalies and paradoxes. How to deal with them?

Time does not permit an evaluation of the many real advances of the past 25 years in our address to such issues. Suffice to say that the concept of development, beset as it is by conceptual and other anomalies and problems of operational definition, has persisted; witness the interest in this conference.

The passing of Piaget, the giant of child psychologists of this century, reminds us that as we move beyond his language and concepts, we sometimes forget his role in establishing the transactional character of the organism–environment relationship. Most of us now accept this concept as a matter of course, a distinct advance over the simplistic notions of S–R Behaviorism of an earlier day.

Developmental psychology's early concern with the person and with behavior in its molar expressions has been continued in the growth of the life-span emphasis. One notes also the recent surge of interest in biographical and autobiographical methods for studying the life course. Such may yet become incorporated into longitudinal method, one of developmental psychology's unique contributions. And as we study behavior over longer reaches of time, we are forced to reconsider, in studying psychological processes, the function of the individual subject's goals or purposes. And in considering the paradoxes and anomalies posed in concepts of development, we come up against issues with which "dialectical developmental psychology" has concerned itself in recent years.

From my long concern with such issues, it is with great satisfaction that I introduce several papers of this conference, to which distinguished investigators bring their mature, seminal thinking. Professor Flavell takes another look at the often disputed but extremely durable notions of stages. He reviews both the arguments and the evidence for the behavioral homogeneity that would establish the concept of stage. He concludes that, whereas one might make some case for the idea, there is a better case for variety rather than homogeneous structure across a child's performance repertoire at a given period. He is more persuaded of relatively homogeneous structure achieved over time in particular performances or skills (behavioral sequences).

Professor Levine reaffirms the need to consider the organism as a whole, not simply as a "functioning gene machine." Although it is necessary to use an intensely analytical approach, one does this most profitably at several levels, as for example the hormonal *and* the behavioral. When one does this, he/she often finds differing pictures of antecedent–consequent relationships, requiring him/her to rethink his/her "theory" in order to achieve some conceptual synthesis of the evidence.

Professor Gibson reviews the emergence of behaviorism from the older functionalism and shows how a reconsideration of a functional approach to behavior, via the concept of "affordances," allows a richer, more productive, transactional view of the organism–environment relationship and takes account of the human organism's ubiquitous "purposefulness." Such a concept also gives more precise meaning to the idea of "potential."

Professor Sameroff supplies what the first conference needed but lacked, a consideration of systems theory, with its promise of furthering our grasp on the knotty issues of organization and of complex, transactional relationships.

Dr. Rutter's extremely clear review and exposition of the place, value, and limits of the correlational versus the epidemological method in establishing causation, and the virtues of longitudinal versus experimental methods in studying "cause" in complex behavioral processes places our principal methodologies in lucid perspective.

It is quite clear now that the first conference 25 years ago was, indeed, not a last-ditch effort to defend an outworn descriptive term. The Concept of Development is alive and well, indeed thriving productively in the broad demesne of psychology.

Dale B. Harris
Professor Emeritus of Psychology
and Human Development
The Pennsylvania State University

Preface

This volume contains the papers of the 15th annual Minnesota Symposium on Child Psychology, held October 30–November 1, 1980, at the University of Minnesota, Minneapolis. As in each of the past 14 years, the faculty of the Institute of Child Development invited a group of scholars to present research programs of current or promised significance in the study of development. This year's program was the first attempt within the series, however, to address the concept of development per se. Thus, the symposium represents both the continuation of a long tradition and a unique scholarly effort, as well.

This symposium on the Concept of Development owes a great deal to an event that took place at the Institute of Child Development 25 years ago. In 1955, Dale Harris, who was then Director of the Institute, organized a conference on the Concept of Development, the papers from which eventually appeared in a classic volume by the same name. The influence of that volume continues today; in 1979, some 60 new copies of Harris's *The Concept of Development* were sold—22 years after it was first published.

The 1955 volume contained a diversity of vantage points on development. There were papers on biological perspectives by J. P. Scott, T. C. Schneirla, and Howard Meredith; on behavioral perspectives by Heinz Werner, Robert Sears, and Wallace Russell; perspectives from history, classics, anthropology, and applications to medicine, psychopathology, social work, and education. Many of these contributions dealt very directly with the concept of development. For example, in the section on philosophical issues, Ernest Nagel specified that the concept of development involved two essential components: (1) the notion of a system with a definite structure and a definite set of pre-existing capacities; and (2) "the notion of a sequential set of changes in the system, yielding relatively permanent but novel increments not only in its structure, but in its modes of operation as well [p. 17]." Nagel discussed the conditions under which deterministic models were and were not compatible with this notion. Schneirla preferred a viewpoint based on adaptation: "The term development, with respect to individual behavior, stresses progressive change in organized adaptive function through ontogeny. Behavioral development on any phyletic level is . . . a new composite leading to a new pattern distinctive of the level [p. 102]."

For the 1980 symposium, by contrast, fewer participants were asked to address the concept of development, and they were invited to do so within the context provided by their own research, or within the particular area in which they work. Thus, John Flavell addresses the concept of structures in the study of cognitive development. Eleanor Gibson proposes that a functionalist spirit is returning to investigations of development and presents evidence relevant to the concept of affordances to give substance to her point. Seymour Levine presents an analysis based on comparative research of the complex causal relationships between hormonal factors and social behavior; he reminds us that the biological substrate of development is more subtle and complex than is generally recognized. Arnold Sameroff's chapter addresses systems analyses of development; Sameroff draws parallels from other disciplines to illustrate the importance of conceptual schemes broad enough to encompass the range of variables that impinge upon development. In Michael Rutter's chapter, the focus is on strategies for isolating and explicating complex developmental relationships through epidemiological and longitudinal research strategies.

In the final chapter of this volume, as in the final, plenary session of the symposium, three distinguished developmental scholars provide commentary on perspectives on the contributed papers and the issues raised in discussions of them during the symposium. Rochel Gelman primarily addresses developmental issues suggested by studies of cognitive and language skills. Robert LeVine addresses issues and perspectives drawn from a cross-cultural vantage on the study of development. Eleanor Maccoby comments on the analysis of development from the perspective of socialization research. As their commentaries make clear, consideration of the issues raised by the authors of this volume point to a number of the central problems with which developmental scholars are struggling in 1980.

Financial support for this 15th Symposium was provided by Public Health Service Grant from the National Institute of Child Health and Human Development, by the Institute of Child Development, and by the Association of Graduate Students in Child Psychology. Additional funds were provided by the University of Minnesota College of Education, in partial observance of the 75th anniversary of its establishment.

A number of individuals at the Institute of Child Development participated in conducting the symposium, and their contributions are acknowledged with appreciation. They were Judith Becker, Ryan Bliss, Helen Dickison, Virginia Eaton, Rebecca Eder, Deborah Garfin, Elizabeth Haugen, Judith List, Michael

Livingston, William Merriman, Catherine Meyer, Frosso Motti, Anne Pick, Herbert Pick, Martha Robb, Christine Todd, and Mary Jo Ward. In addition, Lonnie Christensen provided extraordinarily able and thorough support in every aspect of the symposium's operation. The counsel and cooperation of Lawrence Erlbaum and Art Lizza, Jr., throughout their association with the symposium series has also been valuable.

Finally, the contributors who prepared the papers included in this volume are gratefully recognized. Their talent and their vision are impressive testimony of the vitality and promise of a field devoted to the concept of development.

W. Andrew Collins
University of Minnesota

1 Structures, Stages, and Sequences in Cognitive Development

John H. Flavell
Stanford University

My aim in this chapter is to speculate about certain aspects of childhood cognitive development. The chapter is intended to be an essay or "think piece" rather than a literature review, and thus the coverage and referencing are selective rather than systematic and exhaustive. The aspects of cognitive growth that are discussed mostly fall into the "formal" rather than "functional" category. As Flavell and Wohlwill (1969) have stated:

> The formal aspect has to do with the "morphology" of the process: the sorts of cognitive entities that make up the successive outputs of development and how these entities are causally, temporally, and otherwise interrelated. . . . The other aspect . . . has to do with function and mechanism: the activities or processes of the organism, somehow specified in relation to environmental inputs, by which it in fact makes the cognitive progress that has been formally characterized [pp. 67–68].

Discussion centers on three formal aspects—structures, stages, and sequences—with the discussion of sequences raising questions about functional aspects. An important objective throughout is to make best guesses about how much and what kind of structure or organization there is in human cognitive growth. To what extent and in what ways can it be characterized as orderly, predictable, coherent, regular, consistent, or otherwise nonrandom? To see the range of possibilities, imagine a dimension with minimum developmental order at one end and maximum developmental order at the other. At the minimum-order end, no cognitive-developmental acquisition bears any kind of interesting relation to any other. Acquisitions cannot be meaningfully compared to one

1

another as to similarity of underlying process, structure, or maturity level; they do not influence one another's emergence; they do not consistently appear either synchronously or sequentially, one in relation to another. At this end of the dimension, cognitive development is a chaotic hodgepodge of isolated and unconnected learnings and maturings.

Let us suppose that the other end of the dimension is occupied by some extreme and caricaturish variation of the Piagetian view of cognitive development. Such a development consists of a fixed and universal sequence of stages and substages, each defined by a highly general cognitive structure of the Piagetian *structure d'ensemble* type. Predictability, consistency, and coherence abound. If a child is in a stage or substage at all, he is in it completely, in the sense that all his cognitive activities are tightly governed by that stage's cognitive structure. Thus, at any point in his childhood, the nature and developmental level of his thinking are constant and consistent across all tasks and situations. His mentality undergoes profound qualitative changes in its orderly progression toward its universal adult destination, but it is "homogeneous" (Fischer, 1980) rather than "heterogeneous" at each step in this progression.

Although it is certain that real-life cognitive development differs from both of these extreme portraits, it is by no means clear exactly how much and what sorts of organization can justifiably be attributed to it. We should also like to be able to make guesses as to why cognitive development might have whatever amount and kind of structure we decide it does have. For example, if we were to conclude that human cognitive growth is really not very stage-like after all, we would also like to be able to say why that state of affairs might be just what one would expect, given this fact or that consideration. Focusing exclusively on structures, stages, and sequences cannot give us a complete picture here, because it ignores regularities on the functional side. However, it is a good place to begin—or, in the present case, to begin again (Flavell, 1970, 1971, 1972, 1977; Flavell & Wohlwill, 1969). It is also a good time to begin again, because there now exists a substantial theoretical literature on these and related topics, some of it still in press or in preparation. Writings that I have found particularly useful in thinking about these issues include Brainerd (e.g., 1978a, 1978b, plus commentaries by others on 1978b), Case (1978, in preparation), Damon (1977, in press), C. F. Feldman & Toulmin (1976), D. H. Feldman (1980), Fischer (1980), Gardner (1973), Keats, Collis, & Halford (1978), Klahr & Wallace (1976), Rest (1979), Selman (in press), Siegler (1979, in press), Smedslund (1977), Toulmin (in preparation), Turiel (in press), and Wohlwill (1973).

Before proceeding further, it should be pointed out that psychologists are quite capable of discovering new and important things about childhood cognitive growth without deciding exactly what they believe about structures, stages, sequences, etc.—without pondering "the nature of the big picture of cognitive development" (Fischer, 1980, p. 520). Most of us go about our daily research activities without worrying much about this "big picture." Still, it is probably good for all of us to get out of the trenches occasionally to try to see what the whole landscape looks like. It might even improve our research.

Structures, Structuralists, and Structuralism

Let me begin by trying to define "cognitive structure." Flavell, 1971, has stated:

> the really central and essential meaning of "cognitive structure" ought to be a set of cognitive items that are somehow interrelated to constitute an organized whole or totality; to apply the term "structure" correctly, it appears that there must be, at minimum, an ensemble of two or more *elements* together with one or more *relationships* interlinking these elements. There also appear to be at least two additional secondary properties. One is that such organizations of cognitive items are relatively stable, enduring affairs, rather than merely temporary arrangements. The other, closely related, is that a structure is to be regarded as the common, underlying basis of a variety of superficially distinct, possibly even unrelated-looking behavioral acts; to use Werner's (1937) terminology, structures are akin to the "processes" which give rise to a variety of cognitive "achievements" [pp. 443–444].

With respect to this second property, we could say that cognitive structures are intellectual "forms" that are somewhat abstract in the sense that they can apply to a range of contents. Rough synonyms might include "system," "organization," "network," and "program" (in artificial intelligence).

The terms *structuralist* and *structuralism* are often used in an effort to distinguish among different developmental psychologists' conceptions of what cognitive development is like—of how much and what kind of "organization" it possesses, in the sense described previously. It might therefore be useful to try to convey the meaning of these concepts also. Structuralism and structuralist are applied to the work of a group of (mostly) European scholars in such fields as linguistics, anthropology, literary and art criticism, psychology, psychoanalysis, and philosophy (DeGeorge & DeGeorge, 1972). Marx, Freud, and de Saussure appear to have been the major precursors of the structuralist movement. Contemporary structuralists best known to psychologists would probably be Chomsky, Jakobson, Lévi–Strauss, and Piaget (Piaget, 1970). Although structuralists differ from and disagree with one another, Gardner (1973) has well described what seem to be the core similarities:

> The structuralists are distinguished first and foremost by their ardent, powerfully held conviction that there is structure underlying all human behavior and mental functioning, and by their belief that this structure can be discovered through orderly analysis, that it has cohesiveness and meaning, and that structures have generality (otherwise there would be as many structures as behaviors, and little point in spelling them out) [p. 10].

> The most salient feature of structuralism . . . is the belief that diverse sets of phe-
> nomena can be related to one another, once relevant factors and their relationships
> have been ferreted out [p. 40].

> Each of these scholars [Lévi–Strauss, Piaget, and Chomsky] focuses particularly on
> Man, seeing him as a constructive organism, with generative capacities, who
> nonetheless is preordained to follow certain paths in his intellectual development
> and achievement because of the structure of his own brain and the regulating forces
> in the human environment [pp. 241–242].

It is probably true that reference to "structuralism" and to "structuralist" theoretical approaches that posit the existence of cognitive "structures" in the developing child was once a clear and useful way to distinguish some students of child behavior and development from others. "Structuralist" mainly meant the followers of Piaget, Chomsky, and Kohlberg—and appropriately so. Those not called structuralists mostly subscribed to some variety of behaviorism or S-R theory and were thus loathe to endow the inside of the head with anything complex enough to require the designation "cognitive structure."

However, I believe that there has been a precipitous decline in the usefulness of these terms as the "cognitivization" of psychology has become more and more complete. Piaget, Newell and Simon, Chomsky, and others have now convinced just about everyone that adult and child minds alike are inhabited by exceedingly rich structures of knowledge and cognitive processes. Consider adult cognition about the nonsocial and social worlds, and how it is currently concep-tualized by theorists in the areas of psycholinguistics, cognitive psychology, artificial intelligence, judgment and decision processes, and social cognition or person perception. One sees a variety of models postulating such patently "struc-tural" cognitive structures as sentence and story grammars, schemata, frames, scripts, prototypes, implicit or naive theories, production systems, systematic judgmental and inferential biases, executive processes, organized strategies, knowledge structures, expertise, and semantic networks (Brown, in press; Glass, Holyoak, & Santa, 1979, Nisbett & Ross, 1980). Virtually everyone nowadays agrees with Piaget that we assimilate input to our existing knowledge structures rather than merely copy it—that our learning, comprehension, and other cogni-tive activities are heavily constructive or "top down" in nature.

The same is true of the contemporary field of cognitive development. Almost everyone takes it for granted that there is considerable structure and organization in the infant's and child's knowledge and cognitive processes. How many cogni-tive developmentalists can you think of who do *not* believe that the child's mental contents and processes are complexly organized?

I think there is a very simple reason why we cannot reasonably deny the appellation *structuralist* to today's cognitive psychologists and cognitive devel-opmentalists. It is that anything capable of generating the enormously complex and variegated behavior patterns these scientist routinely observe could not help but have a very complicated structure itself. There is simply no alternative possibility that I can imagine. Read once again the preceding passages from Flavell (1971) and Gardner (1973) and ask what contemporary theories and theorists they do not describe. Doesn't every student of human cognition have an "ardent, powerfully held conviction that there is structure underlying all human behavior and mental functioning, etc.'' (Gardner, 1973, p. 10)? This is not to say, of course, that developmentalists agree on what sorts of cognitive structures to attribute to the child—for example, how abstract, general, and context-free they should be—or even on their role and importance in describing or explaining cognitive development (Brainerd, 1978b, plus commentary by others; Feldman & Toulmin, 1976). However, there is general agreement today that cognition *is* heavily and complexly structured.

I think, therefore, that we should give up using "structuralism'' and "structuralist'' to describe "them'' versus "us'' type differences of opinion about the nature and development of cognition. In my opinion, they have become empty slogans or buzz words that vaguely and imprecisely connote some measure of acceptance of some part or variate of the Piagetian vision of cognitive growth. They actually interfere with communication because they give one only the illusion of understanding exactly what claims about the formal aspects of development are being made. If someone told me 15 years ago that he/she subscribed to a structural or structuralist view of cognitive development, I would assume he was either a Piagetian or a Wernerian. If someone told me the same thing today, I would: (1) have only a rough idea what he meant; and (2) suspect that he might also have only a very rough idea what he meant. (Expressions like "structural transformations'' and "developmental reorganizations'' affect me the same way, although others may find them meaningful.) It is, of course, extremely difficult to communicate clearly to either yourself or others when trying to formulate in a precise, specific way exactly what you believe and don't believe about the morphology of cognitive growth. I think, however, that a moratorium on the use of structuralist in an era of almost universal structuralism of one variety or another would be a help.

STAGES

Consider once again the order–disorder dimension described at the beginning of this chapter. Most developmental psychologists would obviously be happier if real-life cognitive development turned out to be very orderly in this particular sense; that is, cognitive development would clearly be a much more interesting and substantial object of scientific inquiry if it had a lot of internal structure for us to describe and explain. It would go a long way toward being that kind of scientific object if it were highly stage-like in nature.

As Wohlwill (1973, Chapter 9) has shown, "stage'' can mean a number of different things in developmental psychology. In this chapter, I am going to focus only on what Wohlwill called the "horizontal structure" aspects of the stage concept. This means the degree to which the child's thinking at any stage X is all of the same cognitive-developmental level; that is, all "stage X-like" in nature and quality. This focus intentionally neglects other important issues concerning stages, in particular the possible formal and functional relationships between stage X and those immediately preceeding and following it; I return to some of these issues in the section on Sequences, however. For present purposes, then, we say that human cognitive growth is "stage-like" to the extent that the child's mind is at any given point in its development "all of a piece"—constant, consistent, uniform, and homogeneous in its character, quality, and level of cognitive maturity across all tasks, situations, and cognitive domains.[1]

What might incline developmental psychologists to believe that cognitive development is highly stage-like? The most obvious answer would refer to the enormous influence of Piaget's theory and research: We think it is highly stage-like because Piagetians the world over have amassed a great deal of evidence purporting to show that it is. This is probably not the only source of our inclination, however. Another source has already been mentioned; that is, our understandable wish that the object of our scientific study possess significant regularities, with stage-like properties being one class of such regularities.

Another source may be certain basic tendencies of the human mind, which developmentalists and other scientists naturally share with everyone else (Nisbett & Ross, 1980; Schneider, Hastorf, & Ellsworth, 1979). We all try to make the world cognitively manageable by simplifying it as we assimilate and categorize it. We gloss over differences, inconsistencies, irregularities, and other real but complexity-adding features. We lean toward typologies, stereotypes, prototypes, and other complexity-reducing categorizations. When we think about people, these tendencies cause us to be implicit trait theorists. As such, we are inclined to attribute stable and cross-situationally consistent general traits or dispositions to people—perhaps overly inclined (Bem & Allen, 1974; Mischel, 1977). I believe we do this in the cognitive as well as the personality domain; that is, just as we find it easy and natural to think of adult A as "honest" and child B as "independent," so also do we think of adult C as "logical" and child D as "preoperational." On those occasions when cognitive psychologists turn their attention to nonadult minds, their spontaneous leveling and lumping tendencies lead them to form one large, homogeneous category called "children," as in sentences like "Children's thinking is less _____(abstract, inferential, systematic, etc.) than adults'." For the cognitive-developmental psychologist, who is used to seeing impressive age differences in cognitive performance within "children," the

---

[1]One clear weakness in this chapter is the vagueness of the key concepts in this sentence. Can we compare "levels of cognitive maturity" across *all* tasks, situations, and cognitive domains, even in a rough, intuitive way? I am not sure we can and only hope that the analysis presented will be useful even if we cannot.

same tendencies encourage the formation of an ontogenetically ordered set of smaller but equally homogeneous categories. These categories are general and transituational developmental stages (substages, periods) with names like "sensory-motor," "preoperational," "concrete-operational," and "formal-operational." When we try to formulate the gist of the most striking cognitive changes that seem to occur between birth and maturity, either for others (students, parents, teachers, interested others) or for ourselves, the tendency to think in stages can be very compelling indeed. Understandably, our listeners want a *hunger* neat and simple "ages-and-stages" developmental story. But so also do we *or desire* ourselves, I believe—and equally understandably, once one realizes how much *for story* that kind of story runs with everyone's cognitive grain.

All this does not mean that a highly stage-like conception of cognitive development must be incorrect, any more than the layperson's proclivity for attributing stable and transituationally consistent personality traits or dispositions to others means that trait theories of personality must be incorrect. I am somewhat uncomfortable about the fact that I have been presenting an essentially ad hominem rather than data-based argument for why we should be wary of stage-like conceptions of cognitive development. Nonetheless, I cannot help but believe that the argument really does have some force. It is also worth noting that both trait theories of personality (Mischel, 1968) and highly stage-like conceptions of cognitive development (Brainerd, 1978b) have been coming under attack in recent years (although it must be admitted that there have also recently been some impressive defenses of trait theory, Epstein, 1980).

On the developmental side, it is, of course, Piaget's stages and associated structures that have been the principal objects of criticism (Brainerd, 1978a, 1978b, and commentaries; Case, in preparation; Ennis, 1975; Feldman & Toulmin, 1976; Fischer, 1980; Flavell, 1963, 1971, 1977; Keats et al., 1978; Osherson, 1974; Siegler, 1979; Toulmin, in preparation). I think that most of this criticism is well-taken, and that there are very serious problems with Piaget's structures and stages, especially the postinfancy ones. The problems I see are the following. (For an able presentation of a favorable evaluation of Piagetian stages, see Karmiloff-Smith's commentary in Brainerd, 1978b.)

First, Piaget's characterizations of his concrete-operational and formal-operational structures are poor examples of scientific communication. theoretical model building, or both (one cannot always distinguish between the two in Piaget's writings). The structures are not clearly or consistently defined, and their intended relation to both formal logic and subjects' actual cognitive abilities and activities is often obscure. For instance, it is not clear to me *exactly* what is being claimed about a child's cognitive abilities when it is said that she does or does not possess "reversible operations." I do not mean, of course, that the term communicates nothing at all to me, but I do mean it communicates nothing that is satisfactorily precise and specific. It is also the case that some of Piaget's concrete-operational groupings do not even *claim* to model any commonly engaged-in form of thought whatever (Flavell, 1963); that is, there is theoretical vacuity as well as lack of clarity to be found in Piaget's structural models.

I also believe Piaget's structures may model children's thinking incorrectly and incompletely. As to correctness, I am not convinced that classical Piagetian tasks, such as the various conservation problems, are necessarily or even frequently solved by the operations that form the elements of Piagetian structures. As to completeness, it is becoming increasingly certain that the logic-like mental activities suggested by Piaget could at most be but a subset of the ensemble of knowledge, skills, and processes needed to solve Piagetian tasks (Gelman, 1978; Trabasso, Isen, Dolecki, McLanahan, Riley, & Tucker, 1978). More generally, I suspect these activities may actually play a more restricted and limited role in the child's overall intellectual life than has been assumed; that is, Piagetian operations may simply not be the basic, general, and all-pervasive "cardinal traits" of childhood thinking that the theory claims they are (Smedslund, 1977). Also, as the field of cognitive development has grown, researchers have identified new knowledge structures, processes, strategies, and the like in communication, comprehension, memory, attention, social cognition, and other areas. It is only natural that the intellectual attainments described by Piaget will seem to account for progressively "less of the variance" in children's mental worlds as this proliferation of new cognitive acquisitions continues. I also believe, with others (Feldman & Toulmin, 1976; Toulmin, in preparation; Smedslund, 1977), that the use of highly abstract and formal algebraic structures will probably not ever prove to be the best way to model children's developing cognitive competencies. Unlike Keats et al., (1978), I do not think that Piaget has merely proposed the wrong algebraic systems as models and that what we need are simply more adequate ones. Rather, I believe that algebraic systems are just not the general *sorts* of models that have a promising future in cognitive-developmental psychology.

There is also the well-known fact that empirical studies have generally not found as much chronological synchrony or concurrence among same-stage acquisitions as Piaget's stage theory should predict (various commentaries in Brainerd, 1978b; Fischer, 1980; Flavell, 1977, p. 248; Roberge & Flexer, 1979; Siegler, 1979, in press). Diverse abilities and concepts that one would expect the child to acquire at the same time, because they are assumed in the theory to reflect the emergence of the same cognitive structure, often do not appear to develop concurrently. Siegler (1979) and others have described a closely-related difficulty with Piaget's stage theory:

the age norms associated with the knowledge states seem increasingly tenuous: three- and 4-year-olds display conceptual understanding on some tasks that they should not possess until age 6 or 7, and 19- and 20-year-old college students fail to display conceptual understanding that they should have acquired at age 13 or 14 [p. 98].

Thus, the cognitive abilities of young children and adults appear to be less different than the theory would predict.

There are at least two reasons why empirical data on this within-stage synchrony issue are intrinsically difficult to interpret, however. The first has to do with differences in the diagnostic sensitivity of the tasks used to assess the putatively same-stage acquisitions. Flavell (1977) has stated:

> Unfortunately, it is very difficult to determine whether two or more cognitive entities do or do not develop concurrently and interdependently . . . much of the difficulty stems from diagnostic uncertainties. Suppose that, without our knowing it, our test x for development X had extraneous but very taxing performance demands not present in our test y for development Y. That is, test x is harder and less sensitive than test y because of heavy information-processing requirements or other task factors that have nothing intrinsically to do with the cognitive acquisition the test was designed to measure. Accordingly, test x will underestimate the child's level of development of X much more than y will with respect to Y, since it will yield more false-negative type misdiagnoses. This difference in the sensitivities of the two tests could cause developments X and Y to look concurrent when X actually occurs earlier in ontogenesis than Y; conversely, it could make a true developmental concurrence look sequential, with Y seeming to emerge before X [pp. 247–248].

The second reason is that, as suggested previously, Piagetian tasks may not always be solved by means of the operational structures proposed by Piaget. To the extent that this is true, the preceding concurrence-diagnosis problem becomes moot, because the theory simply has no chance of receiving an adequate test from the outset.

In view of what has just been said, trying to decide how stage-like cognitive development is would seem to be a fruitless venture. If the foregoing criticisms are valid, there are several major obstacles to deciding how stage-like it is with respect to Piagetian acquisitions. And for any acquisitions imaginable, the researcher would still undoubtedly be confronted with the difficult methodological problem of differential test sensitivities described earlier.

There is, however, another way to approach the problem. It is simply to think hard about the whole matter, drawing upon any arguments, considerations, knowledge, and guesses that seem helpful. My strategy is the following: I begin by trying to imagine possible considerations, factors, or states of affairs that would make the child look relatively homogeneous and uniform in cognitive level and his/her development correspondingly stage-like. Following this, I do the same with respect to the opposite possibility; that is, of a relatively heterogeneous mind that does not mature according to a sequence of highly general stages. I then try to extract from all these ruminations some best guesses about the psychological reality and scientific utility of the concept of a broad and general cognitive-developmental stage. In what follows, I continue (Flavell,

1971, p. 422) to use the term *item* as a convenient generic term for any sort of cognitive-developmental acquisition or class of acquisitions.

Homogeneity

Some measure of cognitive homogeneity would obtain if two or more items continually lent mutual assistance to one another's development. In such a "reciprocal mediation" process (Flavell, 1972), each small developmental advance in item A tends to facilitate a small developmental advance in item B (C, D, E . . .), which in turn tends to mediate an increment of further progress in A (Flavell, 1972). This process insures that the maturity level or quality of the child's knowledge or thinking will continue to be at least fairly homogeneous or similar across these items as their development proceeds. Reciprocal mediation seems likeliest to occur within knowledge and skill domains that tend to contain rich conceptual interdependencies among their constituent items. School subjects like mathematics and the sciences are obvious candidates. Some reciprocal mediation may also be found in language development, the development of social cognition, and other areas of cognitive growth.

A set of cognitive-developmental items may also look more homogeneous by virtue of the fact that the items possess a common mediator. As used here (in contrast to Flavell, 1972), "common mediator" can refer to a wide variety of things: a prerequisite or facilitative capacity, aptitude, skill, strategy, body of knowledge, or set of experiences. The prototypical common mediator would be a Piagetian stage-specific structure, such as a concrete-operational grouping. If psychologically real, such a mediator would add considerable uniformity and consistency to the child's thinking.

However, one can also think of other possible mediators, some of which would probably make for a lesser degree of cognitive homogeneity than Piagetian structures would. For example, the cognition of the infant is at least homogeneous in the weak sense that it is always and everywhere "sensory–motor" rather than "symbolic-representational" in nature (whatever we shall finally agree that those expressions mean at the process level). In the same way, intellectual performance after infancy is weakly homogeneous across tasks and domains in that it is mediated by and bears the stamp of our basic symbolic-representational capacity (Flavell, 1970, p. 1040).

Various basic skills and knowledge may also lend some measure of homogeneity to the child's cognitive life. For example, there may be homogeneities in cognitive processing that are mediated by learning to read, write, and perform mathematical operations. Similarly, the acquisition of object permanence, self-awareness, the idea of a unit measure, and other fundamental Piagetian and nonPiagetian concepts undoubtedly constrain how heterogeneous in level the child's thought would be across situations. Once such basic skills and knowledge have been acquired, it may even be *impossible* for the individual to think as primitively as he once did in the situations concerned. Once the child learns to read numbers, for instance, he will automatically and involuntarily decode any number that he sees; he no longer *can* respond to them as meaningless scribbles. (We might say that he is completely and homogeneously "in" the "number-reading stage"—in the unambiguous way that we would like to but cannot, I believe, say that an adolescent is "in" the formal-operational stage.)

Related to the foregoing, some homogeneity might be produced by experiences that facilitate the development of two or more items. For example, exposure to formal schooling might foster the codevelopment of, say, the ability to control attention and the ability to think and reflect before answering questions. The degree of similarity in maturity level between the two skills thus engendered might not be very high in absolute terms—merely higher than it would have been without the common mediating effects on each of school experience.

There is another possible common mediator that is interesting because it connects individual-differences and cognitive-developmental approaches to children's thinking. The mediator is the psychometric or information-processing construct variously labeled *ability, aptitude, factor,* or *component* (Sternberg, 1979). There should be some tendency toward homogeneity of cognitive level across all tasks that are heavily dependent on the same mental factor or factors for their solution. Just as one could imagine a Piagetian concrete-operational grouping lending some consistency to the child's cognitive level over all tasks to which that grouping is relevant, so also can one imagine a spatial ability factor, say, doing the same for all tasks on which that ability is highly useful.

The degree of mental homogeneity we see may also depend on when we look as well as where we look. At the beginning of any acquisitional sequence, the child lacks the knowledge and skills needed to solve any task for which that acquisition is requisite, whether easy or hard. As a consequence, he/she fails all such tasks and is, in that respect, cognitively homogeneous (Flavell & Wohlwill, 1969, p. 100). In addition, the cognitive processes that lead to this uniform incorrect responding across tasks may sometimes also be quite homogeneous at this early period. Siegler (in press) asks:

Why might this be the case? A possible explanation, admittedly speculative at this point, involves the notion of "fall-back rules." The basic idea is that people may have certain standard forms of reasoning that they rely on when they lack particular forms of reasoning that they rely on when they lack particular information about a problem. In the present situation [conservation and other Piagetian tasks], five-year-olds may have utilized a fall-back rule that lacking direct information about a task, it is best to rely solely on the values of the single, seemingly most important dimension [p. 79].

When the child is a novice at something, then, he/she may respond to most or all tasks in that area in a relatively more fixed, undifferentiated, sterotypic way—consistently centering on what is most perceptually salient, repeatedly giving the same answer, and so on. This is an understandable tendency, of course, and adults may also follow it in areas where they are totally ignorant (Brown & DeLoache, 1978, p. 13). Unlike adults, however, the very young are novices at virtually everything—"universal novices" in Brown and DeLoache's words (p. 14). As a consequence, there may be more intellectual homogeneity generally very early in ontogenesis. Very young infants will necessarily respond in much the same way to many different inputs because their repertoire of schemes and skills is so limited. A sizable cognitive repertoire may thus be a necessary condition for marked heterogeneity and inconsistency of response level across tasks and contexts.

There is likely to be less homogeneity during the middle phases of any acquisition sequence and, more generally, after the early infancy period. As the child advances in an acquisition process, she/he will begin to succeed on the easier tasks in the area but will continue to fail the harder ones (Flavell & Wohlwill, 1969, pp. 100–101). Faced with the harder tasks, the child may have no choice but to resort to "fall-back rules" (Siegler, in press) or some other overlearned approach. The result is less across-task homogeneity of cognitive level at the intermediate than at the beginning phases of the acquisition process.

As the acquisition process becomes more and more complete, however, the subject's cognition in this task domain should become more and more homogeneous (Flavell & Wohlwill, 1969, p. 101). The relevant cognitive items eventually become reliably evoked and effectively utilized in almost all tasks for which they are appropriate solution aids (Flavell, 1977, pp. 222–227). I have argued elsewhere that maximum across-task homogeneity in the use of a given set of cognitive items may only be achieved subsequent to the "stage" that these items define (1970, p. 1040; 1971, pp. 431–435). There is nothing puzzling or paradoxical about this state of affairs. For example, children in our culture normally acquire concepts of measurement during the early school years. In Piaget's theory, these concepts are associated with the concrete-operational stage. However, the normal, time-dependent process of practice, generalization, differentiation, and integration with other knowledge virtually guarantee that these concepts will be more reliably and skillfully employed across situations by the average 16-year-old than by the average 8-year-old, and still more so by an adult engineer. Flavell (1970) states: "If you really want to study a Piagetian concrete-operational structure in all its power and glory, choose an adolescent as your subject—or better yet, a bright adult! [p. 1040]."

It would be wrong, however, to conclude from the foregoing that the developmental sequence from birth to adulthood is homogeneity → heterogeneity → homogeneity for the cognitive system as a whole. Although the young infant's whole cognitive system may be relatively homogeneous, that of the adult is not. An engineer's use of measurement concepts and other well-practiced components of his engineering knowledge may be highly consistent across a wide variety of problems and situations in that field. However, his level of thinking is *relativity* liable to appear both less mature and less consistently same-level in other *of* areas—areas where he possesses less expertise (Piaget, 1972), where his *traits* learning experiences have been less systematic, coherent, and rational, where affective and cognitive biases (Schneider et al., 1979, Chapter 10) are likelier to *or* intrude, etc. His cognition may thus show a lack of homogeneity in three *abilities* respects: (1) between the engineering domain and other domains; (2) among some of these other domains; (3) within some or many of these other domains.

When in the life cycle are people likeliest to show the *least* homogeneity in their thinking? My guess is between early infancy and whenever formal school- //// ing or other systematic training ends—usually around the beginning of young adulthood (notwithstanding the aforementioned lack of high homogeneity in adult minds). During those childhood years, people are constantly turning their minds toward tasks and situations they partly but do not fully understand; they *child is* are commonly somewhere in the middle game of one learning enterprise or *always* another. Thus, children seem psychologically as well as biologically almost *changing* always in transition, almost never in a steady state. Considerable heterogeneity of cognitive functioning level both within and between domains would seem to *i.e. no* be their natural condition, given that they are constantly learning and changing, constantly being taught and socialized. Because "development" seems to apply *homo-* more naturally to children than to adults (the Life-Span Development movement *geneity* notwithstanding), so also does "developmental stage." Yet, ironically and in seeming paradox, the child's chronically low level of homogeneity and "hori- zontal structure" (Wohlwill, 1973) makes him a particularly unpromising candi- date for the classical broad and sweeping stage-developmental characterization. I find it easier to imagine the neonate, or even the adult, as being consistently "in" one general stage than I do the child or adolescent.

Before examining possible sources of heterogeneity in detail, there is one more guess to make about homogeneity, namely, that there may be individual differences among children (and adults) in how much cognitive homogeneity they exhibit and in what domains. Firstly, some children may tend to develop in a more even, stage-like fashion than others. Exactly how and why can only be guessed. It may be that some children have a greater tendency than others to consolidate and generalize developmentally earlier items before making a start on developmentally later ones. Perhaps because they are sensitive to Piagetian states of cognitive conflict or disequilibrium, they may show less of the heterogeneous and multilevel functioning that Kohlberg and others have called "stage mixture" (Rest, 1979, Chapter 3). They might be likelier than other children to monitor their thinking for consistency across tasks and situations, perhaps because they are more given to remembering and comparing their own cognition from one occasion to the next. Secondly, there could be differences among children as to where their development is most stage-like—in domain A for one child, in domain B for a second, in no domain for a third. Adults may show similar individual differences in patterns of homogeneity and heterogeneity, perhaps largely as a function of differences in occupational and leisure time pursuits (recall the engineer example given earlier).

It might be added that these types of individual differences have their counterparts in social and personality psychology. Some people vary their social behavior greatly from situation to situation, chameleon-like, whereas others tend to be consistently "themselves" no matter what the situation or who is present; Snyder (1974) has called this personality variable "self-monitoring." People may also differ as to the areas of functioning in which their behavior is relatively more cross-situationally consistent or trait-like (Bem & Allen, 1974).

Heterogeneity = non-stage like

The mind and its development would appear heterogeneous and nonstage-like to the extent that many items neither bore any developmental relation to one another nor shared any sort of common mediator. For many pairs of items there may be no reciprocal mediation process (Flavell, 1972) to insure at least rough similarity of cognitive maturity level between pair members at any point in developmental time. Likewise, many items may share no common mediator—no common underlying cognitive structure, process, body of knowledge, concept, skill, ability factor, or facilitating set of experiences. Since the ascendancy of Piagetian developmental psychology, we have come to think of the child's cognitive growth as made up of a network of interwoven, multiply-interconnected developmental paths. I suspect, however, that a surprisingly large number of developments may proceed quite independently of one another, and that the maturity of the child's thinking—however defined—may be quite uneven across these developments (Fischer, 1980).

Even if two items are developmentally related, this state of affairs may not result in any increase in homogeneity. This would be the case where the developmental influence is undirectional rather than reciprocal. Item X might be a necessary or at least frequent mediator of item Y's development. However, Y does not also assist X's development, nor does X continue to develop apace with Y; indeed, it may not develop further at all. For instance, the recognition that addition of elements always increases the cardinal-number value of a set, that subtraction always decreases it, and that doing neither always leaves it unchanged undoubtedly helps children get started in the development of mathematical understanding. The recognition may not itself undergo any further development, however. The two developments are functionally related but occur sequentially rather than synchronously. The fact that they are related in this way lends an increment of "structure" to the child's overall cognitive development, to be sure, but the structure is of the "vertical" (sequential) rather than "horizontal" variety (Wohlwill, 1973, Chapter 9) and therefore does not make that development more "stage-like," as I have been using the term.

There may be considerable heterogeneity at any given age for biological reasons. The ontogenetic time course of different cognitive items may be partly controlled by different biological-maturational processes, and these processes may become active at different ages. Thus, maturational factors could cause the individual to be much more cognitively advanced in one area of functioning than another. I return to this possibility later.

Several developmentalists who find the concept of developmental stage useful in their theorizing agree that we are likely to see stage-like consistency of cognitive level only within cognitive domains, not across them (Damon, 1977, in press; Fischer, 1980; Turiel, in press). Turiel (in press) further argues that whereas some domains of social cognition show a kind of stage-like development, others do not. It may be recalled that even Piaget argued that perceptual development is not a stage-like affair (Flavell, 1963, p. 234). However, how much cognitive homogeneity actually obtains across tasks and situations within the domains that are identified as relatively more stage-like is still open to question, in my opinion. I suspect that the developmental structure to be found within such domains is largely of the sequential, vertical, rather than stage-like, horizontal variety.

Recall the suggestion made at the end of the Homogeneity section that there may be substantial individual differences regarding within- and between-domain homogeneity. Some children may tend to progress evenly on all intellectual fronts. I suspect that most do not, however, and that some children may at any given age be functioning at very different cognitive levels in different areas. Marked intraindividual differences in aptitudes, interests, and experiences across areas could lead to considerable heterogeneity. Imagine, for example, a child or adolescent who is particularly well-endowed with the abilities needed to do computer science, has an all-consuming interest in it, has ample time and opportunity to learn about it, and has an encouraging parent who is a computer scientist (whence much of the aptitude, interest, and opportunity, perhaps). The quality and sophistication of the child's thinking in this area might well be higher than that of most adults in any area. It would also likely be much higher in this area than in most other areas of the child's cognitive life. His level of moral reasoning or skill in making inferences about other people might be considerably less developed, for instance. The heterogeneity could be a matter of time constraints as well as a matter of differential aptitudes and interests; that is, time spent at the computer terminal is time not spent interacting with and learning about people.

A final source of cognitive heterogeneity, already partly covered in previous paragraphs, is variability in the cognitive demands and difficulty levels of tasks. There are several different kinds of task factors and they could collectively engender a great deal of heterogeneity (Flavell, 1977, pp. 114–118). The factors we usually think of are general information-processing ones, such as the variable attentional and memory demands different tasks place on the subject. They are general in that they would presumably affect the performance level of any cognitive organism. In addition, tasks can vary in difficulty for us because we have a human mind rather than some other kind (species-specific heredity), because we were born with this profile of aptitudes rather than that (person-specific heredity), and because we have this particular cultural, subcultural, educational, and other task-relevant experiential background rather than that.

As to species-specific heredity, the general point has been made by Chomsky (1972, 1975) and numerous others: Human beings have evolved to find some kinds of cognition and learning easier and more natural than others. For instance, there appear to be important constraints on the structure of human languages that probably derive from our species-specific learning biases and mechanisms (Newport, 1981). Fodor (1972) has presented a variation on this position that is particularly relevant to the heterogeneity-in-development issue. He begins by describing a very stage-like conception of cognitive development:

> Take a time slice of a child and you will find pervasive and homogeneous limits upon the type of concepts it can form. Developmental stages are to be characterized by reference to such limits; ideally, by the construction of formalisms which express them precisely. The primary goal of theories in cognitive development is thus to exhibit the changing mental capacities of the child in terms of an orderly progression of such formalisms, and to characterize the endogenous and exogenous pressures which occasion transitions between them.
>
> There are, however, alternative views. One might suppose that computational power is quite unevenly distributed among the tasks with which a given child is confronted at a given time. Formally quite powerful computational processes may thus be available to the very young child, though only for the performance of quite specific sorts of computations. For example, no one rational can now doubt the formal power of the mechanisms underlying the acquisition of syntax. What is striking is that the child who is exploiting these mechanisms for language learning apparently does not have analogously powerful systems available for 'general problem solving'. . . . Essentially similar remarks could presumably be made about the power, and the specificity, of the computational procedures underlying the ontogenesis of spatial orientation, face recognition, locomotion, depth perception, object constancy, and so on.
>
> One thus considers the possibility of viewing the mental life of children in a way that is quite alien to the Vygotskyian (or the Piagetian) tradition. Classical developmental psychology invites us to think of the child as a realization of an algebra which can be applied, relatively indifferently, to a wide variety of types of cognitive integrations, but which differs in essential respects from the mathematics underlying adult mentation. The alternative picture is that the child is a bundle of relatively special purpose computational systems which are formally analogous to those involved in adult cognition but which are quite restricted in their range of application, each being more or less tightly tied to the computation of a specific sort of data, more or less rigidly endogeneously paced, and relatively inaccessible to purposes and influences other than those which conditioned its evolution. Cognitive

development, on this view, is the maturation of the processes such systems subserve, and the gradual broadening of the kinds of computations to which they can apply [pp. 92–93].

There is also a growing body of evidence (Nisbett & Ross, 1980; Shaklee, 1979; Schneider et al., 1979; Wason & Johnson–Laird, 1972) that the human mind has a number of systematic shortcomings—information-processing biases of cognitive or motivational origin, proneness to a variety of types of faulty reasoning, etc. I suspect that many of these shortcomings are due more to (human) nature than nurture, although we really do not know at present (Ross, 1981). Whatever their origin, they certainly make our thinking appear much less rational and veridical in some situations than in others. As Wason and Johnson–Laird (1972) put it: "At best, we can all think like logicians; at worst, logicians all think like us [p. 245]."

The other two factors need little further mention. I have already discussed how intraindividual differences in native abilities or aptitudes could help make for cognitive heterogeneity (the case of the budding computer scientist). It is obvious that differences in past experience could do the same. For example, two tasks that appear similar in logical structure and information-processing demands may be approached and dealt with in very different ways by a child who can bring a wealth of relevant and useful previous experiences to bear on one task but not the other. Transfer and generalization is a continuing problem for child and adult alike, not something we can assume will automatically happen. The individual's cultural and educational background is an especially potent determinant of the particular pattern of cognitive heterogeneity he will show (Dasen, 1977).

Conclusions About Stages

In the preceding sections, I have enumerated some possible sources or loci of cognitive homogeneity and heterogeneity. By their very nature as armchair speculations, they permit no firm, sure, scientifically well-grounded conclusions. However, they have suggested what I believe is a reasonable best guess. The guess is that human cognitive growth is generally *not* very "stage-like," in the horizontal-structure, high-homogeneity meaning of the term. I believe that Fischer (1980) is right when he says that: "unevenness is the rule in development [p. 510]." I believe that Wohlwill (1973) is probably attributing too much horizontal structure or homogeneity to human ontogenesis when he asserts that: "behavioral development does not take place in isolated packages or along neatly separated, independent tracks, but along a variety of fronts in close interaction with one another [p. 240]."

It is, of course, possible that cognitive development does have this sort of stage-like quality within some domain—for instance, where there is continuous reciprocal mediation among two or more developing cognitive items. The isolation of such domains might well be a profitable scientific endeavor (Turiel, in press). However, I suspect that there are not many domains of this kind, and also that they may have constraints or limitations that reduce their scientific interest. As two possible examples of such constraints, perhaps only some people's development within the domain looks highly stage-like, and perhaps the number of items or task situations over which such homogeneity obtains is quite small. When stage-like developments are "thin" in this latter sense (few codeveloping items, restricted homogeneity), Wohlwill argues that we should use terms like *step* rather than *stage* (1973, pp. 193-195). Others have also proposed the use of *step* or *level* in these instances (Feldman, 1980, p. 5; Fischer, 1980; Flavell 1963, p. 443; Flavell in Brainerd, 1978b). In such narrow, step-wise developments, the sequential, vertical-structure aspects of the process become of primary interest, because there is relatively little horizontal structure to study; that is, we want to know what develops after what and why, but we have no prior expectations or theoretical commitments as to how generally and consistently "what"-like in cognitive level the child should be at any step in the sequence.

Like Wohlwill (1973, p. 191), I believe that, taken collectively, developmentalists use the term *stage* to refer to an unacceptably wide variety of things. I further suspect that, like structuralist and structuralism, stage is all too often sent and received with neither party to the communicative exchange having a really clear and specific idea what either means by it. I think it should be used sparingly and with its intended meaning very carefully spelled out. I think that the word connotes more homogeneity to most audiences than its user may want to claim—*and* more than actually obtains within the child's mind.

SEQUENCES

Even if cognitive development does not prove to be as stage-like as we once thought, I believe it contains numerous interesting sequences of psychologically related acquisitions (for a contrary view, see Brainerd, 1978b). The study of cognitive-developmental sequences has long been recognized as a highly interesting and worthwhile scientific enterprise (Flavell, 1972), thanks largely to the pioneering work of Piaget. Sequences are the very wire and glue of development. Later cognitive acquisitions build on or are otherwise linked to earlier ones, and in their turn similarly prepare the ground for still later ones. The fact that the components of such sequences may be more accurately characterized as steps or levels than as general stages should not make the sequences less interesting to a developmentalist. To return to an issue raised at the beginning of the chapter, I believe that there *is* considerable structure in human cognitive growth, and that much of it is the "vertical structure" (Wohlwill, 1973) that sequences provide.

There are several reasons why this is a particularly exciting time to study cognitive-developmental sequences. Firstly, new statistical and other methodologies for detecting sequences in developmental data have recently been described (Davison, King, Kitchener, & Parker, 1980; Froman & Hubert, 1980; Jamison & Dansky, 1979; Wohlwill, 1973). Secondly, evidence has recently been adduced for the existence of a wide variety of new and important-looking sequences, many of them in the area of social-cognitive development (Case, 1978, in preparation; Colby, 1979; Damon, 1977; Fischer, 1980, and studies cited therein; Flavell, Everett, Crofts, & Flavell, 1981; Rest, 1979; Selman, in press; Siegler, in press; Turiel, 1978). To illustrate, Selman (in press) has evidence that there are four levels of social perspective-taking knowledge and ability that develop in a fixed order over the course of childhood and adolescence. The following is a very brief and incomplete account of the four levels:

At Level 0, children do not clearly and fully differentiate between the physical and psychological characteristics of persons, nor between their own and other people's conceptual perspectives. At Level 1, these differentiations are clearly made so that, for instance, the child can understand that two people could have different thoughts or feelings about the selfsame situation. At Level 2, the child is further able to step mentally outside himself and take a self-reflective or second-person perspective on his own thoughts and actions, and also knows that others can do the same. This permits him to be aware, for example, both that he knows the other person likes him and that the other person knows he likes him. At level 3, the child can also adopt a more abstract, third-person or generalized-other perspective that permits him to take the interpersonal relationship itself (e.g., friendship) as an object of reflective thought. Additional skills are present at Level 4, including that of considering still more abstract and generalized points of view, such as that of society at large. I believe that Selman's four-level sequence tells a very interesting and plausible developmental story about an ecologically significant type of social cognition and well demonstrates the substantive contribution that a sequential analysis can make.

A third reason to be interested in sequence just now is the recent emergence of two theories of cognitive development in which sequences figure importantly (Case, 1978, in preparation; Fischer, 1980). These are not specific theories about the development of a particular class of acquisitions, as are those of Selman, Damon, Turiel, Siegler, and others cited earlier. Rather, they are more ambitious, general theories like Piaget's. Indeed, their authors see them as building directly on Piaget's theoretical efforts and they are very like Piaget's theory in key respects. Most importantly, they attempt to describe and explain cognitive development as a *whole*—to see "a clear general picture of development" (Case, in preparation) or "the big picture of development" (Fischer, 1980). Whatever the shortcomings of these theories may eventually prove to be, their explicit focus on the overall shape and structure of cognitive development makes them worth our closest attention. Of the two, Fischer's theory has existed in semicomplete form for a longer period of time; Case's systematic presentation of his theory exists only in book chapter drafts at this writing (Case, in preparation). In addition, Fischer's theory has already generated a number of interesting studies of developmental sequences (Berthenthal & Fischer, 1978; Fischer & Roberts, 1979; Hand, 1979; Watson & Fischer, 1977, 1980). For these reasons, I mostly summarize and discuss aspects of Fischer's theory. "Summarize" and "aspects" are used advisedly; neither all of its important details nor all of its strong points and shortcomings can be presented here.

Fischer (1980) interprets cognitive growth as the sequential development of more and more complex cognitive skills. "Skills" are defined very broadly and appear (to me) to include some declarative as well as procedural forms of knowledge (e.g., the knowledge that the total length of a cord remains the same under certain length-irrelevant changes in its appearance). A more obviously procedural-looking skill in Fischer's (1980) system would be the infant's ability to use one sensory–motor scheme as a means to the enactment of another as goal. The following is a brief overview of the theory:

> Skills develop step by step through a series of 10 hierarchical levels divided into three tiers. The tiers specify skills of vastly different types: sensory–motor skills, representational skills, and abstract skills. The levels specify skills of gradually increasing complexity, with a skill at one level built directly on skills from the preceding level. Each level is characterized by a reasonably well defined type of structure that indicates the kinds of behaviors that a person (child or adult) can control at that level. The skills at each level are constructed by a person acting on the environment. She performs several actions induced by a specific environmental circumstance, and the way those actions occur in that circumstance provokes her to combine the actions: The person thus combines and differentiates skills from one level to form skills at the next higher level. The movement from one level to the next occurs in many microdevelopmental steps specified by a series of transformation rules. Notice that the skills develop through levels, not stages: Development is relatively continuous and gradual, and the person is never at the same level for all skills. The development of skills must be induced by the environment, and only the skills induced most consistently will typically be at the highest level that the individual is capable of. Unevenness in development is therefore the rule, not the exception [pp. 479–480].

Fischer's theory makes a number of very strong claims about cognitive-developmental sequences. First, the theory asserts that development in all skill domains is formally similar, in that it always proceeds in the same order through the same four levels. These levels are called *single sets, mappings, systems,* and *systems of systems.* To illustrate their meaning, a skill at the level of single sets during infancy might consist of the ability to look at an object that comes into the infant's field of vision. At the following level of mappings, the infant can coordinate two such single-set skills to form a more complex skill, for instance, using his looking skill to guide his grasping skill. At the next level, subcomponents of one skill are coordinated with subcomponents of another to form a skill system. At the final level, two of these systems become interconnected to constitute a system of systems.

As the previous quotation from Fischer (1980) indicates, these same four levels are said to characterize the development of three different types (cognitive-developmental "levels") of skills, referred to as sensory–motor, representational, and abstract *tiers*. The three tiers are linked together in that the fourth level of one tier also constitutes the first level of its successor. Thus, a system of sensory–motor systems is also a single representational set and a system of representational systems is also a single abstract set. This recurrence of exactly the same four abstractly defined levels at higher tiers is obviously reminiscent of Piaget's concept of vertical décalage (Fischer, 1980, p. 518). However, it appears to represent a considerably stronger and more specific claim about the amount and kind of vertical or sequential structure present in cognitive growth: In Fischer's theory, cognitive development consists of a sequence of three tiers, all of which contain the same subsequence of four levels.

It is interesting to note that Case's (in preparation) theory also attributes a good deal of vertical structure to cognitive development. Moreover, the nature of that structure is similar in some respects to that posited by Fischer. In Case's theory, the developing child acquires *executive control structures* rather than skills, there are four tiers (called *stages*) rather than three, and there are other differences between the theories. However, there are again four sequentially ordered levels (*substages*) within each stage, these four substages are formally similar from stage to stage, and the last substage of one stage essentially comprises the first substage of the following stage.

Fischer (1980) describes five transformation rules or processes that specify how developmental advances in cognitive skills gradually occur within and between levels: *intercoordination, compounding, focusing, substitution,* and *differentiation.* They are summarized as follows:

Intercoordination and compounding specify how skills are combined to produce new skills. Intercoordination describes combinations that produce development from one level to the next (macrodevelopment), and compounding describes combinations that produce development within a level (microdevelopment). Focusing and substitution specify smaller microdevelopmental steps than compounding. Focusing deals with moment-to-moment shifts from one skill to another, and substitution designates certain cases of generalization of a skill. The fifth rule, differentiation, indicates how sets become separated into potentially distinct subsets when one of the other four transformations occurs, but it can also be used separately to predict microdevelopmental steps. The microdevelopmental transformations of differentiation, substitution, focusing, and compounding eventually produce the macrodevelopmental transformation of intercoordination. These five transformations are probably not exhaustive; future research will indicate whether additional transformation rules are required [p. 497].

Fischer believes that most known cognitive-developmental sequences can be explained by his system of levels, tiers, and transformation rules. In addition, he and his coworkers try to use the theory to predict new sequences (Fischer, 1980).

Fischer's ideas about the uses of his theory suggest another reason why we should be interested in cognitive-developmental sequences, namely because they may help us explain cognitive growth. We are accustomed to regarding sequences as descriptions rather than explanations of development. They are descriptions, of course; they describe what develops first, what develops next, and so forth. However, a careful analysis of sequences may give us hints about possible developmental mechanisms or processes that produce these sequential changes. In the area of language development, for example, Clark's (1973) semantic feature theory of lexical acquisition is a theory of developmental process that relied on the order of acquisition of word meanings (thus, sequences) for its support. Exactly what would and would not count as an explanation versus a mere description of mental development is a matter of some dispute among developmentalists (Brainerd, 1978b, and commentaries). However, most would probably agree that we are providing at least a partial explanation whenever we can specify such mechanisms or processes.

How can sequences suggest possible developmental mechanisms? Consider any two-item sequence A–B. If we have clear and specific descriptions of acquisition A and acquisition B we may also be able to formulate one or more ways they are related to one another. For example, the relation might be that of *substitution,* with B replacing A as a solution procedure in a certain class of problem situations, or *inclusion,* with elements of A becoming constituents or components of B; *addition, modification* (in the form of *differentiation, generalization,* or *stabilization*), and *mediation* are some other A–B relationships that have been used to characterize cognitive-developmental sequences (Flavell, 1972; Siegler, in press). To use Fischer's (1980) theory as an illustration, although more than one relationship may obtain between any pair of adjacent levels, one relationship that always holds is that of inclusion: A level A skill always becomes a component of a level B skill.

It is a short step from thinking about an A–B relationship to thinking about the possible processes or mechanisms that caused it to be that particular relationship rather than some other. Indeed, the names of most A–B relationships immediately connote the general sorts of processes that probably brought the child from A to B. For instance, "substitution" suggests the existence of processes that somehow increase the probability that B will be used in a certain set of cognitive circumstances and decrease the probability that A will be used in those same circumstances. One is even more likely to think about processes when the connection between earlier A and later B is described in terms of "developmental principles," like Werner's (1948) *differentiation* and *hierarchic integration.* It seems to me that such developmental principles are really sketches or outlines of process analyses. They indicate what happens during a stretch of ontogenetic time and with what result (M gets distinguished from N, X is now integrated with Y, etc.), but only in a global, nonspecific way. They constrain what the processes could be like by indicating what they must accomplish, but they do not further specify them. The same is largely true, I believe, of Piaget's equilibration process and Fischer's (1980) five transformation rules; that is, they too are more like abstract A–B relationships or developmental principles than like concrete and detailed models of actual developmental process. However, they too could be construed as preliminaries to a more detailed process model. (For a more advanced venture in this direction, see Klahr and Wallace, 1976.)

The strategy of trying to analyze sequences for hints about developmental processes is particularly timely because there is currently a renaissance of interest in learning processes (Anderson, Kline, & Beasley, 1979; Anzai & Simon, 1979; Brown, in press; Neches & Hayes, 1977; Siegler & Klahr, 1979; Simon, 1980). Cognitive psychologists, computer scientists, and other students of what is coming to be called "cognitive science" have recently started to model richly structured intelligent systems that learn and change their cognitive organization as well as just process information. Unlike the sterotypic S–R learning theorist of yesteryear, today's cognitive scientists attribute a great deal of complexity to the system that does the learning, to what it learns, and to the structures and processes that accomplish the learning. Some of the learning processes proposed sound very familiar to a student of developmental sequences and some do not. For example, Anderson et al.,'s (1979) ACT is a computer simulation program that makes use of a propositional network to represent its factual knowledge and a set of productions (condition-action rules) to represent its procedural knowledge. Its learning processes include the familiar mechanisms of *generalization* and *discrimination* and the unfamiliar one of *designation*. Other unfamiliar-sounding processes of cognitive change recently proposed include *reduction to a rule, reduction to results, unit building* (Neches & Hayes, 1977), *consistency detection,* and *redundancy elimination* (Klahr & Wallace, 1976), although some of these at least partly resemble developmental principles that have been described previously (Flavell, 1972).

So, we see on the contemporary scene developmentalists who describe interesting sequences, various types of cognitive scientists who are beginning to model learning processes, and a few people interested in both (Brown, in press; Siegler & Klahr, 1979). I think students of cognitive growth would do well to track both enterprises for clues to developmental mechanisms. Cognitive scientists are accustomed to describing change processes precisely enough to simulate them on the computer, whereas very few developmentalists have ever tried to be anywhere near that precise and specific about developmental principles or processes (Klahr & Wallace, 1976). On the other hand, developmentalists should have a much better purview of what develops—of the many key sequences of acquisitions that normally occur during ontogenesis. They are apt to have a better idea than their kin in cognitive psychology and artificial intelligence of what "job descriptions" the latter's precisely defined change processes ought to have. They know, as cognitive scientists may not, that processes are needed that will do the job of moving the child's mind from A_1 to B_1, or A_2 to B_2, or A_3 to B_3, because those are the significant acquisitional sequences that have been identified on the macrodevelopmental level. Sequences may be used to help specify processes just as processes may be used to help predict new sequences (Fischer, 1980). More cross talk between sequence hunters and learning simulators might thus advance our understanding of the functional as well as the formal aspects of cognitive development.

However, the problem of specifying developmental processes is too difficult and tricky to permit such a cheery, come-let-us-reason-together ending to this essay. I believe that the thinking about processes in both camps has been too narrow and simplistic. In the developmental camp, for instance, Fischer (1980) appears to claim that all cognitive development can be construed as the development of "cognitive skills," that all cognitive skill development proceeds via the same four-level sequence, and that the processes that generate this development consist of only five transformation rules. In the cognitive science camp, likewise, Anderson and his colleagues (1979) believe that: "a single set of learning processes [four in number] underlies the whole gamut of human learning—from children learning their first language by hearing examples of adult speech to adults learning to program a computer by reading textbook instructions [p. 278]."

I strongly suspect that learning and development are more complex—more "heterogeneous," to reintroduce an earlier term—than Fischer's and Anderson's theories would have it. I think they are more heterogeneous in two related respects (Flavell, 1978). Firstly, I believe that the cognitive entities or items we acquire are more diverse and variegated than is generally recognized. Secondly, this greater variety in what gets acquired suggests the possibility of correspondingly greater variety in acquisitional processes.

On the first point, we surely acquire things that cannot be called "cognitive skills" under any reasonable interpretation of "skills." According to Flavell (1978), we acquire and elaborate in the course of childhood: "all manner of attitudes, beliefs, aspirations, fantasies, and feelings regarding the social and nonsocial world [p. 104]." We acquire metacognition about cognition as well as cognition about things. We acquire specific pieces of declarative and procedural knowledge, but also fuzzy ideas of large compass; "major changes in perspective . . . or paradigmatic shifts of theory or world view (Brown, in press, p. 22)." Some cognitive acquisitions are more biologically prepared for or preprogrammed than others; not all cognitive development is cognitive learning, nor is all cognitive learning of a single type (Brown, in press).

The corollary possibility is as yet undreamed-of heterogeneity in the realm of developmental processes or mechanisms. Even now, there are many more proposed change processes in the literature than can be found in any single theory, suggesting that the single theories are probably incomplete. I believe the list of candidate processes will grow much longer as we continue to search for effective mechanisms of change, and, especially perhaps, when we take due account of the large variety of possible developables. Some of the differences in process may be due to differences in the subject's level of cognitive maturity—what "tier" he/she is in Fischer's (1980) sense. For example, it is hard for me to believe that the actual, real-time processes by which we "intercoordinate" (Fischer, 1980) two cognitive entities to form a new whole could be the same at 6 months, 4 years, and 18 years. It is hardly original to claim that part of what gets acquired during ontogenesis must consist of new processes of acquisition; we learn *how* to learn as we learn *what* we learn. Preschooler novices probably do not acquire expertise by means of exactly the same acquisitional processes adult novices use. For instance, Brown (in press) says: "the adult knows how to set about becoming an expert in new domains [p. 33]." I conclude this point and this essay by the time-honored persuasive technique of appealing to authority. To add to the persuasive impact I remind you that the authority is that rarest of species—a psychologist who won the Nobel prize. Anzai and Simon (1979) state that:

> Learning takes place in a wide variety of situations and probably by a number of different processes. This article proposes a theory of the specific processes that enable a student to learn while engaged in solving a problem. No claim is made that the theory embraces all possible kinds of learning by doing [p. 124].

ACKNOWLEDGMENT

I am very grateful to Sophia Cohen for her thoughtful and astute critique of the first draft of this chapter.

REFERENCES

Anderson, J. R., Kline, P. J., & Beasley, C. M. A general learning theory and its application to schema abstraction. In G. H. Bower (Ed.), *The psychology of learning and motivation* (Vol. 13). New York: Academic Press, 1979.

Anzai, Y., & Simon, H. A. The theory of learning by doing. *Psychological Review*, 1979, *86*, 124–140.

Bem, D. J., & Allen, A. On predicting some of the people some of the time: The search for cross-situational consistencies in behavior. *Psychological Review*, 1974, *81*, 506–520.

Berthenthal, B. I., & Fischer, K. W. The development of self-recognition in the infant. *Developmental Psychology*, 1978, *14*, 44–50.

Brainerd, C. J. *Piaget's theory of intelligence*. Englewood Cliffs, N.J.: Prentice-Hall, 1978. (a)

Brainerd, C. J. The stage question in cognitive-developmental theory. *Behavioral and Brain Sciences*, 1978, *2*, 173–213. (b)

Brown, A. L. Learning and development: The problem of compatibility, access, and induction. *Human Development*, in press.

Brown, A. L., & DeLoache, J. S. Skills, plans, and self-regulation. In R. S. Siegler (Ed.), *Children's thinking: What develops?* Hillsdale, N.J.: Lawrence Erlbaum Associates, 1978.

Case, R. Intellectual development from birth to adulthood: A neoPiagetian interpretation. In R. S. Siegler (Ed.), *Children's thinking: What develops?* Hillsdale, N.J.: Lawrence Erlbaum Associates, 1978.

Case, R. *Intellectual development: A systematic reinterpretation.* In preparation.

Chomsky, N. *Language and mind* (enlarged edition). New York: Harcourt Brace Jovanovich, 1972.

Chomsky, N. *Reflections on language.* New York: Pantheon, 1975.

Clark, E. V. What's in a word? On the child's acquisition of semantics in his first language. In T. Moore (Ed.), *Cognitive development and the acquisition of language.* New York: Academic Press, 1973.

Colby, A. *A longitudinal study of moral judgment.* Paper presented at the meeting of the Society for Research in Child Development, San Francisco, March, 1979.

Damon, W. *The social world of the child.* San Francisco: Jossey-Bass, 1977.

Damon, W. The nature of social-cognitive change in the developing child. In W. F. Overton & C. Reese (Eds.), *Knowledge and development* (Vol. 4). New York: Plenum, in press.

Dasen, P. R. (Ed.). *Piagetian psychology: Cross-cultural contributions.* New York: Gardner, 1977.

Davison, M. L., King, P. M., Kitchener, K. S., & Parker, C. A. The stage sequence conception of cognitive and social development. *Developmental Psychology,* 1980, *16,* 121–131.

DeGeorge, R. T., & DeGeorge, F. M. *The structuralists: From Marx to Lévi-Strauss.* Garden City, N.Y.: Doubleday, 1972.

Ennis, R. H. Children's ability to handle Piaget's propositional logic: A conceptual critique. *Review of Educational Research,* 1975, *45,* 1–41.

Epstein, S. The stability of behavior: II. Implications for psychological research. *American Psychologist,* 1980, *35,* 790–806.

Feldman, C. F., & Toulmin, S. Logic and theory of mind. *Nebraska Symposium on Motivation,* 1976, *23,* 409–476.

Feldman, D. H. *Beyond universals in cognitive development.* Norwood, N.J.: Ablex, 1980.

Fischer, K. W. A theory of cognitive development: The control and construction of hierarchies of skills. *Psychological Review,* 1980, *87,* 477–531.

Fischer, K. W., & Roberts, R. J., Jr. *Development of classification skills in preschool children.* Unpublished manuscript, University of Denver, 1979.

Flavell, J. H. *The developmental psychology of Jean Piaget.* New York: Van Nostrand, 1963.

Flavell, J. H. Concept development. In P. H. Mussen (Ed.), *Carmichael's manual of child psychology* (Vol. 1). New York: Wiley, 1970.

Flavell, J. H. Stage-related properties of cognitive development. *Cognitive Psychology,* 1971, *2,* 421–453.

Flavell, J. H. An analysis of cognitive-developmental sequences. *Genetic Psychology Monographs,* 1972, *86,* 279–350.

Flavell, J. H. *Cognitive development.* Englewood Cliffs, N.J.: Prentice-Hall, 1977.

Flavell, J. H. Comments. In R. S. Siegler (Ed.), *Children's thinking: What develops?* Hillsdale, N.J.: Lawrence Erlbaum Associates, 1978.

Flavell, J. H., Everett, B. A., Croft, K., & Flavell, E. R. Young children's knowledge about visual perception: Further evidence for the Level 1-Level 2 distinction. *Developmental Psychology,* 1981, *17,* 99–103.

Flavell, J. H., Omanson, R. C., & Latham, C. Solving spatial perspective-taking problems by rule versus computation: A developmental study. *Developmental Psychology,* 1978, *14,* 462–473.

Flavell, J. H., & Wohlwill, J. F. Formal and functional aspects of cognitive development. In D. Elkind & J. H. Flavell (Eds.), *Studies in cognitive growth: Essays in honor of Jean Piaget.* New York: Oxford University Press, 1969.

Fodor, J. Some reflections on L. S. Vygotsky's thought and language. *Cognition,* 1972, *1,* 83–95.

Froman, T., & Hubert, L. F. Application of prediction analysis to developmental priority. *Psychological Bulletin, 1980, 87,* 136-146.

Gardner, H. *The quest for mind: Piaget, Lévi-Strauss, and the structuralist movement.* New York: Knopf, 1973.

Gelman, R. Cognitive development. *Annual Review of Psychology,* 1978, *29,* 297-332.

Glass, A. L., Holyoak, K. J., & Santa, J. L. *Cognition.* Reading, Mass.: Addison-Wesley, 1979.

Hand, H. H. *The development of children's understanding of opposites in their behavior: How children develop the capacity to rationalize their niceness and meanness.* Paper presented at the meeting of the Society for Research in Child Development, San Francisco, March, 1979.

Jamison, W., & Dansky, J. L. Identifying developmental prerequisites of cognitive acquisitions. *Child Development,* 1979, *50,* 449-454.

Keats, J. A., Collis, K. F., & Halford, G. S. *Cognitive development: Research based on a neoPiagetian approach.* Chichester, England: Wiley, 1978.

Klahr, D., & Wallace, J. G. *Cognitive development: An information-processing view.* Hillsdale, N.J.: Lawrence Erlbaum Associates, 1976.

Mischel, W. *Personality and assessment.* New York: Wiley, 1968.

Mischel, W. On the future of personality measurement. *American Psychologist,* 1977, *32,* 246-254.

Neches, R., & Hayes, J. R. *Progress towards a taxonomy of strategy transformations.* Unpublished manuscript, Carnegie-Mellon University, 1977.

Newport, E. L. Contraints on structure: Evidence from American Sign Language and language learning. In A. Collins (Ed.), *Minnesota Symposium on Child Psychology* (Vol. 14). Hillsdale, N.J.: Lawrence Erlbaum Associates, 1981.

Nisbett, R., & Ross, L. *Human inference: Strategies and shortcomings of social judgment.* Englewood Cliffs, N.J.: Prentice-Hall, 1980.

Osherson, D. N. *Logical abilities in children* (Vols. 1 & 2). Hillsdale, N.J.: Lawrence Erlbaum Associates, 1974.

Piaget, J. *Structuralism.* New York: Basic Books, 1970.

Piaget, J. Intellectual evolution from adolescence to adulthood. *Human Development,* 1972, *15,* 1-12.

Rest, J. R. *Development in judging moral issues.* Minneapolis: University of Minnesota Press, 1979.

Roberge, J. J., & Flexer, B. K. Further examination of formal operational reasoning abilities. *Child Development,* 1979, *50,* 478-484.

Ross, L. The "intuitive scientist" formulation and its developmental implications. In J. H. Flavell & L. Ross (Eds.), *Social cognitive development: Frontiers and possible futures.* New York: Cambridge University Press, 1981.

Schneider, D. J., Hastorf, A. H., & Ellsworth, P. C. *Person perception* (2nd ed.). Reading, Mass.: Addison-Wesley, 1979.

Selman, R. L. *The growth of interpersonal understanding: Developmental and clinical analyses.* New York: Academic Press, in press.

Shaklee, H. Bounded rationality and cognitive development: Upper limits on growth. *Cognitive Psychology,* 1979, *11,* 327-345.

Siegler, R. S. Children's thinking: The search for limits. In G. J. Whitehurst & B. J. Zimmerman (Eds.), *The functions of language and cognition.* New York: Academic Press, 1979.

Siegler, R. S. Developmental sequences within and between concepts. *Monographs of the Society for Research in Child Development,* in press.

Siegler, R. S., & Klahr, D. *When do children learn: The relationship between existing knowledge and the acquisition of new knowledge.* Unpublished manuscript, Carnegie-Mellon University, 1979.

Simon, H. A. Cognitive science: The newest science of the artificial. *Cognitive Science*, 1980, *4*, 33-46.

Smedslund, J. Piaget's psychology in practice. *British Journal of Educational Psychology*, 1977, *47*, 1-6.

Snyder, M. Self-monitoring of expressive behavior. *Journal of Personality and Social Psychology*, 1974, *30*, 526-537.

Sternberg, R. J. *Components of human intelligence*. (NR 150-412 ONR Technical Report No. 19.) New Haven: Department of Psychology, Yale University, 1979.

Toulmin, S. *Human understanding* (Vol. 2). In preparation.

Trabasso, T., Isen, A. M., Dolecki, P., McLanahan, A. G., Riley, C. A., & Tucker, T. How do children solve class-inclusion problems? In R. S. Siegler (Ed.), *Children's thinking: What develops?* Hillsdale, N.J.: Lawrence Erlbaum Associates, 1978.

Turiel, E. The development of concepts of social structure: Social convention. In J. Glick & A. Clarke-Stewart (Eds.), *The development of social understanding*. New York: Gardner, 1978.

Turiel, E. Domains and categories in social cognitive development. In W. F. Overton (Ed.), *The relationship between social and cognitive development*. Hillsdale, N.J.: Lawrence Erlbaum Associates, in press.

Wason, P. C., & Johnson-Laird, P. N. *Psychology of reasoning: Structure and content*. Cambridge, Mass.: Harvard University Press, 1972.

Watson, M., & Fischer, K. W. A developmental sequence of agent use in late infancy. *Child Development*, 1977, *48*, 828-836.

Watson, M. W., & Fischer, K. W. Development of social roles in elicited and spontaneous behavior during the preschool years. *Developmental Psychology*, 1980, *16*, 483-494.

Werner, H. Process and achievement. *Harvard Educational Review*, 1937, *7*, 353-368.

Werner, H. *Comparative psychology of mental development* (rev. ed.). New York: Follett, 1948.

Wohlwill, J. H. *The study of behavioral development*. New York: Academic Press, 1973.

Comparative and Psychobiological Perspectives on Development

2

Seymour Levine
Stanford University

This chapter undertakes a necessary, but difficult task. It seeks to examine the conceptual and theoretical assumptions that define developmental psychobiology, and, further, to examine the contribution of the developmental psychobiologist to understanding the ontogeny of behavior. As a research area, developmental psychobiology has never been formalized; it does not consist of a specific theory, nor is it a specific discipline in the sense that it has a single focus of study. In fact, what makes it difficult to evaluate the contributions of developmental psychobiology to the understanding of behavioral development is that it does cover an enormous range of content areas. In spite of these problems, there is one very basic assumption that underlies the biological approach to behavioral development; that is, that an understanding of behavioral development is not possible without a fuller understanding of the functional and structural aspects of the organism's physiology.

Perhaps the best single definition of the approach that characterizes developmental psychobiology is given by Cairns (1979) when he states that

> there is a need to consider the organism and its behavior as a whole, not as a functioning gene machine that is made up of confederations of genetic elements nor as a discrete social entity that serves an assigned role for society. According to the orientation of the developmental psychobiologist, behavior is appropriately viewed as an integral function of the biological-social system; hence, the key to understanding development lies in understanding how biological, interactional, and social components become fused during the course of ontogeny [p. 321–322].

Although this statement, which represents what Cairns has labeled "holistic theory," is eloquent in its simplicity, it does place an enormous burden on the

29

developmental psychobiologist. All features of biological development become essential for understanding how behavioral development occurs, and, further, an appreciation of many aspects of the environment is also essential to understand how behavioral development unfolds. Thus, the developmental psychobiologist is forced to view the organism and its environment as an interacting system in which, in order to understand development, all aspects of the system must eventually come under scrutiny. Because of its insistence that behavior can only be viewed as one component of an organismic system, the burden is placed upon the developmental psychobiologist to be, of necessity, interdisciplinary. The developmental psychobiologist can be no less attentive to subtleties in the environmental dynamics in which the living organism develops than he can avoid being cognizant of the importance of the neurobiological substrates underlying the expression of behaviors.

Although, as we stated earlier, developmental psychobiology is not in itself a theory, it does contain certain very specific guiding principles. A most thoughtful analysis of these principles and the most formalized statement of them has been presented by Cairns in his chapter entitled "The Psychobiological Foundations of Social Development." Although these are entitled Guiding Principles, they do indeed contain within them some of the basic concepts of development that underlie developmental psychobiology. To quote Cairns (1979), the psychobiological orientation can be described by the following six principles:

1. Behavior, whether social or nonsocial, is appropriately viewed in terms of an organized system and its explanation requires a holistic analysis.

2. The system of which behavior is a part is not merely organismic but for some functions, particularly social behavior, it must be expanded to include the acts of other organisms and the reciprocal relationships that are formed with them. Bidirectional and feedback effects can potentially occur across several levels. Behavior development is probabilistic, not fixed by genes or by early experience.

3. There is a continuity in development, such that the organization at one stage provides the basis for organization at the next succeeding stage. This does not mean, however, that all processes persist throughout life, nor does it mean that behaviors must remain stable across stages. On the contrary, development is essentially a dynamic process that promotes reorganization and adaptation across time.

4. The need for multiple levels of analysis—this need is a direct corollary to the assumption that there are interlocked systems associated with the control of behavior, from neurobiological events to sociocultural events. The investigator must be prepared to operate simultaneously on different levels of analysis in order to achieve an adequate account of behavioral phenomena.

5. Comparison across species, or across time, requires polythetic analysis—(attention to the dissimilarities as well as the similarities of the function that a given pattern plays in social organization of which it is a part).

6. The organism is continuously adaptive and active throughout the course of development, not merely in its early stages. Hence, development continues to be bidirectional and probabilistic throughout the lifespan [pp. 325-326].

Perhaps the best way to illustrate these principles and how they operate within the framework of an experimental program that is psychobiological in its orientation is to take a specific problem and show how it is attacked utilizing the theoretical tenets of developmental psychobiology. During the last decade, our laboratory has been involved in an extended psychobiological analysis of mother–infant relationships. This program has studied several species and has included both biological and behavioral analysis. It seems appropriate, therefore, to use this as an illustration, although a number of other problem areas could clearly have served just as effectively. For example, the psychobiological approach to understanding sex differences has resulted in major changes in the understanding of the development of gender roles (Harris, 1964). Similarly, understanding the influence of early malnutrition on development has profited enormously by using a psychobiological approach (Levine & Wiener, 1975). The mother–infant studies do, however, illustrate dramatically the importance of multiple levels of analysis and how the utilization of this approach provides information that is almost impossible to achieve by any single-method approach to the study of mother–infant relationships. Further, the very nature of mother–infant relationships is interactional. The mammalian infant is not only profoundly influenced by its social, physical, and biological world, but the concept of the passive infant organism is dramatically changing, and there is a growing body of information (Lewis & Rosenblum, 1974) that indicates that the infant, in turn, influences its world. One of the primary functions of the infant is to modify the behavior of the caregiver, and although the method by which the infant manipulates its environment is species-specific, the absence of the ability of the organism to deal effectively with an interactional system does have profound long-term consequences.

It is important to note that there are some problem areas that have concerned psychologists for many years that have proven to be more amenable to study using biological variables than studying the organism's behavior. In particular, the measurement of states such as fear, anxiety, stress, and arousal have been behaviorally elusive. It is not surprising, therefore, that the psychobiologist and psychophysiologist have emphasized the use of biological measures as the dependent variables that are most suitable for measuring changes in state. In a recent paper (Hennessy & Levine, 1979, pp. 133-178), we proposed that the pituitary–adrenal system is part of the arousal system and may prove to be an extremely reliable and sensitive measure of arousal, in addition to its more traditional use as a measure of stress. Arousal encompasses a wider range of independent and dependent variables. Stress refers primarily to the effects of tissue damage, painful stimulation, and toxins upon certain physiological organ systems. Arousal, on the other hand, deals with the effects of: (1) psychophysical stimulus variables; (2) the psychobiological aspects of the gratification of needs and the withdrawal from irritants (ecological variables); and (3) the collative variables (requiring comparison) of novelty, uncertainty, and conflict (Berlyne, 1960). Stimulators of arousal are measured in behavioral as well as physiological terms. The concept of stress, then, might be subsumed under the umbrella of arousal theory. For example, most of Selye's stressors are aversive and produce behavioral consequences in that animals can learn to avoid these events, including the illness associated with the administration of toxins (Garcia, Hankins, & Rusiniak, 1974). Further, both stress and arousal can be considered as representing "state" phenomena.

A distinction has been drawn between stimulus response (S-R) or motor systems with direct pathways through the brain, and "state" or arousal systems with diffuse central nervous system connections (Berlyne, 1960). This proposition was originally derived from the studies of response plasticity within S-R systems. When a motor response is evoked, both S-R and arousal systems are activated. These two types of systems are independent, yet interaction is possible. For example, arousal systems tend to contribute to the vigor of skeletal motor responses. Because S-R and arousal systems may be subject to the effects of different parameters of stimulation, dissociation between the two are possible. In fact, dissociations between the traditional measures of behavioral arousal and the physiological measures by which we infer the state of arousal frequently occur, and a number of examples of this dissociation appear throughout this chapter. The initial reaction on the part of the behaviorally oriented psychologists is that if behavior and physiological responses are dissociated, how does one then interpret the physiological responses? Dissociation is, however, a biological fact and the two-process model of Groves and Thompson (1970) would not only effectively handle the neurological basis for this dissociation but actually predict that under certain circumstances the more diffuse physiological arousal systems would be activated, whereas no apparent response should occur in the motor systems. Certain behavioral responses, as we hope to demonstrate, are very situationally specific, whereas the physiological response appears to be more diffuse and more capable of being activated under a variety of environmental changes.

RODENT STUDIES

Our initial concern with mother-infant interactions and, more specifically, our concern with the influence of the infant stimuli on the mother derive from three somewhat independent areas of investigation. Firstly, the most accepted theory to account for the long-term effects that infantile stimulation has upon the subsequent psychophysiological function of adult rodents is that manipulating the infant in the laboratory environment alters the nature of the mother-infant relationship, and that the changes in the mother's behavior have long-term consequences for the developing infant (Smotherman, Wiener, Mendoza, & Levine, 1976, pp. 5–25). Secondly, in our studies on malnutrition, one of the major effects of early malnutrition in rodents is a marked disturbance in the normal patterns of the mother–infant relationship. A third series of studies, which more directly relates to the series of studies we are going to describe, investigated the reactivity of lactating mother rats to disturbance and stress (Stern & Levine, 1974).

It was observed in these studies that the lactating rat shows what we have termed a "buffered" response to environmental change. In a variety of conditions, lactating females demonstrated a marked reduction in pituitary–adrenal responses when compared to nonlactating animals exposed to the same conditions. Reduction (altered tonicity) in pituitary–adrenal activity under conditions of stress as a consequence of lactation, therefore, minimizes the physiological response to stress. However, the lactating mother shows a selective responsiveness to cues from her pups. When an infant is separated from the mother, the infant shows a marked increase in ultrasonic vocalizations. Further increases in vocalizations can be induced when the infant rat is handled, shocked, or exposed to cold during separation (Bell, Nitschke, Bell, & Zachman, 1974). The more intense the stimuli that the infant is exposed to, the more vigorous the vocalizations appear to be. These ultrasonic vocalizations are extremely important in eliciting maternal behavior, and retrieval on the part of the lactating female rat is induced by these ultrasonic vocalizations. Thus, we are faced with a paradox— that the lactating rat appears to be less sensitive to environmental stimuli with regard to induction of the pituitary–adrenal activity but appears to be more sensitive to pup-related stimuli. This leads to the conclusion that the lactating rat, although hyposensitive, may be selectively responsive to stimuli elicited by her pups. Such a system would be highly adaptive, because the primary function of the lactating female is to maximize those behavioral responses and physiological responses that would ensure the highest rate of survival.

Insofar as these experiments do require a period of separation of the infant from the mother, an experiment was designed to examine the effects of separation upon the pituitary–adrenal activity of lactating females. In this experiment (Smotherman, Wiener, Mendoza, & Levine, 1977), changes in the plasma levels of corticosterone were used to evaluate the response of lactating rats to the loss of their infants. Mothers on Day 7 and Day 14 of lactation were removed from the home cage for a 2-minute period. During this time, the pups were either removed prior to the return of the mother and the mother was returned to an empty cage (R condition), or the pups were undisturbed and the mother simply returned to her cage (C condition), thus serving as a control for the disturbance of handling. The mothers were then blood sampled 15, 30, 60, or 180 minutes later. Both mothers that were returned to an empty cage and those that were returned to their pups showed an initial elevation in steroids. The fact that there was no difference between groups R and C suggested that this elevation was due to the disturbance caused by removing the lactating female from her home cage. Separation from the young did not result in an additional increment in plasma corticosteroid levels.

In an extension of the separation experiment described previously, differentially treated litters were returned to their mothers following a 3-hour separation. Prior to return, pups were either mildly shocked or handled. The pups were returned to their mother in a wire mesh basket in order to prevent direct mother–infant interaction, thus allowing a determination of whether or not rat mothers are capable of discriminating the stimulus quality of their pups. Mothers were assigned to one of three experimental groups, depending on treatment prior to blood sampling: return of Handled Pups, Shocked Pups, or an empty basket (Basket Control). An additional group of mothers was blood sampled to determine corticosterone levels after the 3-hour period of separation. These procedures were conducted on postpartum Days 7 and 14 with mothers being tested under the same conditions on both days. Mothers were sampled immediately after the end of the separation period (to provide postseparation resting levels), 20 minutes after reunion with their litter, or after introduction of an empty basket.

The results of this experiment (Fig. 2.1) revealed that rat mothers do respond selectively to pup-produced cues, as shown by the difference between mothers in the basket control condition and those mothers who were returned handled pups. In addition, the rat mothers were capable of discriminating the state of their pups as evidenced by the greater corticosterone response when returned to shocked pups as compared to handled pups. This differential response to pup cues has also been demonstrated following brief separation (2 min) and reunion (Smotherman, Brown, & Levine, 1977).

Rosenblatt (1969) has demonstrated that patterns of maternal behavior change during the preweaning period: An initial phase of intense maternal behavior (i.e., during the first postpartum week), initiated primarily by the mother and cued by stimuli from the pups (Smotherman, Bell, Starzec, Elias, & Zachman, 1974), is followed in the third postpartum week by a period during which the pup initiates contact with the mother; the contact is controlled by stimuli emanating from the mother (Moltz & Leon, 1973). Furthermore, there exist ontogenetic changes in the cues (e.g., ultrasonic vocalizations) provided by the infant rat (Noirot, 1972; Okon, 1971). These cues, as stated previously, coordinate sequences of maternal behavior. In addition, the pituitary–adrenal responsiveness of the lactating female to stressors (Stern & Levine, 1974) varies as a function of the stage of her lactation.

For these reasons, we examined the ontogeny of the mother rat's differential pituitary–adrenal responsiveness to her pups (Smotherman, Mendoza, & Levine, 1977). Again, the separation–manipulation–reunion procedure was used with individual groups of mothers being exposed to their pups after the pups had been

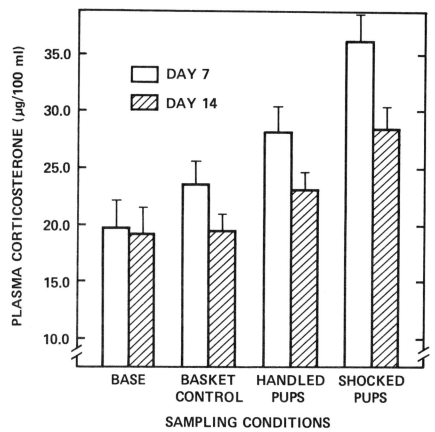

FIG. 2.1.   Mothers' plasma levels of corticosterone after reunion with handled or shocked pups or an empty basket. Pups were returned after 3 hr of separation and mothers were sampled 20 min after the reunion. Entries are means ($\pm$SEM); n's = 8 mothers per bar (Smotherman, Wiener, Mendoza & Levine, 1977).

handled or shocked. Mothers were tested with their litters twice during lactation, the second treatment 9 days after the first. Thus, each mother was tested on postpartum Days 2 and 11, 5 and 14, or 8 and 17 (Fig. 2.2). We found ontogenetic changes in the corticosterone response. Mothers showed equally high corticoid concentrations in response to shocked pups throughout lactation. However, on Days 2 and 5 of lactation, the amount of corticosterone released in response to handled pups was as great as the amount evidenced by females in response to shocked pups. Not until Day 8 of lactation did we see the differential responsiveness to handled and shocked pups that we observed in previous experiments. Early in lactation (during the first 5 postpartum days), mothers showed a maximal corticoid response to pups *independent* of which treatment the pups had

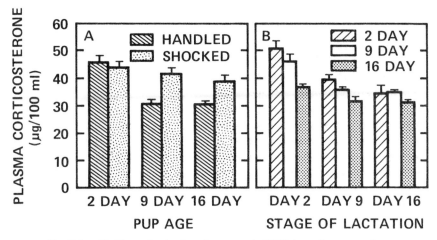

Fig. 2.2.   (A) Plasma levels of corticosterone (±SEM) in mothers exposed to
pups aged 2, 9, or 16 days that had been handled or shocked; (B) Plasma levels of
corticosterone (±SEM) collected at 3 stages of lactation (Days 2, 9, or 16) from
mothers exposed to pups aged 2, 9, or 16 days (Smotherman, Mendoza & Levine,
1977).

undergone. These data parallel closely the behavioral data (e.g., the initial stage
of the intense maternal responsiveness during the first week after parturition)
reported by Rosenblatt (1969).

Thus, we have observed that the lactating rat had what we have called a
buffered response to environmental change (stress). Under a variety of conditions, lactating females invariably demonstrate a marked and significant reduction in the pituitary–adrenal activity that is normal in nonlactating animals experiencing these conditions. The reduction in pituitary–adrenal activity is due to
various factors including a suppression of the secretion of corticotropin from the
pituitary (indicating a modulated central nervous system response to stress) and
reduced adrenal output that ensures in effect a reduction in the plasma concentration of corticoids during lactation. In contrast, we have demonstrated that the
lactating female is hypersensitive to stimuli emitted by her pups. The lactating
mother is more responsive than nonlactating females when the pups are disturbed, either by shocking or simply by handling.

Early in development, shock and handling are not differentiated by the
mother; and she responds equally to both of these conditions imposed on her
pups. However, later in development, she continues to respond vigorously in
terms of pituitary–adrenal activity to shocked pups but not to pups that are handled.
Possibly early in development, the pups emit equally strong signals regardless of the
treatment imposed on them, or, conversely, the mother is incapable at that time
of discriminating between different stimuli. It appears, therefore, that the buffering of the stress response provides a condition whereby the mother filters out

irrelevant stimuli that would normally arouse her. This allows her sensitivity to specific stimuli related to the pups to change. These stimuli now become more arousing and cause the mother to give greater attention to the offspring, particularly in conditions where her offspring are in distress, thereby ensuring the survival of more offspring in the litter.

Although we have demonstrated that the lactating rat is highly responsive to stimuli emitted by the pup, and that the rat emits highly organized and specific behavior patterns that are related to the caregiving function, there appear to be several major differences between certain aspects of rat maternal care as compared with those observed in primates and humans. In establishing the criteria for attachment, Ainsworth (1972, pp. 97-137) described three basic requirements: (1) an ability to recognize the object of attachment; (2) a preference for the attachment figure; and (3) a response to removal of the object of attachment. Although this chapter is not specifically directed to attachment theory per se, it is apparent that rodent mother–infant relationships are different from those observed in primates and humans in the sense that the rodent does not show these particular aspects of mother–infant relationships. The evidence suggests that neither recognition nor preference play a primary role in maternal behavior in the rat. Rat mothers indiscriminately retrieve and show maternal behavior to pups of any litter (Moltz, 1971, pp. 263-313). In addition, maternal behavior in rats can be indefinitely extended by continually replacing older pups with pups from another litter of a younger age (Rosenblatt, 1965, pp. 3-45). Although there are reports that indicate specificity of response of a given rat mother to her young in wild populations (Beach & Jaynes, 1956; King, 1939), if the maternal diet is held constant, the specificity of the response of mother to young, as well as young to mother, is no longer apparent (Leon, 1975). Moreover, although infant rats do respond to brief periods of separation from the mother, if the infant is provided with compensatory stimuli (e.g., warmth and contact) normally provided by the mother, the separation response is eliminated (Hofer, 1975).

PRIMATE STUDIES

The principle of polythetic (see Principle 5 earlier) analysis led directly into a series of studies examining the psychobiology of mother–infant relationships using a primate species that shows some of the characteristics of attachment relationships. The primate we chose to study was a small South American primate, the squirrel monkey. Squirrel monkey infants have been shown to be capable of recognizing their mothers when given a choice between mother and familiar or unfamiliar adult females (Kaplan & Schusterman, 1972; Rosenblum, 1968). Squirrel monkey mothers also show preference for their own infants over infants at a comparable stage of development (Rosenblum, 1968, pp. 207-233). In addition, as early as 4 weeks of age, surrogate-reared infants have been shown to be capable of discriminating their own surrogate from a perceptually identical clean surrogate (Kaplan & Russell, 1974). Both squirrel monkey mothers and infants, then, are capable of recognizing a specific member of the dyad as shown by the active preference shown when presented with a choice.

Because mother–infant interactions are species-specific, it is often difficult to compare the behaviors between these species in a meaningful way. However, it appeared likely that we could contrast the nature of mother–infant relationships in the rat with those of the squirrel monkey by assessing an equivalent biological response following similar experimental manipulations. The ability to compare species using a biological response, which although may be quantitatively different is qualitatively similar in terms of the stimuli that elicit it, is yet another case in point for the power of the psychobiological approach to the study of development. Thus, a technique is available for cross-species comparisons that is often difficult using behavioral responses that are species-specific. Before discussing the endocrine responses of infants and mothers to manipulations in the mother–infant relationship, I would like to describe some of the salient features of the mother–infant relationship in the squirrel monkey.

Infants are born in a precocious state after a gestation of approximately 160–170 days (Goss, Popejoy, Fusilier, & Smith, 1968, pp. 171–192). At birth, the infant climbs onto the mother's back with minimal assistance and remains continuously in contact with her until the onset of independent activities. Nursing is accomplished by the infant shifting to the mother's ventrum and rooting for the nipple, a technique that is usually mastered by the second day of life. As is the case in most primate species, the biological mother is typically the primary caregiver. The mother shows a specific recognition of her infant after the first day and will usually not accept another infant, although some females will transfer maternal caregiving following the death of their infants.

Infant selectivity does not develop as rapidly, but experimental tests indicate the ability of the infant to discriminate the maternal figure by several weeks (Kaplan & Russell, 1974). The rapid formation of a mother–infant bond appears to occur through the performance of caregiving behavior by the mother and the concomitant expression of behavioral reflexes on the part of the infant. These reflexes include clinging, rooting, and suckling and are initially expressed nonspecifically toward any object of appropriate stimulus characteristics, including claspability and warmth. The expression of the reflexes appears to be reinforcing, and, when directed repeatedly toward the same object, it becomes a specific focus of attachment.

The nature of the relationship in the squirrel monkey begins to change rapidly, however, as the developing infant becomes attracted to other aspects of the environment. After having been exclusively in ventral and dorsal contact with their mothers during the first weeks of life, the infants begin to make initial attempts to leave their mother at 1 month of age. Contact between mothers and infants declines sharply in the succeeding months and stabilizes at low levels at around 4-5 months of age. The time spent in suckling also drops after the first month; weaning efforts usually begin between 2.5 and 3.5 months of age and are completed between 6 and 7 months. The period between 3 and 5 months is the time of greatest instability in the mother–infant relationship because of the conflicting approach–leave tendencies in both members of the dyad. The mother that was retrieving her departing infant at 2-3 months of age is now removing the infant from her back. Similarly, at 2-3 months of age, the infant frequently attempts to return and reestablish contact during times of heightened distress, but later it regularly leaves the mother to investigate the physical or social environment. Of importance, however, is the observation that even older infants that are spending considerable time away from their mother will, when the environment changes dramatically (such as the appearance of a stranger or other disturbance) rapidly seek proximity and reestablish contact with the mother.

The most widely used technique for studying mother–infant relationships has been the response to separation. Both the behavioral and physiological responses of mothers and infants have been studied in response to the absence of either figure from the normal environment. The initial response to loss of the mother can be described as protest and involves agitated activity and distress vocalizations. Upon sustained separation, however, the infant's behavior may change from protest to a response that has been described as despair or depression, which is manifested by extremely low levels of activity, general lethargy, and apparent withdrawal from the environment. Although the protest reaction appears to be invariant, the depression response is dependent on conditions of separation (Mineka & Suomi, 1978). Depression is most likely to occur when the infant remains behind in the social group after the mother has been removed.

In almost all the research that has examined a response to separation, however, the primary emphasis has been on the behavioral responses of the infant. Yet, attachment theorists and other theorists who have dealt with mother–infant relationships have repeatedly pointed out that the mother–infant relationship is a system. We would therefore expect that the responses of the mother to separation should be as profound as the responses of the infant. Therefore, we have chosen in our laboratory to investigate the effects of separation on the endocrine response of both mother and infant squirrel monkeys. By using this different level of analysis, examining the hormonal responses, we proposed that we could demonstrate that separation was effective in eliciting a distress response in both members of the dyad.

Our initial experiment (Mendoza, Smotherman, Miner, Kaplan, & Levine, 1978) was designed to determine whether we could effectively use the endocrine response as a measure of disturbance in the mother–infant relationship. Thus, the pituitary–adrenal response in both mother and infant squirrel monkeys was examined after a brief separation. Each dyad was subjected to each of three experimental conditions. The first involves obtaining a base sample in which mother and infant were quickly removed from their home cage, separated, anesthetized immediately, and blood samples obtained. The second was a separation condition in which mother and infant were removed from the cage, the mother returned to her cage, and the infant placed in an identical holding cage in a different room. Thirty minutes following separation, mothers and infants were anesthetized and a blood sample again obtained. The third condition was designed as a control condition to assess the effects of disturbance without separation. For this condition (Separation–Reunion), the mother and infant were removed, separated, immediately reunited and returned to their home cage. Thirty minutes following this procedure, both mother and infant were anesthetized and blood sampled. A similar paradigm was used to evaluate the response to separation and reunion in surrogate-reared infants. These infants had been raised on inanimate surrogates beginning at 1 week of age. A complete description of this surrogate-rearing condition in squirrel monkeys is presented by Kaplan and Russell (1974). The results of this initial experiment were most encouraging and indicated that mothers, infants, and surrogate-reared infants respond to a brief separation with a substantial increase in plasma cortisol (Fig. 2.3).

In contrast to the rat, the predominant corticosteroid released from the squirrel monkey adrenal is cortisol. Further, the squirrel monkey, for reasons as yet unknown, appears to produce and release exceptionally high levels of circulating cortisol (Brown, Grota, Penney, & Reichlin, 1970). Values obtained in the Separation–Reunion conditions did not differ significantly from basal values in any of the three groups, suggesting that the pituitary–adrenal activation is a direct effect of separation and not a result of the disturbance involved in the separation procedure. The response of surrogate-reared infants following separation from their surrogates was not different from the response of normal infants following separation from their mothers and suggested initially that surrogate-reared infants develop a bond to the surrogate that is similar to that between normal infants and their own mothers. The cortisol response to separation, both in the mother and the infant, has proven to be highly reliable, and, in several studies that have now been performed, the mother and the infant both respond to separation with increased cortisol responses; however, as we indicate later, the behavioral responses to separation are extremely dependent on the specific conditions under which separation occurs.

It should be noted that in this initial study the infant was removed from its mother and placed in a novel environment, and, although the mother was clearly responding to the loss of her infant, it is difficult to assess whether the increased levels of plasma cortisol in the infants were a consequence of separation per se or confounded by an additional variable of novelty by being separated into a novel environment. Subsequently, we attempted to partition out the effects of separation from the effects of novelty (Coe, Mendoza, Smotherman, & Levine, 1978). In this experiment, mother and infant pairs living in a social group were tested under the standardized conditions utilized in our laboratory for studying the effects of separation. These conditions, as previously described, involved obtain-

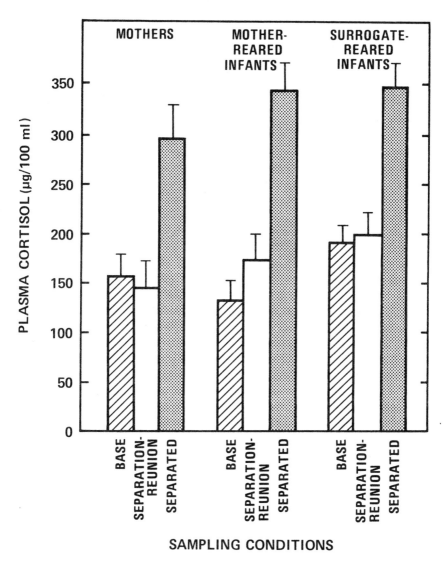

Fig. 2.3. Mean ($\pm$SE) plasma cortisol concentrations for mothers and infants for each experimental condition (Mendoza et al., 1978).

ing a basal sample, a separation sample, and a separation–reunion sample. However, for this experiment, two separation samples were obtained: (1) when the mother was removed, leaving the infant in the group; (2) when the infant was removed, leaving the mother in the group with her social partners. Under certain conditions, female squirrel monkeys that do not have infants will show maternal behavior in that they will permit the infants to ride dorsally and will frequently attempt to retrieve infants. This behavior is particularly prevalent in late pregnant females. In this particular group of monkeys, there was one late pregnant female who, when the mother was removed, aunted the separated infants. The infants, when aunted by the female, showed no sign of the usual protest behavior observed immediately following separation.

The results of this experiment indicated that, under all conditions of separation, both mother and infant showed an elevated cortisol response. However, this cortisol response was present in the infant whether or not behavioral agitation was expressed. The phenomenon of reduced behavioral agitation when an infant is with an aunt has been interpreted by Rosenblum (1972) as indicating that aunting reduces the effect of separation. This interpretation is indeed valid when one examines only the behavioral responses to separation. However, if one examines the physiological response to separation, it appears that the behavioral agitation is specific to conditions where the infant is either isolated or in a novel environment, but that the adrenal response to the loss of the mother appears to be independent of these environmental constraints affecting the behavior. In a more recent study (Vogt & Levine, unpublished data), we have also demonstrated that behavioral agitation, as manifested by increased vocalization and increased activity, was not present if social partners were available. However, once again removal of the mother did lead to an elevated cortisol response on the part of the infant. Thus, the behavioral response to loss of the mother is extremely dependent on the environmental conditions under which separation occurs, and the behavioral responses, particularly vocalization, appear to be more specifically related to isolation rather than to maternal loss.

Another example (Coe, Wiener, & Levine, unpublished data) of the dissociation between behavioral and physiological responses to separation was observed in an experiment in which we were evaluating the behavioral and hormonal responses to a separation of considerably longer duration than we had previously used. Mothers and infants were separated for 6 hours. The behavioral manifestations of distress were very marked during the first several hours following separation, but, by the sixth hour, the infants' distress vocalizations and agitated activity were considerably reduced. However, when one examined the hormonal response, adrenocortical secretion following 6 hours of separation was considerably higher than we had ever seen in infant squirrel monkeys. Thus, the hormonal response appeared to reflect progressively greater distress over time, whereas the behavioral response suggested a habituation. It appears as though the animal may be unable to sustain an intense behavioral response to separation, but it is quite capable of maintaining continued heightened pituitary–adrenal response (Fig. 2.4).

This is yet another example of the value of multiple levels of analysis. The behavior alone would lead us to conclude that the initial response to separation is one of distress and agitation, but eventually the animal learns to habituate to its surroundings and to separation. The hormonal response alone would have indicated that the animal was extremely responsive, and thus we would have con-

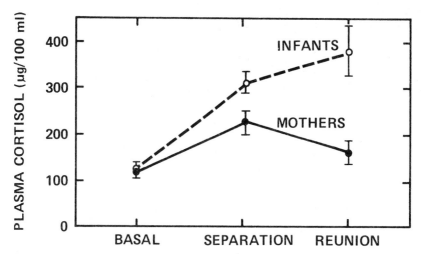

Fig. 2.4.   Mean (±SE) plasma cortisol concentrations for mothers and infants for each experimental condition (Levine et al., 1978).

cluded that the behavioral response might be increasing equally in intensity. However, with both sets of observations, we are able to conclude that the behavioral response does appear to have a finite time course, and that this does not necessarily represent a failure of the animal to continue to respond to prolonged separation.

Although thus far we have focused extensively on the effects of separation and the stress- or arousal-inducing consequences of separation, a finding embedded in this series of studies that appears to be even more informative in terms of the functional consequences of mother–infant relationships is not the effects that were observed under separation, but the results that were obtained under our Separation–Reunion condition. Recall that the Separation–Reunion condition involved removing the mother and infant, briefly separating them (which clearly seems to be disturbing in view of the distress vocalizations emitted by infant and mother), and immediately reuniting the pair and returning them to their home cage. Under these circumstances, we observed no change in plasma cortisol in either the mother or the infant, even though the procedure appeared overtly disturbing. These data were indeed surprising, because we had previously demonstrated (Mendoza et al., 1978) that removing a nonlactating female from her cage and immediately returning her to her home cage does lead to a significant elevation of plasma cortisol when measured 30 minutes later. Two hypotheses were proposed to account for these data. The first is that the mother and infant have the capacity to buffer each other from stress, and, therefore, the presence of the mother and the infant under some circumstances is the primary mechanism whereby the infant has the capacity to modulate its arousal levels. However, an alternate explanation of these data is that cortisol levels in both mother and infant

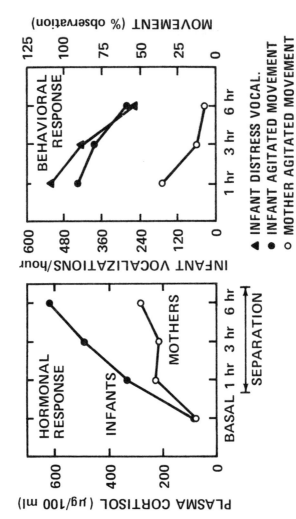

Fig. 2.5. Hormonal and behavioral responses during prolonged mother–infant separation (Levine & Coe, in press).

44

could have been significantly elevated initially but by 30 minutes may have returned to basal levels. Thus, the Separation–Reunion procedures may indeed constitute a stress; however, contact between mother and infant following immediate reunion could have reduced the extent of their response to the stressors and permit a return to basal levels by 30 minutes.

A study designed to evaluate this question (Levine, Coe, Smotherman, & Kaplan, 1978) indicated that the first hypothesis more accurately described the process. Blood samples were obtained from mothers and infants under the Separation–Reunion condition 5, 10, and 30 minutes after being reunited. Under no circumstances did the observed rises of plasma cortisol approach that seen under 30-minute separation. These data indicated that the mother and infant serve a mutual function to reduce the response to stress under the experimental circumstances used in this situation. Another aspect of this experiment also demonstrated a functional consequence of being reunited. Following 30 minutes of separation, when both mother and infant showed elevated cortisol levels, the infant was reunited with the mother, and 30 minutes later another blood sample was taken. These data indicated that the infants continued to show elevated cortisol levels as high as after 30-minute separation, but that the mother actually showed a reduction. These data were difficult to interpret until the results of the prolonged separation experiments were obtained. Although the infant does not appear to return to basal level as quickly following being reunited, it does not continue to show elevations that were observed following prolonged separation. The mother, in contrast, shows a significant drop, whereas following a prolonged separation she tends to maintain elevated levels. It therefore appears that even following a brief separation, being reunited can once again modulate and reduce the response that was observed as a consequence of separation (Fig. 2.5).

These data suggest that the nature of the mother–infant interaction leads to differential effects on each member of the dyad. The effects of reunion are more immediately observable in the mother following a 30-minute period of separation. It appears as though the mother's plasma cortisol returns to basal level during the period of time in which the infant is still showing a vigorous pituitary–adrenal response. This interpretation has some appeal from an ethological point of view, because it may be argued that the stability of the mother is essential in maintaining the mother–infant relationship. If the mother were to remain disturbed following reunion, her capacity to provide adequate care to the infant could indeed be impaired.

SURROGATE–INFANT STUDIES

These data on both the response to separation and the absence of response following the separation–reunion procedures are relevant not only to the understanding of mother–infant interactions but also lead to a specific set of hypotheses as to what are some of the major consequences of mother–infant relationships that lead to normal adaptive behavior in adulthood. We hypothesize that under conditions of stress, proximity and contact with the mother results in a modulation and reduction in infant arousal levels. Theories that are related to coping indicate that control is an important mechanism for reducing stress (Weinberg & Levine, 1980, pp. 39–59). Proximity-seeking behavior that results in arousal reduction can best be viewed within the context of coping. It therefore appears that for the infant the primary experience with coping occurs in the context of mother–infant interactions. Although the mother certainly imposes a degree of control over the infant's behavior, there is more and more evidence that indicates that the infant, by use of certain specific signals, is also capable of controlling its mother's behavior. The neonatal rodent emits very specific ultrasonic signals that lead to an increase in certain aspects of maternal behavior. Because the infant rodent is limited in its motoric capacity, it may therefore require a different set of stimuli that are capable of modifying the mother's behavior. In the primate, the more advanced motor development permits the infant to actively seek proximity and achieve contact in addition to emitting vocal signals that elicit both retrieval in the mother and proximity-seeking behavior on the part of the infant. Thus, the infant functions in a contingent environment in which it can control outcomes through the specific responses it emits. The infant very early in development learns to control its environment by developing contingent relationships between its responses and outcomes, which at this early stage of development normally involve modification of maternal behavior.

Seligman (1975) and Watson (1967) have also proposed that the infant is involved in a contingency analysis of the relationship between its responses and their outcomes. This particular hypothesis bears directly on the interpretation of the long-term consequences of surrogate rearing. The original paper by Harlow and Zimmerman (1959) disproved the hypothesis that rhesus infantile attachment was based solely on the pleasures of feeding. This experiment argued that the overriding factor in such attachment was contact comfort and was based on the finding that young monkeys formed a clear preference for cloth surrogates over wire surrogates, regardless of which surrogate was involved with feeding. However, all the evidence available appears to indicate that surrogate rearing results in long-term deficits in a whole variety of behavioral parameters. This information has been reviewed extensively by Sackett and Ruppenthal (1974, pp. 163–185). When one examines this data closely, what is apparent is that the infant appears to have a failure to deal with even subtle changes in the environment when reared on surrogates. A very elegant demonstration of this process was presented in an experiment by Sackett (1972). He demonstrated that when young rhesus monkeys are presented with a series of visual stimuli ranging from very complex to most simple, the mother-reared infants spent more time exploring the more complex stimuli. In contrast, surrogate-reared animals spent most of their time exploring the least complex of the stimuli.

If one examines the nature of the responses of the infant to the surrogate, one sees very clear differences between the surrogate-reared infant's response to its surrogate and loss of its surrogate when compared to the response of mother-reared infants. A recent experiment (Hennessy, Kaplan, Mendoza, Lowe, & Levine, 1979) indicates that, in contrast to mother-reared infants, the removal of the surrogate from the home cage resulted in a significant increase in behavioral agitation, but under no circumstances did the infant exhibit a change in plasma cortisol levels. The surrogate-reared infant squirrel monkey does have the capacity to show significant elevations of plasma cortisol when exposed to novelty but does not appear to show changes in plasma cortisol following removal of the surrogate from its home environment. Here again, we have an interesting dissociation between behavior and the physiological response. This dissociation is paradoxical to the dissociations we have reported upon previously. Here we have indications of behavioral distress with no indications of physiological arousal (Figs. 2.6 and 2.7).

Other investigators have also shown similar differences between mother and surrogate rearing. Using other physiological measures, Reite, Short, and Seiler (1978) found an increase in heart rate and body temperature compatible with a state of hyperarousal in separated group-living pigtail monkeys. When infant pigtail monkeys were reared on surrogate mothers, and the surrogate mothers were then removed, the changes in the physiological responses observed were quite different. These animals failed to show any of the physiological changes

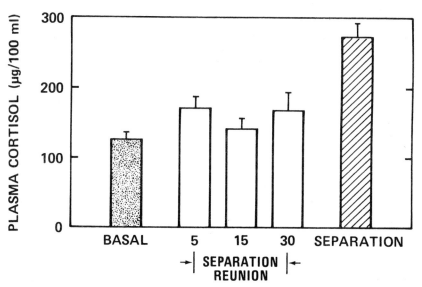

Fig. 2.6.   Mean (±SE) plasma cortisol values for each experimental condition (Levine et al., 1978).

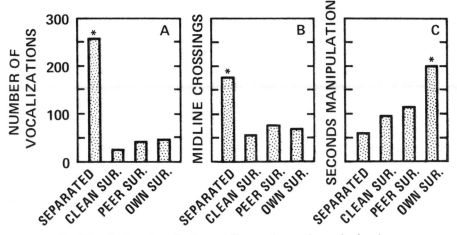

Fig. 2.7.   Number of vocalizations, midline crossings, and seconds of environmental manipulation by infants in experimental conditions (SUR = surrogate)
(Hennessy et al., 1979).

that were observed when mother-reared infant pigtails were separated from their
mothers.

There is another aspect of these separation studies that indicates a marked
difference between surrogate- and mother-reared infants. In the studies reported
on the surrogate-reared squirrel monkeys, a number of experimental conditions
were imposed following removal of the surrogate. These conditions were imposed in order to determine the specificity of the response of the infants reared on
surrogate cloth mothers. Thus, following removal of the surrogate, either the
infant was left alone, or on separate occasions one of a variety of surrogates was
placed in the cage—its own surrogate, a clean cloth surrogate, or a surrogate
from another infant. All these surrogates were capable of reducing behavioral
agitation in response to surrogate removal, although the presence of the strange
surrogate was not sufficient to reduce a plasma cortisol response in the
surrogate-reared infant (Fig. 2.8). In contrast, mother-reared infants, even when
in proximity to their mothers and not showing behavioral agitation, do show a
marked elevation of plasma cortisol when exposed to a stranger. This cortisol
response was present only in the infant, not in the mother (Vogt & Levine,
1980).

It is not of particular relevance in this discussion to worry the question as to
whether or not surrogate-reared infants become attached to their surrogate. There
is sufficient evidence that many aspects of the attachment process are present in
surrogate-reared infants. What is important is the major difference in the environment between the surrogate-reared and mother-reared infants. A number of
functions of the mother can be clearly provided by the surrogate (e.g., the

nurturant function and the contact comfort function). The one important aspect of mother–infant relationships that cannot be assumed by an inanimate object is the availability of contingent relationships. Contingency is important for two reasons: it shapes the acquisition of specific behaviors and it enables the child to develop a motive—the basis for future learning. The infant's belief that his actions can affect his environment is the main characteristic for this motive. Because the contingency between the infant's behavior and the mother's responses enables the infant to learn that his behavior has consequences, the mother's role is especially important (Lewis & Goldberg, 1969). Mason (1978, pp. 233–251), in discussing the difference between infant rhesus monkeys that were reared with stationary surrogates and infant rhesus monkeys raised with dogs, comments:

> I believe that the critical distinction between attachment figures in these experiments is the presence or absence of contingent stimulation. Stationary surrogates and hobby horses surely provide few opportunities for the developing individual to experience the fact that his behavior has effects on the environment and to learn that the events going on around him are amenable to his control. Inert mother substitutes make no demands, occasion no surprises, do not encourage the development of

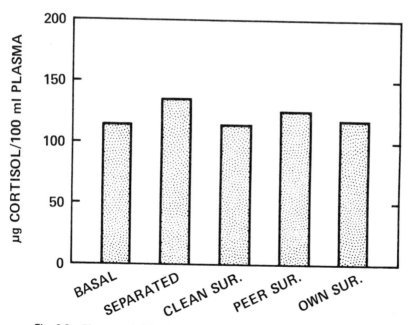

Fig. 2.8. Plasma cortisol levels of infant squirrel monkeys in each of five experimental conditions: *Basal; Separated; Clean Surrogate Substitute* (CLEAN SUR.); *Peer Surrogate Substitute* (PEER SUR.); *Own Surrogate* (OWN SUR.) (Hennessy et al., 1979).

attentional processes and the acquisition of simple instrumental behaviors that are the fabric of social interaction [p. 249].

That mothers are the prime source of contingent stimulation in the primate needs little elaboration. These early contingent relationships are required in order for the infant to learn certain cogent aspects of its environment that permit it to acquire adaptive coping responses. These early coping responses appear to be essential for normal infant development and also permit the infant to become an adaptive functioning adult as compared to surrogate-reared infants who show many behavioral aberrations as adults.

Although the differences between mother–infant relationships between rodents and primates has been emphasized, it is important to point out that there are also striking similarities. Both rodent and primate infants possess complex signaling mechanisms that permit the infant to influence the mother's behavior. The stimulus properties of these signals do elicit arousal as evidenced by an increased pituitary–adrenal response in the mother when these signals are emitted. Further, permitting the mother to interact with her infant reduces the signal production of the infant (Brown, Smotherman, & Levine, 1977) and reduces the level of maternal arousal. Although attachment is traditionally defined may be different in rodents and primates, both infants appear to be involved in a contingency analysis of the relationship between its responses and their outcomes.

CONCLUSION

In this chapter, three tasks were undertaken. Firstly, to describe and define the psychobiological approach to development and to attempt to specify the concepts of development that are inherent in the approach used by the psychobiologist. Secondly, to illustrate the use and power of the psychobiological approach in establishing new hypotheses in a specific content area, namely, mother–infant relationships. Thirdly, to describe a body of information on mother–infant relationships that have been derived by using psychobiological principles. If there is a problem in psychobiology, it is that the process is almost endless. The use of multiple levels of analysis invariably leads to other levels of analysis. We represented one level of analysis that utilizes the biological response—pituitary-adrenal activation—to answer certain psychological questions. In one sense this level is very simplistic; it leads to further levels of analysis that ask about neuroanatomical and neurochemical control of these hormonal responses, and how these systems are ultimately affected by the environmental context in which they develop. In spite of these difficulties, the basic assumption of the psychobiologist is that the key to understanding development lies in understanding how biological, experiential, environmental, and social components become fused during the course of development.

ACKNOWLEDGEMENTS

This research was supported by MH-23645 from NIMH, HD-02881 from NICH&HD, and Research Scientist Award MH-19936 from NIMH.

REFERENCES

Ainsworth, M. D. S. Attachment and dependency: A comparison. In J. L. Gewirtz (Ed.), *Attachment and dependency*. Washington, D.C.: V. H. Winston, 1972.

Beach, F. A., & Jaynes, J. Studies on maternal retrieving in rats. I. Recognition of young. *Journal of Mammalogy*, 1956, *37*, 177–180.

Bell, R. W., Nitschke, W., Bell, N. J., & Zachman, T. A. Early experience, ultrasonic vocalizations, and maternal responsiveness in rats. *Developmental Psychobiology*, 1974, *7*, 235–242.

Berlyne, D. E. *Conflict, arousal, and curiosity*. New York: McGraw-Hill, 1960.

Brown, C. P., Smotherman, W. P., & Levine, S. Interaction-induced reduction in differential maternal responsiveness: An effect of cue-reduction or behavior? *Developmental Psychobiology*, 1977, *10*, 273–280.

Brown, G. M., Grota, L. J., Penney, D. P., & Reichlin, S. Pituitary–adrenal function in the squirrel monkey. *Endocrinology*, 1970, *86*, 519–529.

Cairns, R. B. *Social development: The origins and plasticity of interchanges*. San Francisco: Freeman, 1979.

Coe, C. L., Mendoza, S. P., Smotherman, W. P., & Levine, S. Mother–infant attachment in the squirrel monkey: Adrenal response to separation. *Behavioral Biology*, 1978, *22*, 256–263.

Coe, C. L., Wiener, S. G., & Levine, S. Unpublished data.

Garcia, J., Hankins, W. G., & Rusiniak, K. W. Behavioral regulation of milieu interne in man and rat. *Science*, 1974, *185*, 824–831.

Goss, C. M., Popejoy II, L. T., Fusilier, J. L., & Smith, T. M. Observations on the relationship between embryological development, time of conception, and gestation. In L. A. Rosenblum & R. W. Cooper (Eds.), *The squirrel monkey*. New York: Academic Press, 1968.

Groves, P. M., & Thompson, R. F. Habituation: A dual process theory. *Psychological Review*, 1970, *77*, 419–450.

Harlow, H. F., & Zimmerman, R. R. Affectional responses in the infant monkey. *Science*, 1959, *130*, 421–432.

Harris, G. W. Sex hormones, brain development, and brain function. *Endocrinology*, 1964, *75*, 627–648.

Hennessy, J. W., & Levine, S. Stress, arousal, and the pituitary–adrenal system: A psychoneuroendocrine hypothesis. In J. Sprague & A. Epstein (Eds.), *Progress in psychobiology and physiological psychology* (Vol. 8). New York: Academic Press, 1979.

Hennessy, M. B., Kaplan, J. N., Mendoza, S. P., Lowe, E. L., & Levine, S. Separation distress and attachment in surrogate-reared squirrel monkeys. *Physiology and Behavior*, 1979, *23*, 1017–1023.

Hofer, M. A. Infant separation responses and the maternal role. *Biological Psychiatry*, 1975, *10*, 149–153.

Kaplan, J., & Russell, M. Olfactory recognition in the infant squirrel monkey. *Developmental Psychobiology*, 1974, *7*, 15–19.

Kaplan, J., & Schusterman, R. J. Social preferences of mother and infant squirrel monkeys following different rearing experiences. *Developmental Psychobiology*, 1972, *5*, 53–59.

King, H. D. Life processes in gray Norway rats during fourteen years in captivity. *American Anatomical Memoirs*, 1939, *17*, 1–72.

Leon, M. Dietary control of maternal pheromone in the lactating rat. *Physiology and Behavior*, 1975, *14*, 311-319.

Levine, S., & Coe, C. L. Social modulation of endocrine function. *Scientific American*, in press.

Levine, S., Coe, C. L., Smotherman, W. P., & Kaplan, J. N. Prolonged cortisol elevation in the infant squirrel monkey after reunion with mother. *Physiology and Behavior*, 1978, *20*, 7-10.

Levine, S., & Wiener, S. A critical analysis of data on malnutrition and behavioral deficits. *Advances in Pediatrics*, 1975, *22*, 113-136.

Lewis, M., & Goldberg, S. Perceptual-cognitive development in infancy: A generalized expectancy model as a function of the mother-infant interaction. *Merrill-Palmer Quarterly*, 1969, *15*, 81-100.

Lewis, M., & Rosenblum, L. A. (Eds.). *The effect of the infant on its caregiver*. New York: Wiley, 1974.

Mason, W. A. Social experience in primate cognitive development. In G. M. Burghardt & M. Bekoff (Eds.), *The development of behavior: Comparative and evolutionary aspects*. New York: Garland, 1978.

Mendoza, S. P., Smotherman, W. P., Miner, M. T., Kaplan, J., & Levine, S. Pituitary-adrenal response to separation in mother and infant squirrel monkeys. *Developmental Psychobiology*, 1978, *11*, 169-175.

Mineka, S., & Suomi, S. J. Social separation in monkeys. *Psychological Bulletin*, 1978, *85*, 1376-1400.

Moltz, H. The ontogeny of maternal behavior in some selected mammalian species. In H. Moltz (Ed.), *The ontogeny of vertebrate behavior*. New York: Academic Press, 1971.

Moltz, H., & Leon, M. Stimulus control of the maternal pheromone. *Physiology and Behavior*, 1973, *10*, 69-71.

Noirot, E. Ultrasounds and maternal behavior in small rodents. *Developmental Psychobiology*, 1972, *5*, 371-387.

Okon, E. E. The temperature relation of vocalizations in infant golden hamsters and Wistar rats. *Journal of Zoology*, 1971, *164*, 227-237.

Reite, M., Short, R., & Seiler, C. Physiological correlates of maternal separation in surrogate-reared infants: A study in altered attachment bonds. *Developmental Psychobiology*, 1978, *11*, 427-435.

Rosenblatt, J. S. The basis of synchrony in the behavioral interaction between the mother and her offspring in the laboratory rat. In B. M. Foss (Ed.), *Determinants of infant behaviour III*. London: Methuen, 1965.

Rosenblatt, J. S. The development of maternal responsiveness in the rat. *American Journal of Orthopsychiatry*, 1969, *39*, 36-56.

Rosenblum, L. A. Mother-infant relations and early behavioral development in the squirrel monkey. In L. A. Rosenblum & R. W. Cooper (Eds.), *The squirrel monkey*. New York: Academic Press, 1968.

Rosenblum, L. A. Sex and age differences in response to infant squirrel monkeys. *Brain, Behavior, and Evolution*, 1972, *5*, 30-40.

Sackett, G. P. Exploratory behavior of rhesus monkeys as a function of rearing experiences and sex. *Developmental Psychology*, 1972, *6*, 260-270.

Sackett, G. P., & Ruppenthal, G. C. Some factors influencing the attraction of adult female macaque monkeys to neonates. In M. Lewis & L. A. Rosenblum (Eds.), *The effect of the infant on its caregiver*. New York: Wiley, 1974.

Seligman, M. E. P. *Learned helplessness: On depression, development, and death*. San Francisco: W. H. Freeman, 1975.

Smotherman, W. P., Bell, R. W., Starzec, J., Elias, J., & Zachman, T. Maternal responses to infant vocalizations and olfactory cues in rats and mice. *Behavioral Biology*, 1974, *12*, 55-56.

Smotherman, W. P., Brown, C. P., & Levine, S. Maternal responsiveness following differential pup treatment and mother–pup interactions. *Hormones and Behavior,* 1977, *8,* 242–253.

Smotherman, W. P., Mendoza, S. P., & Levine, S. Ontogenetic changes in pup-elicited maternal pituitary–adrenal activity: Pup age and stage of lactation effects. *Developmental Psychobiology,* 1977, *10,* 365–371.

Smotherman, W. P., Wiener, S. G., Mendoza, S. P., & Levine, S. Pituitary–adrenal responsiveness of rat mothers to noxious stimuli and stimuli produced by rat pups. In K. Elliott & D. W. Fitzsimons (Eds.), *Breast-feeding and the mother,* Ciba Foundation Symposium 45. Amsterdam: Elsevier, 1976.

Smotherman, W. P., Wiener, S. G., Mendoza, S. P., & Levine, S. Maternal pituitary–adrenal responsiveness as a function of differential treatment of rat pups. *Developmental Psychobiology,* 1977, *10,* 113–122.

Stern, J. M., & Levine, S. Psychobiological aspects of lactation in rats. *Progress in Brain Research,* 1974, *41,* 433–444.

Vogt, J. L., & Levine, S. Response of mother and infant squirrel monkeys to separation and disturbance. *Physiology and Behavior,* 1980, *24,* 829–832.

Vogt, J. L., & Levine, S. Unpublished data.

Watson, J. B. Memory and "contingency analysis" in infant learning. *Merrill–Palmer Quarterly,* 1967, *17,* 139–152.

Weinberg, J., & Levine, S. Psychobiology of coping in animals: The effects of predictability. In S. Levine & H. Ursin (Eds.), *Coping and health.* New York: Plenum Press, 1980.

3

The Concept of Affordances in Development: The Renascence of Functionalism

Eleanor J. Gibson
Cornell University

It is a matter of common agreement among scientists that not many ideas are new. Physicists find new particles, evolutionary biologists and geneticists move toward new models of speciation and evolutionary change (Lewin, 1980), but the discoveries and new views always have a past. Still, over the decades or at least centuries, it appears to most of us that science progresses, sometimes in spurts and sometimes slowly, to new understandings. Often, this happens because a way of viewing the phenomena of some scientific discipline, once discarded as worn out and unproductive, appears in a new light; reclothed and fresh, its new vitality shows us the way out of traps in which our thinking had become stalled and stereotyped, allowing us to take a naive look at what we are trying to understand, unfettered by paradigms that had slowly taken the place of the original problems.

My chapter focuses on a concept that seems to me new and fresh, with great possibilities for offering insights into development. It is not a theory of development, but I think it has broad implications for one and that it is capable of generating hypotheses with consequences that can be tested experimentally. The concept is that of *affordance,* taken from a way of thinking about perception and the world to be perceived that was recently described by my husband, James Gibson, in his last book, *The Ecological Approach to Visual Perception.* This way of thinking has a past in the early flourishing of a peculiarly American psychology, the psychology of *functionalism,* as opposed to the structuralism characteristic of the British empiricists and many German psychologists, which found its ultimate elaboration and also its nadir in Titchener's laboratory. Functionalism died in the finally fossilized and unproductive blind alley of S–R theory. But its earlier beginnings tie in remarkably well with modern notions of ecology and the mutual, reciprocal relations of living creatures and their environments.

In the recent flurry of seeking one's roots, there have been many addresses titled ''Something-or-other Revisited.'' I am not talking about revisiting, in the sense of dragging an old idea out of a trunk and dusting it off. I see a possible new vitality, a new expression, a new set of implications, a new impetus for research in a new functionalism, and a radical departure from what I consider the current focus of structuralism (''construction'' theories). It seems appropriate to begin with the past and then move toward the future.

First, however, let me define the concept of affordance, best done in the words of James Gibson (1979):

> The *affordances* of the environment are what it *offers* the animal, what it *provides* or *furnishes*, either for good or ill. The verb *to afford* is found in the dictionary, but the noun *affordance* is not. I have made it up. I mean by it something that refers to both the environment and the animal in a way that no existing term does. It implies the complementarity of the animal and the environment. The antecedents of the term and the history of the concept will be treated later; for the present, let us consider examples of an affordance.
>
> If a terrestrial surface is nearly horizontal (instead of slanted), nearly flat (instead of convex or concave), and sufficiently extended (relative to the size of the animal) and if its substance is rigid (relative to the weight of the animal), then the surface *affords support*. It is a surface of support, and we call it a substratum, ground, or floor. It is stand-on-able, permitting an upright posture for quadrupeds and bipeds. It is therefore walk-on-able and run-over-able. It is not sink-into-able like a surface of water or a swamp, that is, for heavy terrestrial animals. Support for water bugs is different [p. 127].

The description just given sounds like a physical description, and so it is. But notice that it is also relative to the animal. The properties that define the affordance have unity only ''relative to the posture and behavior of the animal being considered.'' The mutuality of the affordances of the environment and the behavior of the animal is the essential thing. J. J. Gibson (1979) continues:

> An important fact about the affordances of the environment is that they are in a sense objective, real, and physical, unlike values and meanings, which are often supposed to be subjective, phenomenal, and mental. But, actually, an affordance is neither an objective property nor a subjective property; or it is both if you like. An affordance cuts across the dichotomy of subjective–objective and helps us to understand its inadequacy. It is equally a fact of the environment and a fact of behavior. It is both physical and psychical, yet neither. An affordance points both ways, to the environment and to the observer [p. 129].

Notice that the animal's behavior and perception are both involved here. The animal behaves in accordance with the affordances of the environment; and this depends on his perceiving them. We are at once concerned, as psychologists, with what he can do and also with what he can perceive. Acting appropriately implies perception of the affordances offered. As a developmental psychologist, a rather grand program immediately opens up before me: I need to find out what the environment offers in the way of affordances—how to describe them, what the appropriate behaviors are—and also whether and where they are perceived as affordances. As there are appropriate behaviors, I ask in my experiments on perception whether different affordances are differentiated by appropriate behaviors.

Perceiving an affordance implies perception that is meaningful, unitary, utilitarian, and continuous over time to the extent that environmental events that pertain to the observer may require. To what extent must young creatures (human or otherwise) learn to perceive them? And if they must learn, how is it done? One thing more I take from my husband's concept—affordances are not invented or read into events by the perceiver. They are there to be perceived. A lever affords facilitation of moving something, even in the case of a small child who is as yet ignorant of its utility. He simply does not perceive its affordance. A mailbox affords mailing a letter, even if it is red and cylindrical and called a "pillar box," and even if I do not know what it is or do not want to mail a letter. I do know that when I know what it affords, I perceive its affordance quite directly, as directly as I perceive its color. I come back to this later.

FUNCTIONALISM AND THE CONCEPT OF AFFORDANCE

The concept of "affordance" cannot be found in William James or John Dewey, but I believe that the underlying assumptions of a functional psychology are vastly extended by it. Functionalism,[1] as I have always thought of it, is closely tied to the doctrine of evolution, to the notion of the adaptation of a species to its environment, and to the mutuality of animal and environment. Early students of animal behavior, now dubbed ethologists (although we tend to connect that term with a German origin), illustrate this aspect of functionalism. They have been very interesting to me, especially Spalding (1875),[2] who was one of the earliest to exploit the method of controlled rearing for the study of what we can now call "perceived affordances." He wrote:

---

[1]In the course of refreshing my knowledge of the American functionalists, I reread the excellent chapter on functionalism by Edna Heidbreder (1933) and was pleased to note that she wrote this chapter at the University of Minnesota, where she was an associate professor at the time. I am glad to be in such good company.

[2]I am afraid that Spalding was British, but there were Americans of his kind; for example, Craig, and even Lashley and Watson in the early days when they studied the noddy and sooty terns.

Two years ago I shut up five unfledged swallows in a small box, not much larger than the nest from which they were taken. The little box, which had a wire front, was hung on the wall near the nest, and the young swallows were fed by their parents through the wires. In this confinement, where they could not even extend their wings, they were kept until after they were fully fledged. . . . On setting them free, No. 3 and No. 4 "never flew against anything, nor was there, in their avoiding objects, any appreciable difference between them and the old birds. No. 3 swept round the Wellingtonia, and No. 4 rose over the hedge, just as we see the old swallows doing every hour of the day. I have this summer verified these observations. Of two swallows I had similarly confined, one, on being set free, flew a yard or two close to the ground, rose in the direction of a beech tree, which it gracefully avoided; it was seen for a considerable time swerving round the beeches and performing magnificent evolutions in the air high above them [p. 187].

The "topographical significance" (James' term, *Principles*, Vol. 2, 1890, p. 406) of the layout with its affordance of paths for flight and obstacles to be avoided, was fully grasped by them at once.

A second, quite different aspect of functionalism was its denial of the structuralists' view that meaning must be sought in some form of compounding, such as adhesions of memories or associated feelings of pleasantness or unpleasantness. I like this statement from William James (1890):

The fundamental conceptions of psychology are practically very clear to us, but theoretically they are very confused, and one easily makes the obscurest assumptions in this science without realizing, until challenged, what internal difficulties they involve. When these assumptions have once established themselves (as they have a way of doing in our very descriptions of the phenomenal facts) it is almost impossible to get rid of them afterwards or to make any one see that they are not essential features of the subject. The only way to prevent this disaster is to scrutinize them beforehand and make them give an articulate account of themselves before letting them pass. One of the obscurest of the assumptions of which I speak is *the assumption that our mental states are composite in structure, made up of smaller states conjoined*. This hypothesis has outward advantages which make it almost irresistibly attractive to the intellect, and yet it is inwardly quite unintelligible. Of its unintelligibility, however, half the writers on psychology seem unaware [Vol. 1, p. 145].

James (1890) wrote explicitly, again and again, of the artificiality of sensations. "No one ever," he said, "had a simple sensation" (Vol. 1, p. 224). In the *Principles*, he starts with the "stream of thought," goes on to "consciousness of self," "attention," "discrimination and comparison," and so on, and only in the second volume takes up sensation, which he considered an abstraction. He said, rather inconsistently, that "pure sensations" are only realized in the earliest days of life. But even this "sensation" he supposed to have some kind of meaning (James, 1890):

The first sensation which an infant gets is for him the Universe.... In his dumb awakening to the consciousness of *something there,* a mere *this* as yet (or something for which even the term *this* would perhaps be too discriminative, and the intellectual acknowledgement of which would be better expressed by the bare interjection 'lo!'), the infant encounters an object in which (though it be given in a pure sensation) all the 'categories of understanding' are contained. *It has objectivity, unity, substantiality, causality, in the full sense in which any later object or system of objects has these things* [Vol. 2, p. 8].

Is there a kind of foreshadowing here of James Gibson's contention that affordances are perceived directly, without the intermediary of underlying constituent sensations?

Other, later, acknowledged functionalists criticized the atomism of the structuralists' approach, the best known of them Dewey and J. R. Angell. Dewey's criticism is especially interesting, because he did not limit himself to criticizing the analysis of mental content into elements of structure. In his classic paper, "The Reflex Arc Concept in Psychology" (1896), he stressed that he saw in the S–R distinction the beginnings of a new kind of atomism. And how right he was! The so-called Chicago school of functionalists for the most part eschewed consciousness as their subject matter, because they were interested in activities—process, not content—but it turned out that even a so-called process can be stalled and treated as a kind of element of structure. That was certainly true of S–R learning, which has only recently been revitalized with a functional look by the work of Garcia (1981) and his colleagues, who showed that what was conditioned to what was not an arbitrary matter but depended on species-selective constraints that fit an animal for living in its own ecological niche. I think we see another example of elementarism today in the so-called information-processing approach. The term *process* does not prevent it from having a curiously static look; the processes turn out to be mental structures with elements of content after all ("memory store," for example). Functionalism at Chicago dwindled away finally into studies of memory, retreating again to the laws of association (with Robinson and McGeoch). The nonsense syllable returned in force with all its deadening respectability, and the emphasis on utility that had been a prominent characteristic of functionalism was gone.

Utility was indeed a key principle of functionalism, deriving from the underlying assumptions of evolutionary theory and adaptation to an environment. Biological processes had a function in adapting a species to its environment, mental processes as well as bodily ones like digestion and respiration. They led to practical consequences and needed to be considered in terms of their function in attaining a goal. It was a tenet of Dewey's, especially, that psychological investigation should keep to the natural environment in which behavior occurred as much as possible, a tenet that suited his times and the American spirit of looking for practical applications very well.

With the concept of affordance, a functional psychology of perception becomes realizable, both comprehensible and experimentally feasible. Affordances relate the utility of things, events, and places to the needs of animals and their actions in fulfilling them; not merely their immediate desires, but the needs that arise in keeping them in touch with their environment and taking from it (or giving back) what is essential for the kind of life they lead. Affordances themselves are perceived and, in fact, are the essence of what we perceive. We do not perceive stimuli or retinal images or sensations or even just things; what we perceive are things that we can eat, or write with, or sit down on, or talk to.

One more tie-in with functionalism is a philosophical one—an emphasis on realism and the release from a mind–body dualism. The animal and his habitat are a unity of reciprocity, and activities like picking and assimilating and perceiving food are equal in their role of making the reciprocity possible. These exchanges are forward-going events, with continuity over changes, a reason for insisting on a dynamic and functional account of any psychological process, but particularly perceiving. Moreover, to account for the continuity of perceptions, one must provide an account of on-going information in the environment, itself having continuity, or the reciprocity of man and environment is lost. This is exactly what ecological optics[3] attempts to do. The "ambient optic array" and "optical transformations" are examples of concepts introduced for this purpose. Natural events occur over time, and they have affordances, as do places and other animals, that call for appropriate behavior. Both the affordances and the continuity are specified in the world. They may or may not be detected by the perceiver, but it is the same world that he exists in.

Carr, in an essay on functionalism in Murchison's *Psychologies of 1930* said: "There is no functional psychology; rather there are many functional psychologies" (p. 60). The tone of his essay implied that even then functional psychology was moribund, and Carr himself did not manage to infuse its spirit into the psychology of perceiving in his book on space perception. But its spirit—man acting in reciprocity with his environment, keeping in touch with a real world, and perceiving the utility of what that world offers—is present in the notion of affordance.

ANTECEDENTS OF THE CONCEPT OF AFFORDANCE

James Gibson pointed out that this concept had some fairly close antecedents in Gestalt psychology, which emphasized the perceived value of things. Koffka wrote (1935): "To primitive man each thing says what it is and what he ought to

---

[3] "Ecological optics" is James Gibson's formulation of information in the optic array and the way it specifies ongoing events in the world (Gibson, 1979).

do with it: A fruit says, 'Eat me'; water says 'Drink me'; thunder says 'Fear me'; and woman says 'Love me' [p. 7]." These things have what Koffka called "demand character." Lewin had another term, "Aufforderungscharakter," translated generally as "valences." These terms are certainly relatives of "affordance," but they are by no means the same. They were intended as subjective, phenomenal, the contributions of the observer. The notion of the complementarity of man and environment is not in them. But for Gibson (1979): "An affordance is not bestowed upon an object by a need of an observer and his act of perceiving it" (p. 139). He thought that the affordances of things for an observer are specified in stimulus information—a contention that I have been examining developmentally and experimentally.

Curiously enough, we find another related concept in the writing of a self-declared behaviorist, Edward Tolman, in what he called "behavior-supports." Behavior-supports were "characters in the environment required by behavior-acts in order that they may go off without disruption." They included discriminanda, manipulanda, and means–end relations. The definition of manipulanda by Tolman (1932) comes closest to affordance:

> Manipulanda are the characters of objects which support motor activity. They derive in character from the independent physical character of the environmental object and from the response-organ make-up of the given organism. They are such properties of environmental objects as lengths, widths, weights, resistances, solidities, fluidities, etc. But they are these properties defined not as such, and in themselves, but in terms of the range and refinements of manipulations which they will support in the given organism. They are stand-on-able-nesses, pick-up-able-nesses, sit-in-able-nesses, etc., etc. [p. 448].

Here is the reciprocity between the creature as an actor with a purpose and an environment that offers something to support his needs. I have sometimes thought of Tolman as carrying the banner of functionalism through the 30s and 40s though he never declared that he was doing so (as Hull, on the other hand, did).

Finally, I want to acknowledge a paper by one of my colleagues, T. A. Ryan, that I found, well-marked, in going through my husband's files (Ryan, 1938). It is a discussion of "dynamic, physiognomic, and other neglected properties of perceived objects." It is relevant because it emphasizes the immediacy of perception of such properties:

> Thus the weather is 'threatening' and a building is 'gloomy,' 'cheerful,' or 'forbidding.' Such dynamic properties as the use of an object may also be classed here. The dollar bill is an object with which I can pay, a book may be a 'weight to hold my papers down' and a hammer 'a thing for pounding' [p. 642].

Furthermore,

We have contended that the physiognomic characters may be directly inherent in the objects themselves and that they are not 'projected' any more than color and shape themselves are projected. All are properties of a single, unitary object or product [p. 648].

None of these predecessors carries the entire meaning of affordance, but each emphasizes some aspect of it.

EXAMPLES OF AFFORDANCE

Consider now what some important affordances might be. The environment of a living creature is described by Gibson as consisting of the medium, surfaces and their layout, and substances of which surfaces and objects in the layout are composed. All these have affordances, different ones in different combinations. Air, the medium we live in, affords breathing. It affords walking or driving through, and seeing through, at least in communities that are free of smog. Surfaces, if they are extended, flat, and rigid, afford support. If they are opaque and properly illuminated, they provide optical information for supportability. When they are upright, they may afford collision. Substances may be solid, rigid, and hard, or they may be liquid, elastic, soft, or deformable, all properties with characteristic affordances like strikability or manipulability or chewability. Objects have surfaces and are composed of substances. A detached object has a closed surface with characteristic texture, substance, and size. These properties, combined in innumerable ways, give objects typical affordances like grasp-ability. To be graspable, an object must be of a certain size and weight and rigidity. Objects may have many affordances as tools, affordances that we may or may not perceive. How we come to perceive the affordance of a tool is an interesting problem in the study of cognitive development. I have been able to find very little about it in our current developmental journals, but Köhler (1925) wrote about it in *The Mentality of Apes,* as you will remember from pictures of Sultan making a stick long enough to rake in a banana, climbing on some boxes to reach one, or vaulting in the air with a long pole as he seized his prize. The utility of the stick, the piled boxes, and the pole were clearly perceptible to him. Perception of causal relations generally seems to involve as a basis the perception of an affordance.

Places have affordances, like places to hide and places to swim, and places *not* to step over, like a cliff. Events have affordances, like an event affording imminent collision (e.g., the approach of a car or a missile hurled toward one). Sometimes the velocity, size, and path of the missile afford catching, and a ballplayer may be magically and wonderfully accurate in placing his hands in exactly the right place at the right time to meet it. He apparently perceives in the event the velocity and the trajectory of the missile directly and without calculation.

Other people have affordances of immensely varied kinds, and we acquire considerable skill in perceiving what another person's behavior or expressive gestures may afford. Man-made symbols like writing have affordances. A printed word affords reading, and there is information for its meaning that is perceived remarkably directly. If I tell you to name the color of the ink as you look at names of colors nonconcordant with the ink,[4] you will find it difficult, because the meaning of the word is perceived so quickly. The affordance of the word is obviously learned, in this case, so a very young viewer may or may not detect it, but the information is there, in the light.

THE DEVELOPMENTAL STUDY OF AFFORDANCES

Some affordances seem to be perceived, by some animals, without the necessity of learning of any kind. A newly hatched chick perceives the peckability of a bit of grain at once. Spalding's swallows perceived the open vistas for flight paths despite having been reared inside a small box. But as for human creatures, we know little or nothing about the development of perception of affordances. It has been fashionable for psychologists, in our recent past at least, to assume that all the meanings (in the sense of information for action) that I have been calling affordances must be learned through association with action, though there has been little agreement about how that might happen. Luckily, the present state of our technology for studying perceptual development in infancy is sufficient to permit us to pursue serious investigations of how perception of various affordances develops. The question I am asking is this: Where there is invariant information that specifies an object, a place, or an event, and that affords information for action, is the affordance detected by an infant? If so, when, and how does the perception of affordances develop? It makes sense to begin with affordances of events involving objects, surfaces, and properties like substance that seem to be pretty basic for the young human creature. The direct way of asking the question is to choose a significant event for display, in which invariant information for the environmental event can be specified, and to see whether appropriate behavior ensues. Does the infant act in accord with the specified consequences (in the sense that the final trajectory of the ball is specified for the catcher earlier in the transforming flight path)?

A less-direct way of asking my question is to look for appreciation of intermodal relations in an event. Affordances have intermodal consequences that

---

[4]The so-called "Stroop test."

imply *abstract* relations. Knowledge of these, if it can be demonstrated, seems to me to imply perceived meaning, not mere sensory processing of proximal stimuli. Evidence of this kind is more controversial, I admit.

My plan for the remainder of this chapter is to select from the research of the last 2 decades a few examples of the investigation of affordances in infants. Some of the research comes from my own laboratory, but at least as much from others.

The Affordance of a Surface of Support

About 20 years ago, Richard Walk and I devised an experimental setup that we dubbed (not very felicitously) a "visual cliff." We were set on investigating the detection of what we referred to as depth at an edge, and the method had two great advantages. The information for differentiating affordances (though it never occurred to us then to use that word) was easily specified, and the opportunity for behaving appropriately (or inappropriately) was available. The cliff offers, as I would now put it, information for a solid surface of support for the animal on the near side, but not the far. The two surfaces are specified by optical information for gradients of texture, and by transformations in the ambient array when the animal moves its head or locomotes. Perspective transformations of the patterned texture specify that the surface is rigid, and the depth of the dropped surface on the far side is specified by occlusion of texture under the edge between the two as the perceiver moves his head. Information supplied by disparity gradients may also be available.

The main thing is that there is information for a surface that is "walk-on-able," that can be stepped on or crawled on, on one side, but a place that does not afford support or affords falling off on the other. Precocial animals like chicks and baby goats have been shown to perceive these affordances at once, and so do rats that have been reared in the dark for an appreciable time. Human infants mostly perceive the affordance by the time they can locomote (crawl) on their own.

Whether human infants could perceive the depth at the edge before they were able to crawl was a moot question for some time. In an effort to answer it, Campos and his colleagues (Campos, Hiatt, Ramsay, Henderson, & Svejda, 1978) decided to use a different measure of the baby's responsiveness, the change in its heart rate when it was placed on a plexiglass surface and allowed to view a surface directly under it, affording support as compared with one 4½ feet below. The notion was that if the baby perceived danger when there was no underlying surface of support, its heart rate should accelerate as compared with the "safe" side, indicating an emotion of anxiety. Infants under 5 months gave no indication of an accelerated heart rate, but, in fact, there was a relative deceleration, a change that is generally thought to accompany rapt attention in infants. Indications of acceleration began to appear only after about 9 months, well after most infants respond appropriately in the cliff situation.

This disjunction of action and a presumed indicator of emotion underlines another aspect of affordances. They are *not* the attachment of feelings of pleasantness or unpleasantness to a perception. They are information for behavior that is of some potential utility to the animal. A road may afford crossing (if the lights are green), but it does not necessarily give one pleasure to observe this, especially if one does not wish to cross the road. I doubt that a mountain goat peering over a steep crag is afraid or charged up with any kind of emotion; he simply does not step off. Many people do become afraid of heights at some point, but this fear is probably learned long after motor patterns for responding appropriately to surfaces of support have developed. This point has been clarified recently in some elegant research by Rader and her colleagues (Rader, Bausano, & Richards, 1980).

Graspability and Palpability: Affordances of Objects

Objects and the substances they are made of have innumerable affordances, but one of the simplest ones to describe and to observe in an infant is graspability. An object of a certain size (not too big and not too small in relation to the infant's hands), not too far away for the length of the baby's arms, and having the property of substantiality—that is, more or less opaque and rigid—provides optical information in the ambient lighted array for graspability. Size, distance, and texture are optically specified in well-understood ways, as is opaqueness as contrasted with transparency. Optical information for rigidity is specified when slight movements of the object occur.

This information must be detected by an infant for an object's affordance of graspability to be observed. We can note that it has been when an infant reaches appropriately for an object and adjusts the shape of its hands during the reach so as to grasp it. There has been considerable research on reaching and grasping in recent years, with some disagreement as to the time of onset of successful reaching and grasping. But the evidence now is fairly conclusive that by 3 months or so, infants are not likely to reach toward an object that is too far away or not of a graspable size. Field (1977) tested infants at 2 and 5 months with objects of varied sizes at variable distances. At 2 months, infants distinguished objects that were too far away from ones within reach by appropriate arm adduction (even when the retinal image was held constant). But judgments of observers with respect to gradual adjustment were unreliable. At 5 months, however, there was evidence of adjusted reaching for objects at variable distances.

Bruner and Koslowski (1972) varied the size of objects presented to infants from 2½ to 5 months. Objects of graspable size were differentiated by different arm and hand movements by 3 months. Objects within reach but too large to grasp were approached with different hand and arm movements than ones of graspable size.

It is even more interesting to consider the affordance of a moving object. Infants are notoriously very interested in moving things and watch them attentively as neonates. But when are they perceived as something graspable, when the information for velocity and trajectory must be perceived, as well as that for size, substantiality, and so on? Fortunately, there is available some really remarkable research on the baby as a catcher by von Hofsten and Lindhagen (1979). They presented seated infants beginning about 14 weeks with an attractive moving object (a fishing lure). It was mounted on the end of a sort of boom that swung round on a pivot so that it came occasionally within the baby's reach. Infants successfully reached for and caught this object at about 18 weeks, the same time that they had mastered reaching for stationary ones. Von Hofsten (1980) later analyzed the infants' arm movements during reaching, over the period from 18 to 36 weeks of age. The movements improved in skill over this time, becoming more economical (fewer separate small movements) and more ballistic. But even at the beginning, the babies put a hand out to catch the object *not where it was seen at a given instant* but *where it would be,* predicting the object's trajectory. The information for this act is not easy to describe except in rather abstract mathematical terminology. Later on, some of the infants used a hand to trail the object and chase it, speeding up for the catch, but I am most impressed by the earliest reaction, being ready for the catch in the right place at the right time. Von Hofsten's (1980) results imply a basic human capacity to coordinate one's behavior temporally with external events, as he says: ''to foresee in one's actions future locations of moving objects [p. 381].'' The timing consideration is overwhelming proof, it seems to me, of a perceived affordance.

Objects not only afford (or do not afford) grasping; They afford activities having to do with variable properties of the substance they are made of, properties discoverable by palpating but also potentially visible when the object is moved or palpated in appropriate ways. Of course, surfaces have substantial properties too, even when they are not surfaces of detached objects. Some substances afford walking on or pounding with or being pounded; others afford drinking or bathing; and others afford squeezing and all kinds of contact comfort. We refer to them by such terms as ''rigid,'' ''fluid,'' ''elastic,'' or ''spongy.'' Information for perceiving these substances visually, in particular the difference between rigid and elastic substances, is given only by motion. These are important properties of things at a very early age. The earliest activities of a baby include a lot of chewing and mouthing and, a little later, a lot of throwing and banging. I have been very interested in early differentiation of the affordance of rigid as contrasted with deformable, elastic substances and with some young colleagues have done a number of experiments on their detection (Gibson, Owsley, & Johnston, 1978; Gibson, Owsley, Walker, & Megaw-Nyce, 1979; Walker, Gibson, Owsley, Megaw-Nyce, & Bahrick, 1980).

The question addressed in the first of these experiments was whether an infant not only discriminates an object moving rigidly from a deforming object, but whether it perceives different rigid motions as having an invariant property, an abstract property of rigidity. We started out, in other words, looking for evidence of perception of invariant information for rigidity, which would have to be detected if the affordance of rigidity were to be detected. If it were, there was a good chance, we thought, that the affordance was perceived too, and in any case we were interested in whether infants detected the invariant as such.

Information for rigidity is specified in the perspective transformations projected by a moving rigid object. This information is constant over an event, because proportions and cross-ratios underlie the transformations, so that the flow of the optic array as the object (or the observer) moves does not destroy the structure beneath the flow. There is invariant information for both constant shape of the object and for its rigidity. To quote from a recent paper by Johansson, von Hofsten, and Jansson (1980):

> In the geometry specifying perspective transformations, i.e., projective geometry, metrics has no meaning. Instead certain relations, the socalled projective properties, which remain invariant under perspective transformations of a figure, are abstracted. One sample of such an invariance under form change is the cross ratio between sets of elements (points) along a straight line. When the line is rotated relative to the eye (either by locomotion of the perceiver or by motion of the object), the metric distances of the projection of any four points on a picture plane (representing the retina) of course will change very much. The cross ratio between these points on any such projection will remain constant, thus carrying mathematical information about the *constant* distances of the moving line [p. 31].

To test our hypothesis that an infant detected invariant information for rigidity when watching the movements of a rigid object, we habituated infants to three different rigid motions of an object (a circular spotted disc made of foam rubber). The rigid motions displayed were rotation in depth around the vertical axis, rotation in depth around the horizontal axis, rotation in the frontal plane, and translation in depth on the axis perpendicular to the infant. All the motions were cyclic. After habituation, half the infants were presented with a fourth rigid motion of the same object, and half with a deforming motion (squeezing) of the same object. This was followed by the alternative motion in each case. If the infants detected invariant information for rigidity over the three rigid transformations, habituation should persist for the fourth, unhabituated one; but we expected that the infants should dishabituate or attend afresh to the deforming motion. They were given a preference test for the two types of motion before habituation. Looking time was the response measure throughout, and each infant set its own criterion for habituation. The infants in this first experiment were 5-months old.

The data (looking times) were transformed to log scores to normalize the distributions, and backward habituation curves were plotted to show the course of habituation and dishabituation. Figure 3.1 depicts the curve for infants who were shown a deformation following habituation, and then a fourth rigid motion. The curve for the group shown a fourth rigid motion first rose also when the deformation was presented. Dishabituation to the deforming motion was pronounced compared to presentation of any of the four rigid motions following habituation. So infants at 5 months not only discriminated a rigid motion from a deforming one; they perceived a property that was invariant over different rigid motions.

In our next experiment, we chose younger subjects (3 months). We repeated the habituation to several rigid motions and followed it with exposure to a new rigid motion, a deformation, or simply continued exposure to the already habituated rigid motions. But we also varied the shapes of the objects during habituation to see whether detection of rigid motion was invariant over shape change. The shapes (circles, triangles, and squares of spotted foam rubber) were changed from trial to trial. Despite changes in shape and forms of rigid motion, habituation occurred, and there was pronounced dishabituation for the deforming

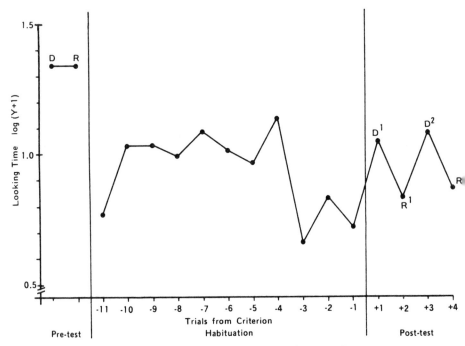

Fig. 3.1.   Backward habituation curves, pretests and posttests for groups presented with three rigid motions for habituation and either a new rigid motion (R) or a deformation (D) following habituation. Subjects were 5-month-old infants.

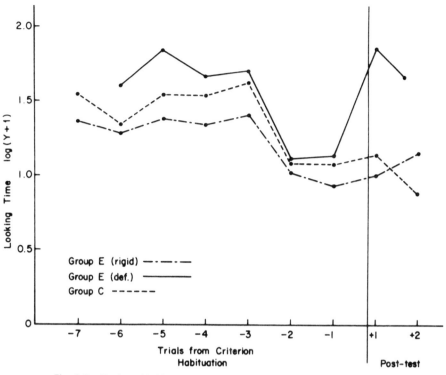

Group E (rigid) — · —— · —
Group E (def.) ————————
Group C — — — — —

Trials from Criterion
Habituation   Post-test

Fig. 3.2.   Backward habituation curves and posttests for groups presented with two rigid motions and varied shapes for habituation, and with either a new rigid motion, a deformation, or no change following habituation. Subjects were 3-month-old infants.

motion, as Fig. 3.2 shows. The curve of looking time after habituation was the same for a new rigid motion as for the control group that continued to see the same motions.

Another experiment varied the rigid motions during habituation but did not vary the shape of the object at that time. Following habituation, however, the shape was changed (or not), although displaying the same rigid motions. The change in shape was noticed, as the curves in Fig. 3.3 shows. There was dishabituation following a shape change, but not when the shape was unchanged, so motions characteristic of rigid objects are perceived as having an invariant property at the same time that a change in shape is noticed.

We wondered whether deforming motions of the kind occurring when an elastic object is squeezed are also perceived as specifying an invariant property. Deforming motions are difficult to describe and classify in terms of optical information specifying some property (although there is new work on this problem by Mark, Todd, & Shaw, in press), but we could at least describe our family

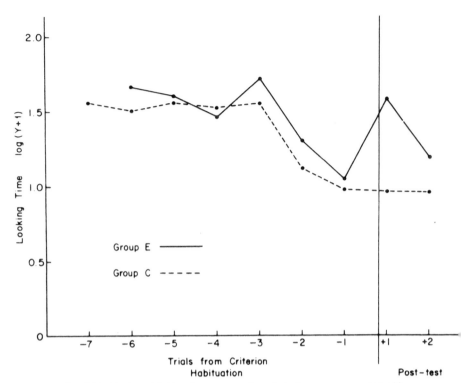

Fig. 3.3. Backward habituation curves and posttests for groups presented with different rigid motions and same shape for habituation, and with either a different shape or no change following habituation. Subjects were 3-month-old infants.

of deforming transformations objectively in terms of their production. Using one of our sponge rubber dappled objects, we produced (by applying pressure at specific spots for which finger holes were burned out) three deforming motions: a ripple, a horizontal fold, and a vertical fold. In other words, when force was applied at particular points, three quite different patterns of stretching were produced, giving different patterns of change in the optic array. These displacements did not maintain invariance of the surface structure.

In an experiment parallel to the previous ones, we habituated infants 3 months of age to two of these deforming motions. Following habituation, one group of infants was presented with a third deforming motion, one with a rigid motion of the same object, and one with a continuation of the two habituated deformations (control group). Figure 3.4 shows the curves of habituation and dishabituation. Dishabituation followed habituation when the rigid motion was presented, but not for the other two groups.

It seems reasonable to conclude that infants at this age are indeed extracting the information in the ambient optic array that specifies invariants of rigidity and elasticity of substances. But one might ask (and people do) whether this is evidence enough that the affordances of rigid and elastic substances are perceived. Would the infants behave in some way that we would agree is appropriate in addition to differentiating them by looking behavior? To answer this question, we resorted to one of our two strategies for investigating affordances, the intermodal paradigm. Would the infants anticipate intermodal consequences?

Substances are best known by handling and palpating them and by watching them undergoing motions produced by handling and palpating. Babies also get haptic information about substance by mouthing. In any case, the information for substance is generally extracted haptically and visually (actually, there may be acoustic information for substance too, but I leave that for the present). With several colleagues, I have been trying for some time now to set up an experiment to find out whether infants anticipate intermodal consequences for rigid and elastic substances. The experiment turns out to be difficult to perform, because until they are about 12 months old, infants have very little skill in palpating and manipulating objects by hand and pay little attention to even the slight information they get this way. Furthermore, they are quite determined to see what they are handling. I can therefore report no tidy results as yet on this problem.

However, after numerous methodologically false starts, we have two experiments now underway that appear to be going to yield results of one kind or another. In one, with infants of 4 weeks, an object (either hard or spongy but of

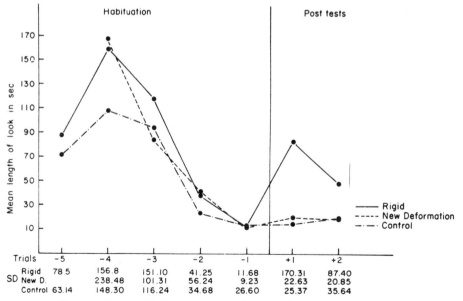

Fig. 3.4. Backward habituation curves and posttests for groups presented with two deforming motions for habituation, and with either a new deforming motion, a rigid motion, or no change following habituation. Subjects were 3-month-old infants.

the same surface texture, in either case) is inserted into the infant's mouth and shielded from sight while it is mouthed for 60 seconds. Following the mouthing, the infant is given a looking preference test. Two objects that look alike in shape and texture are displayed side by side, one moving rigidly and one in a deforming pattern. Will the infant show us, by a preferential pattern of looking, that he recognizes the one he has mouthed? I don't know yet.

In the second experiment, older infants (10 to 12 months of age) are seated on their mothers' laps in a totally dark room. A couple of objects of the same substance are placed on a table before them, detectable visually only by a spot of luminescent paint on each one. It is hoped that the baby will seize an object and manipulate it, possibly carrying it to his/her mouth as well. This behavior is videotaped in infrared light, and an experimenter watching the performance on a television screen in an adjoining room signals an on-the-spot experimenter when the infant has manipulated the object for 60 seconds. Then it is time for the second stage of the experiment. So far, we have tried only one condition, in which the experimenter substitutes on the table a new pair of objects, one like the old one and one of the other substance, and hopefully manipulation in the dark continues. When the babies pick up the new object, they do indeed handle it differently. Whether we can code the tapes so as to tell reliably that the baby recognizes one as new and one as old, I don't know, but perhaps that doesn't matter.

The other condition, following manipulation of only one substance in the dark, is visual. Without turning on the lights, two films of the object moving in characteristic patterns of rigid or deforming motion are back projected on a small screen in front of the infant, and preferential looking behavior is observed (the film provides enough light for the observers behind the screen to monitor looking). Will the babies look preferentially at the novel substance? Again, I don't know. If they do, I think it would be fair to say they have knowledge of intermodal consequences. I would like to do the experiment the other way round (visual presentation followed by haptic), but I am going to have to learn more about palpating behavior in infants first.

Obstacles and Passages: Affordances of Events

Actually, all the evidence we have reviewed so far for the perception of affordances of surfaces and objects depended on the occurrence of presentation of some kind of event, often one produced by the perceiver himself/herself. Affordances of substances, for example, can be detected visually only when the surface or the object is moved or subjected to pressure, and tactually only when they are manipulated in some way by the observer. Even detection of surfaces of support that can or cannot be walked on depends on information from events like looking around or changing one's position, if it is to be reliable and veridical. But there is one experimental situation, now much investigated, that has been recognized and studied as an event from the beginning; that is, the so-called "looming'' experiment, in which the perceived affordance is that of imminent collision. The information for this event was described by James Gibson 30 years ago, when he suggested that optical information for the spatial layout consisted of spatio–temporal flow fields, rather than a sequence of static retinal images (*Visual World,* 1950). In a paper on visually controlled locomotion (Gibson, 1958), he wrote:

> Approach to a solid surface is specified by a centrifugal flow of the texture of the optic array. Approach to an object is specified by a magnification of the closed contour in the array corresponding to the edges of the object. A *uniform* rate of approach is accompanied by an *accelerated* rate of magnification. At the theoretical point where the eye touches the object the latter will intercept a visual angle of 180°; the magnification reaches an explosive rate in the last moments before contact. This accelerated expansion in the field of view specifies imminent collision, and it is unquestionably an effective stimulus for behaviour in animals with well-developed visual systems. In man, it produces eye blinking and aversive movements of the head, even when the stimulus is a harmless magnification of a shadow on a translucent screen [p. 188].

In 1965, Schiff published a monograph describing research on looming with several species of animal (monkeys, fiddler crabs, frogs, chicks, kittens, and an occasional human). The loom was produced with a shadow cast on a screen, and the inverse transformation, a minification of the shadow, was used as a control. The subjects all demonstrated some form of avoidance behavior, however different their visual and response systems, to the flow pattern of accelerated magnification.

Some years later, several independent groups of researchers began to study the sensitivity of human infants to optical information for impending collision. Bower, Broughton, and Moore (1970) reported that very young infants responded with avoidance behavior that included head withdrawal, eye widening, and raising the hands between the object and the face. Both a real approaching object and a magnified shadow were displayed. Ball and Tronick (1971) reported similar behavior in 1-month-old infants with both types of display and compared the collision condition (symmetrical expansion) with an asymmetrical optical expansion pattern that provided information for a ''miss'' course. The infants in this case tracked the display to the side rather than exhibiting avoidance behavior. Hruska and Yonas (1971) monitored heart rate in infants (2- to 10-months old) shown a film of an object approaching or withdrawing. But a differential heart rate, showing acceleration to the collision display and not to withdrawal, occurred only with older infants after 8 months. Avoidance responses, in this case as well as the cliff, are apparently not necessarily accompanied by physiological indicators of fear or anxiety.

Since that time, a number of experiments using more refined response measures have been performed with looming displays, and careful longitudinal comparisons have been made (recently reviewed by Yonas, in press). Yonas' own experiments on sensitivity to optical information for collision have made particular use of blinking, a response that can be very reliably observed, and have been extended to the study of preterm and postterm infants, as well as full-term ones (Petterson, Yonas, and Fisch, 1980). The latter experiments provided evidence that maturation plays an important role in the development of the perceived affordance of optical information for impending collision. Defensive blinking to appropriate displays was advanced in postterm 6-week-old infants as compared with full-term infants at 6 weeks.

Now I would like to describe some research of my own (with John Carroll and James Ferwerda) that extends the usefulness of the concept of affordance in the analysis of how appropriate ways of acting develop in response to optical information about the layout of the environment. The paragraph I quoted from Gibson (1958) described the information for approach of an object as "magnification of the closed contour in the array corresponding to the edges of the object." But this is only part of the story. There are obstacles with which one may collide, but there are also paths that open up and afford locomotion through a passageway. In both cases, there are contours or edges, but the affordance for locomotion varies with the presence or absence of other information. Quoting Gibson (1958) again:

> In short, the lay of the land, the jumping-off places, the interspaces, barriers and obstacles, as well as the level stretches, are given by the geometry of the optic array. Depending on the locomotor capacities of the animal, this terrain provides definite possibilities or impossibilities for crawling, walking, climbing and the like. And if the animal can discriminate the textural variables it can discriminate among potential paths for locomotion. A potential path is a stretch of surface extending away from the animal which affords the kind of locomotion for which the animal is equipped. A barrier or obstacle is a surface which does not afford locomotion [p. 192].

This description emphasizes the role of textural variables, but Gibson had not yet combined this variable with information deriving from flow patterns produced as a creature moved forward along a path or toward an obstacle, or as an obstacle or a contour around an opening moved toward him/her. What is the optical information for approaching an opening that has to be steered through, as opposed to an obstacle with the same contours that will bar locomotion and afford collision? According to Gibson (1979), when an opening is to be entered, movement toward it is accompanied by "opening up of a vista," by "magnification or gain of structure inside the contour and not loss outside" (p. 234). As a barrier is approached (or an obstacle approaches one), it occludes more and more of the background structure until it is lost entirely at 180°.

Our experiment undertook to contrast these two situations with infants as subjects.[5] Do infants, before they achieve independent locomotion of any kind,

---

[5]This experiment is described in detail in a Final Report to the Spencer Foundation, which in part supported the research (Gibson, Carroll, & Ferwerda, 1980).

differentiate between a path ahead that provides an opening vista and might afford passage from an obstacle that progressively occludes more and more of the background structure, even as its own textured structure is magnified? To put it another way, if a rectangular contour is approaching or approached by an animal, when is it perceived as affording a barrier that makes stopping obligatory and when is it perceived as a vista, an opening or aperture that affords passing through? What is the information for the affordance in either case, and when is the affordance detected?

We chose to present the two situations in the form of something moving toward the infant, as is done in the looming experiment. An obstacle or an aperture of the same measurements was moved toward the stationary subject. The optical flow pattern of accelerated expansion of the contour as it approached is the same as if the infant approached it, and deletion or accretion of background structure would also be the same. The optical expansion pattern of the contour of the obstacle and of the aperture would be identical to one another. Panels providing an obstacle or an aperture condition were moved toward an infant in approach trials and were moved away in withdrawal trials. The infants' behavior was recorded on videotape, and pressure of the subject's head against a foam rubber headrest was measured. The subjects in this experiment were approximately 3 months old.

The infant sat at the rear of a booth surrounded by curtains on three sides, all textured with the same pattern. A flat table extended in front of the subject. At the far end of the booth could be placed either of two movable panels, both covered with the same textured material as the walls of the booth, so that, when flush with the rear wall, they covered it and tended to fade into it. Movement of either panel resulted in optical information for edges at the contours of the obstacle or the opening. The panels were supported on invisible carts that were moved toward or away from the subject by an unseen experimenter, at a constant velocity. A panel's approach trip began at the rear wall and ended just short of the infant's face. The movement of the panel lasted approximately 6 seconds.

Each infant took part in four conditions of the experiment: (1) 10 trials with the obstacle approaching (Obstacle Approach); (2) which were alternated with 10 trials with the obstacle withdrawing; and (3) 10 trials with the aperture approaching (Aperture Approach); (4) alternated with 10 trials with the aperture withdrawing. The order of the main condition (obstacle or aperture) was alternated from one subject to the next.

The results indicated that these infants definitely differentiated between the two approach conditions, although no infant cried or became alarmed as the obstacle approached (this finding agrees with all the more recent research on looming, which the obstacle condition resembled in its arrangements). The results of change in head pressure are especially interesting. We calculated a mean curve of head pressure change for every infant in all four conditions, and also a composite group curve for each of the four conditions. The group curves may be seen in Fig. 3.5. Approach trials in both main conditions are grossly different

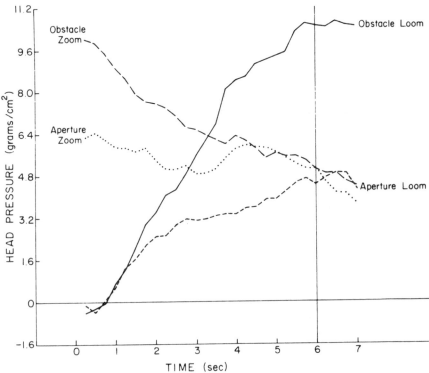

Fig. 3.5. Changes in head pressure as an obstacle or an aperture approached (loom) or withdrew (zoom). Subjects were 3-month-old infants.

from withdrawal trials, with positive slopes for approach (increasing pressure of the head against the headrest) and negative slopes for withdrawal, where the infants' postures relaxed and backward head pressure was released. However, curves for the two approach conditions differ from one another. Head pressure increases very rapidly in the "Obstacle Approach" condition, rising steeply until the cessation of the panel's movement. In the "Aperture Approach" condition, head pressure increases for the first 3 seconds of the panel's movement and then shows little change. Typically, infants in this condition seemed to track the top edge of the opening upward at first, but, as it came closer, they turned their heads toward a side of the opening.

Regression coefficients were calculated for the slopes of each of the four mean curves for all the individual infants, and these bear out the group trends. For example, the coefficient of the positive slope for "Obstacle Approach" is higher than for "Aperture Approach" for 12 of the 16 infants. In an analysis of variance performed on these coefficients, the effect of approach condition was significant (p = <.018), but the interaction of condition and order was not, so the two conditions differed no matter which came first.

Differences in head pressure are only part of the story, however. A much more complex pattern of behaviors differentiated the two approach conditions. The videotapes of each infant were analyzed and coded for a number of different behaviors. Behaviors that differed significantly and reliably in frequency of occurrence (more frequent for the obstacle's approach) were reaching toward the panel, excited movement, arms up, head turned to avoid, anticipation, frowning, and head withdrawal. Blinking came close to significance. Two behaviors, head turning to track and passive interest were noted significantly more often as the aperture approached. Reaching and touching were especially notable as the obstacle approached, frequently with pressure exerted on the surface of the obstacle. The beginning of the reach more often resembled the "placing" response of a kitten extending its forepaws as it is moved toward a surface, than a defensive response of hands raised before the face.

Altogether, the patterns of behavior and the differences appeared to be appropriate indicators of the affordances of the two situations, approach of an impassable surface or obstacle in one case and a vista or passageway in the other. Potential paths for and barriers to locomotion may be differentiated early in life, before self-initiated locomotion has begun.

Affordance of Expressive Behaviors of Another Person

The affordances I have considered are quite primitive ones, such as a surface of support, graspability of something, substances of things, and the contrasting affordances of barriers and passageways. But affordances of things and events can be much more complicated, especially when we enter the realm of social events and what other people afford. I believe it is useful to consider the information specified by other people's actions as providing potentially perceptible affordances, too, affordances that may or may not be detected, especially early in life. The facial and vocal expressions of another person frequently afford information to an adult perceiver about that person's intentions and probable actions in relation to him/her. It is beyond the scope of this chapter (and my ability) to describe in detail the information in another person's behavior that specifies affordances for nurturance and play, as contrasted with neglect or rough handling. But I would like to finish by summarizing briefly research performed by a young colleague, Arlene Walker (1980), on perceiving different affordances of the expressive behavior of another person. Her subjects were about 5 and 7 months old.

To study detection of different affordances in infants, she used the strategy of observing intermodal knowledge. Affordances of expressive behaviors are specified not only in the optic array but in the acoustic array as well. A sophisticated perceiver can detect them visually or aurally, but normally in both ways at once. There is invariant information, specified in both arrays. If infants detect the invariant information, they presumably know something abstract and amodal that we identify with the affordance. Like the experiments on detection of differences in substance, we need to ask first whether intermodal invariants are detected, and then whether they are responded to meaningfully and differentially.

Walker adopted the method of Spelke (1976, 1978, 1979) presenting two sound films side by side to her subjects and playing the sound track, centrally located between the two, of only one of them. The question is, whether the subjects show pick-up of the information common to one film and its accompanying sound by looking preferentially at the correct one. The infants' eye movements were monitored during exposure of the films, which lasted typically for 2 minutes. Babies heard and saw an episode with one sound track for 2 minutes, and then the sound track was changed to the one appropriate for the other film. A search procedure, after acquaintance with the films, was also used. Measures included preferential looking time, and where the infant looked first.

Walker filmed, in sound, episodes of a woman behaving in a very happy fashion, smiling, and speaking in "warm" and pleased tones; of the same woman behaving and speaking in a flat, neutral manner; of the woman behaving in a depressed, sad manner; and of the woman exhibiting angry behavior and vocal patterns.

I simply summarize the results of several experiments by saying that the infants preferred, in any pairing of the films, to look at the "happy" event. But when the filmed event was accompanied by the appropriate sound track, looking time to that film rose significantly even when the event was neutral, or sad, or angry. In short, infants even at 5 months show evidence of recognizing congruence of facial and vocal behaviors as part of a unified expressive event, presumably carrying invariant information about the affordance of the event.

What carries information for congruence of the seen and heard event? One candidate is synchrony of visually and aurally perceived aspects of the event. But is there anything more than synchrony? Walker presented 7-month-old infants with paired films accompanied by the sound track appropriate to one or the other but played out of synchrony with it. In everyday language, one might say that the "mood" of the vocal expression was appropriate for the facial expressions and movements depicted in one of the films, but the vocal recording was offset at some randomly chosen point. The infants appeared to be disturbed initially by the asynchrony (as an adult would be) and did a lot of looking back and forth. But eventually, they settled down to looking longer at the film that was concordant in meaning. There is a long program of research ahead to find out just what the information for this concordance was, but it seems clear that the common affordance of facial and vocal expressions was perceived.

A question that logically follows is whether the infants showed their perception of the differential affordances of the expressive behaviors in some observable behavior of their own. Because infants of 5 and 7 months cannot tell us, we must find some other way of getting an answer. Walker showed infants (7 months old) single films of either happy or sad behavior, accompanied by the appropriate sound track. This time, the infants themselves were videotaped as they watched. Later, observers were shown randomly selected bits of the videotape records taken of these infants and required to judge which of the two films an infant had been watching. Five naive observers (i.e., naive as regards infant research and videotapes of infants) were quite unable to tell and judged at chance levels. But five observers experienced in research with infants judged significantly more correctly than chance. Infants' own expressions are quite difficult to read, partly because their facial structure and musculature is so different from adults' or older children's. Inexperienced judges apparently looked for stereotyped indicators of expression that were not there, but there was some evidence that the infants were differentiating with appropriate responses what the events afforded for them in the behavior of another.

CONCLUSION

In concluding these remarks, I want to return briefly to the topic of the symposium, the "Concept of Development." I have talked about another concept, but I believe it is one rich with implications for the way we should think about development and plan our observations of it. I was asked to characterize the general perspective on development from which my work emerges. In seeking a term with historical antecedents, I have referred to functionalism, but I have also tried to elucidate some of the meanings that that term has for me, and to introduce a concept that seems to me to give the functionalist perspective a new meaning and a new prospect for the study of development.

Here are some meanings that I have tried to emphasize. Development is best viewed in the context of an organism in a relationship of mutuality with its environment. Perception serves the function of keeping an animal in touch with the information in his environment about its affordances for actions, like going places and making use of the objects around him in ways that serve his needs. Evolution of the species has done a lot to provide an individual with the means for accomplishing this, but in the development of an individual, we need to study the way these means are refined by ongoing differentiation of perceived affordances, of actions, and the way the two are related.

A functionalist perspective keeps in mind the utility of actions for supporting a creature's needs. But the creature, human in the case that interests me most, is at once an actor and a perceiver. He cannot act adaptively without perceiving the affordances of his habitat. But on the other hand, he cannot perceive effectively without acting. We are, even as infants, active seekers of information, and as we perform actions, we put ourselves in a position to obtain more information. The flow of perceiving and acting is continuous and unbroken.

This point brings me to another, very important, facet of a functionalist view. It shuns atomism in any form. It does not seek components or final particles of any kind, whether stimuli, or sensations, or memory traces, or responses. The flow of information around us that our environs provide is continuous and the things that it specifies, the surfaces and places and people, are unitary and have meaning for us. It is those meanings that we need to extract. The complementarity of the animal and its environment is a whole thing and needs to be studied as such. The more we try to decompose this complementarity by looking for elements, the more likely we are to sacrifice the meanings we are looking for.

It is a sort of corollary of these points that we should try to study development in the most life-like possible surroundings. I do not think that means that we should shun the laboratory, but rather that we should make conditions of our experiments as much like real ones as possible. The research I have been describing seems to me to do that by attempting to simulate real situations without sacrificing control. I have already alluded to the program of research that this perspective encourages. The study of affordances of the things and places of the world, how they are perceived and lead to action is the way to proceed. Primitive affordances in the young infant are being studied, and some appear to be tuned in innately, but perception is bound to action, as I just said, and most affordances must be extracted in the course of action. New actions become possible, as development progresses, and thus new information for affordances is continually becoming available, giving us more to study.

The old functionalists were essentially pragmatists, and at one point this pragmatism led to formulation of the goal of psychology as the prediction and control of behavior. I have never liked this slogan, because it was not clear who was going to do the controlling. It is control of one's own behavior that is important. Behavior occurs in an environment, and adaptive control requires perceiving the affordances of that environment. My goal is to press toward an understanding of how that comes about.

REFERENCES

Ball, W. A., & Tronick, E. Infant responses to impending collision: Optical and real. *Science,* 1971, *171,* 818–820.

Bower, T. G. R., Broughton, M. M., & Moore, M. K. Infant responses to approaching objects: An indicator of response to distal variables. *Perception and Psychophysics,* 1970, 9, 193–196.

Bruner, J. S., & Koslowski, B. Visually prepared constituents of manipulatory action. *Perception,* 1972, *1,* 3–14.

Campos, J. J., Hiatt, S., Ramsay, D., Henderson, C., & Svejda, M. The emergence of fear on the visual cliff. In M. Lewis & L. Rosenblum (Eds.), *The development of affect.* New York: Plenum, 1978.

Dewey, J. The reflex arc concept in psychology. *Psychological Review,* 1896, *3,* 357–370.

Field, J. Coordination of vision and prehension in young infants. *Child Development,* 1977, *103,* 48–57.

Garcia, J. Tilting at the paper windmills of Academe. *American Psychologist,* 1981, 36, 149–158.

Gibson, E. J., Carroll, J., & Ferwerda, J. Differentiation of an aperture as contrasted with an obstacle under conditions of optical motion. In *Final Report to the Spencer Foundation*, August 1, 1980.

Gibson, E. J., Owsley, C. J., & Johnston, J. Perception of invariants by 5-month-old infants: Differentiation of two types of motion. *Developmental Psychology*, 1978, *14*, 407-415.

Gibson, E. J., Owsley, C. J., Walker, A., & Megaw-Nyce, J. Development of the perception of invariants: Substance and shape. *Perception*, 1979, *8*, 609-619.

Gibson, J. J. *The perception of the visual world*. Boston: Houghton-Mifflin, 1950.

Gibson, J. J. Visually controlled locomotion and visual orientation in animals. *British Journal of Psychology*, 1958, *49*, 182-194.

Gibson, J. J. *The ecological approach to visual perception*. Boston: Houghton-Mifflin, 1979.

Heidbreder, E. *Seven psychologies*. New York: Century, 1933.

Hofsten, C. von Predictive reaching for moving objects by human infants, *Journal of Experimental Child Psychology*, 1980, *30*, 369-382.

Hofsten, C. von & Lindhagen, K. Observations on the development of reaching for moving objects. *Journal of Experimental Child Psychology*, 1979, *28*, 158-173.

Hruska, D., & Yonas, A. Developmental changes in cardiac responses to the optical stimulus of impending collision. *Paper presented at the meeting of the Society for Psychophysiological Research*, St. Louis, October 1971.

James, W. *Principles of psychology*. New York: Holt, 1890.

Johansson, G., von Hofsten, C., & Janssen, G. Event perception. *Annual Reviews of Psychology*, 1980, *31*, 27-63.

Koffka, K. K. *Principles of Gestalt psychology*. New York: Harcourt, 1935.

Köhler, W. *The mentality of apes*. New York: Harcourt, 1925.

Lewin, R. Evolutionary theory under fire. *Science*, 1980, *210*, 883-887.

Mark, L. S., Todd, J. T., & Shaw, R. E. The perception of growth: A geometric analysis of how different styles of change are distinguished. *Journal of Experimental Psychology: Human Perception and Performance*, in press.

Murchison, C. *Psychologies of 1930*. Worcester, Mass.: Clark University Press, 1930.

Petterson, L., Yonas, A., & Fisch, R. O. The development of blinking in response to impending collision in preterm, full-term, and postterm infants. *Infant Behavior and Development*, 1980, *3*, 155-165.

Rader, M., Bausano, M., & Richards, J. E. On the nature of the visual-cliff-avoidance response in human infants. *Child Development*, 1980, *51*, 61-68.

Ryan, T. A. Dynamic, physiognomic, and other neglected properties of perceived objects: A new approach to comprehending. *American Journal of Psychology*, 1938, *51*, 629-650.

Schiff, W. The perception of impending collision: A study of visually directed avoidant behavior. *Psychological Monographs*, 1965, *79* (Whole No. 604).

Spalding, D. A. Instinct and acquisition. *Nature*, 1875, *12*, 507-508.

Spelke, E. Infants' intermodal perception of events. *Cognitive Psychology*, 1976, *8*, 553-560.

Spelke, E. *Intermodal exploration by 4-month-old infants: Perception and knowledge of auditory-visual events*. Unpublished PhD thesis, Cornell University, 1978.

Spelke, E. Perceiving bimodally specified events in infancy. *Developmental Psychology*, 1979, *15*, 626-636.

Tolman, E. C. *Purposive behavior in animals and men*. New York: Century, 1932.

Walker, A. S. *The perception of facial and vocal expressions by human infants*. Unpublished PhD thesis, Cornell University, 1980.

Walker, A., Gibson, E. J., Owsley, C. J., Megaw-Nyce, J., & Bahrick, L. Detection of elasticity as an invariant property of objects by young infants. *Perception*, 1980, *9*, 713-718.

Yonas, A. Infants' responses to optical information for collision. In R. N. Aslin, J. Alberts, & M. Peterson, (Eds.), *Sensory and perceptual development: Influences of genetic and experiential factors*, in press.

4

Development and the Dialectic: The Need for a Systems Approach

Arnold J. Sameroff
Institute for the Study of Developmental Disabilities
University of Illinois at Chicago Circle

The growth of developmental psychology has been accompanied by an increasing uneasiness. This discomfort is centered on the limitations of most current conceptual frameworks for dealing with change and transformation. Early studies had been embedded in a speculative context made possible by a lack of empirical data. The behaviorist tradition acted as a corrective to such speculations by developing an operationalism that accepted as data only consensually validated relationships between observable phenomena. This corrective, however, included an egocentrism that argued that philosophical debates over the nature of science were irrelevant; the facts would speak for themselves. This position could be maintained as long as facts and their interrelationships could be considered to exist independently of the scientific lens through which they are viewed. However, this positivism was antithetical to a discipline that took as its subject matter, development (i.e., the manner in which facts and their interrelations change over time).

Outside psychology, philosophers of science were beginning to expand their perspective from testing truth or falsity of eclectically derived, arbitrary theories (Popper, 1973) to studying the evolution of theories themselves (Foucault, 1970; Kuhn, 1962). This perspective is now finding a place inside psychology. The increase in the historical study of psychological issues (Aries, 1962; Buss, 1975; Riegel, 1976a) and the critique of the assumption that science is value-free has led to the view that the nature of psychological explanation changes as society changes.

A corollary development was the observation that the way in which the facts of the world are interpreted varies as a function of the individual's personality and stage of development. For example, the development of intelligence is not now seen as the learning of increasing numbers of facts or habits but rather as a change in how facts and habits are organized and interpreted. The psychoanalytic model of development originated by Freud, despite its speculative foundations, had an important impact by focusing attention on the way in which the basis of the child's organization of the world changed during development. But it was left to Piaget to produce a theory sufficiently documented by empirical observations to provide a strong basis for arguing that organization of knowledge was rooted in the activity of the child and not solely in the surrounding world. Once the constructive role of the developing child was acknowledged in intellectual realms, it was only a short step to begin speculating about the constructive role of scientists in explaining their adult domains of interest.

If one examines the major turning points in scientific theory that have reshaped our understanding of the universe, one finds that these advances have been based on stepping back from limited domains and placing the object of inquiry into a broader context. For example, in physics, two of the most notable advances were those of Copernicus and Einstein. Copernicus caused us to step back from seeing our own perspective from earth as the center of the universe to seeing our perspective as only one view of a system that had its center elsewhere. We were only part of an existing system rather than the originators of the system. Similarly, Einstein's theory of relativity forced us to step even further back by demonstrating the necessity of including the observer in the system along with the observed. The only absolute in the system was that the system's properties must be regarded as relative.

Social scientists, on the other hand, somehow have managed to keep themselves convinced that they can attain an objective interpretation of their universe of interest while maintaining a stance outside the system. What has come to be called the "cognitive revolution" in psychology is at heart the realization that no one can remain outside the system, because each in our own way adds something to that which we are observing. Piaget spent decades demonstrating that our knowledge of the world is constructed, not received. Despite the fact that children apparently live in the same material world as adults, that world is understood differently depending on the cognitive level of the cognizer. Gibson's (1981) work in perception has placed a central emphasis on what the perceiver brings to the perceived. And most recently in that realm of psychology that comes closest to engaging the complexity of our everyday lives, social psychology, researchers have been caught up with various forms of attribution theory. Two observers experience reality quite differently depending on what they bring to the situation, what they attribute to their perceptions.

LeVine (1980) has pointed out that the area of research that would give us the greatest appreciation of the relativity of our absolute judgments is that of cross-cultural research. This area, however, is probably the most poorly represented in current developmental work. LeVine made the startling observation that our theories of the role of extrinsic reinforcements, such as praise and approval in learning, may be a culture-specific generality closely tied to our socialization needs of producing adults who would be directed toward innovation rather than acceptance. More traditional cultures can use imitation and informational feedback as intrinsic reinforcers, because children are expected to continue in the ways of the past. In Western cultures, our adult model is one of an individual who can go beyond the past, as well as the present, to produce new integrations for which no models exist.

Another view of this same point is nearly presented in the recent television production of the book, *Shogun* (Clavell, 1975), which contrasted Japanese and Western views of social roles. For the Japanese, the role is presented as being central to social functioning. An individual's prime responsibility is to do what is expected of him or her within a very clearly defined social role, including the act of suicide. Individuality can only be expressed in the gaps between roles, but never as an interference with the obligations of the role. In Western cultures, just the opposite obtains. Roles are seen as things we are forced into by the requirements of social interaction, but we try to avoid them as much as possible. Our Western essence is to be expressed in individuality. Our value system is based on being different. We frequently laugh at the need for adolescents to express their uniqueness by the same fad as all the other adolescents who need to express their uniqueness. As adults, however, we have forgotten to continue laughing at our continuing illusions that we are not part of a system.

What is needed for the advancement of this kind of science is a perspective that forces the scientist to question continually the context of his observations, an approach that keeps reminding the investigator that he is not observing absolute phenomena, but rather phenomena that exist in a particular setting. Such a perspective would not prevent scientists from investigating variables in limited domains, because that is where most major empirical advances occur, but would emphasize that such studies represent a *decision* to ignore the other contexts. What happens all too frequently is that these choices are justified by a belief that the context issue is irrelevant, for example, that a social science can be discovered that will have truth outside of a particular cultural, political, and historical setting. Such a truth may be found that does generalize across more than one context, but only if the contexts are included in the theory. A universal theory of cognition could not be found that focused only on within-culture tests of cognition. Such a theory might be found, however, if it included an analysis of the interaction between a range of cultural contexts and individual cognitions.

What we need in developmental psychology is just such an approach. We need an understanding, not only of the development of basic units of behavior such as a conditioned reflex, a concept, or a perception, but of the organization of behavioral systems that incorporate these units and give them meaning as well. In the birth-complications realm, it is not a baby's cerebral palsy alone that condemns him to a low IQ, but rather the denial of entry into the educational system that could allow the child to transcend the physical handicap. And that denial is not only a function of the educational system but is also a function of a particular political system, in a particular historical epoch (Kessen, 1979).

Too often our research efforts result in surprise endings. In my own work, it seemed only logical that continuities and stabilities should be found in an individual's behavior across time. Initial deficits in biological and behavioral functioning should result in deficits in later functioning. Why is it so hard to find such relationships (Sameroff, 1975)? In a similar vein, it seems intuitively obvious that traits should generalize across situations. Why is it so hard to find such generalizations (Mischel, 1977)?

Historical analyses of childhood have found that our concepts of children, our treatment of children, and maybe even the behavior of children have changed dramatically over the centuries. We are distressed that this generation of adolescents is not behaving in the same way as the last one or even my generation before that one. What's changed to produce all these secular effects?

Prior to the 1960s, one moved from adolescence to adulthood. Keniston (1970) discovered a period of development that intervened between the two that he called youth. He defined this period as occurring after maturity and before responsibility. Life-span psychology suddenly illuminated a whole series of developmental changes that occurred during adulthood (Levinson, 1978). Did these adult phases antedate life-span psychology, or have they recently come into existence? Is there place in current developmental psychology to even ask these questions?

We have reached the point in our development as a science where we should resist surprises that keep forcing us to take perspective on our enterprises, by incorporating these surprises into the system. There are two kinds of surprises we can treat this way. The first kind are the surprises of context, and the second are the surprises of evolution. To avoid the first kind of surprise requires a mapping of the universe that allows us to see that each of our observations is made in a specific context by a specific observer. This problem requires a view of the hierarchy of contexts from which we act. Any given psychological trait or function must be seen, not as inhering in a particular individual, but a particular individual in a particular setting.

To avoid the second kind of surprise related to evolution, one needs a theory of development that is open-ended. Frequent criticisms of both theories of ontogeny and phylogeny are that they are teleological, in that they both end with the adult human being. *Homo sapiens adultus* is seen not as a relative end-product within a specific geographic and historical niche but as the absolute end product. Critics of both modern capitalist society as the final stage of civilization and Piaget's formal operations as the last stage of cognition share the view that if one is to be consistent, one must have a theory that not only explains how we got where we are but points in the direction in which we may be going. Any trait or function must be seen as not absolute to humans but as relative to a member of particular species on a particular rung of the phylogenetic ladder at a particular stage of development.

To provide the mapping of contexts to help us avoid the surprises of the first kind, I turn to general systems theory. To provide a theory of evolution that will help us avoid surprises of the second kind, I turn to a theory of development based on dialectics and especially the notion of contradiction.

GENERAL SYSTEMS THEORY

At the outset, we must make a distinction between systems approaches and general systems theory. A systems approach is generally treated synonymously with an interactionist position; that is, that one cannot examine the bits and pieces of behavior in isolation. Our field's evolution out of the atomistic days of the S-R learning theorists into the social learning and cognitive emphases of today have placed great importance on this theme. In its most extreme definition, it leads to a potentially nihilistic position of saying that everything is related to everything else, and therefore nothing can be studied in its own right.

On the other hand, a general systems approach incorporates this wholistic interactionist position but goes on to make a theory of systems. Systems, whatever their specific contents or scientific domains, are seen as having some general properties, which can be studied in their own right independent of their concrete manifestations. General systems theorists have concerned themselves with a number of these general properties.

General systems theory has come to describe a level of theory midway between highly generalized constructions of pure mathematics and the specific theories of the specialized disciplines. Boulding (1956) saw a need for theoretical constructs about the general relationships of the empirical world, which would lie between: "the specific that has no meaning and the general that has no content" (p. 197). He saw the lowest level of ambition for such a theory to be the pointing out of similarities in the theoretical constructions of different disciplines. At a higher level of ambition was the development of a spectrum of theories that may produce a system of systems that would illuminate gaps in theoretical models and even point the way toward methods for filling the gaps, much like Mendeleyev's periodic table of the elements did for chemistry.

Boulding suggested two approaches to such theorizing. The first was to look for general phenomena that could be found in many disciplines, whereas the second approach was to arrange the empirical fields into a hierarchy of complexity. Examples that might evolve from the first approach are that almost all disciplines deal with populations of elements to which new ones are added or born, and old ones are subtracted or die. These elements interact with some kind of environment and express some form of behavior. Among these behaviors are growth and, of most interest from an organizational framework, transmission of information between the elements. The integration of such universal phenomena across disciplines could potentially lead to a general field theory of the dynamics of action and interaction.

As an example of the second approach, Boulding organized the elements of concern to the various disciplines into a hierarchical arrangement emphasizing nine levels. The lowest level, labeled *frameworks,* refers to static descriptions of the relationships of elements in space; the highest level, labeled *transcendental systems,* reflects the necessity for a level to contain ultimates, absolutes, and inescapable unknowables. Along the way, Boulding passes through the level of *clockworks,* which are simple dynamic systems with predetermined movements; the level of *thermostats,* which are cybernetic systems that can transmit and interpret information; the level of the *cell,* where life is differentiated from nonlife by adding the property of a self-maintaining structure; the level of the *plant,* in which the cells have a division of labor into various tissues, as well as the separation between genotype and phenotype; the level of the *animal,* which has specialized information receptors, a central structure for information process-ing in the brain, and self-awareness; the level of the *human,* in which there is a self-reflective quality added to brain structures and the ability to produce, absorb, and interpret symbols; and the *societal* level, in which the unit is not the person but the role that is tied into a network by channels of communication that can deal with value systems in addition to semantic and symbolic systems.

Boulding recognized that such a hierarchy in itself adds little to our under-standing of science, but through it, one can recognize deficiencies in both empir-ical and theoretical analyses. Adequate *theoretical* models currently exist only to the level of the cell. The organismic model in developmental psychology would be at this level (Reese & Overton, 1970). *Empirical* knowledge is deficient at all levels of the hierarchy.

If one examines the explanatory systems applied by workers in the social sciences, one finds that, although they are working at the eighth level of com-plexity, most theories are at the second level moving toward the third; that is, theories at the level of complexity of clockworks and thermostats are used to explain the phenomena of social systems. Although theorizing at any level is better than nothing, eventually, a level of theorizing appropriate to the level of complexity will be a necessity.

Of course, the contrary position has been that of the reductionists, who see no problem with reducing the complexity of higher levels to the principles of lower levels. Given the large body of literature debating this issue, I touch only briefly on this point here and later in the chapter. To help clarify this issue, Anderson (1972) subdivided reductionism into two varieties. Few of us disagree with what might be called *up-reductionism,* which argues that the functioning of higher levels of complexity is based upon and cannot violate the laws of functioning of lower levels of complexity. Our biological functioning cannot violate the laws of chemistry and physics that apply to our constituent atoms and molecules. On the other hand, there would be vigorous debate against a concept of *down-reductionism,* which attempts to argue that higher levels of complexity can be explained by the laws of the lower levels. The laws of chemistry and physics do not explain biological functioning. The genetic code is a good example of this point. The structure of DNA cannot violate the constraints placed upon it by its chemical structure; the laws of chemistry, however, do not explain the genetic code (Polanyi, 1968). The code by which the four bases of the molecule are translated into the 20 amino acids is a biological law that has only an arbitrary connection to its chemical substrate. There is no chemical reason why any specific combination of bases should translate into any specific amino acid.

These hierarchies, although of interest to the general systems theorists, are less so to those of us whose specialty is developmental psychology. We are of necessity interested in the general point of the importance of directing our explanatory efforts toward an appropriate level of analysis, but these efforts must be captured by the processes that may emerge from general systems theory rather than the structures. An overview of such processes must begin with the work of von Bertalanffy.

The idea of a general systems theory is generally attributed to Ludwig von Bertalanffy (1968), who recognized the need to view biology, at least, as an organized system. In the 1930s, Bertalanffy promulgated an interdisciplinary doctrine that elaborated principles and models that apply to systems in general, irrespective of the particular kind of elements and forces involved. He saw classical science, represented by the diverse disciplines of chemistry, biology, psychology, and the other social sciences, as trying to isolate the elements of the observed universe—chemical compounds and enzymes, cells, sensations, habits, and individuals, as the case may be—and expecting that by putting these elements together again, the whole would be intelligible.

von Bertalanffy argued that to understand science, one needed to understand not only the elements but, more importantly, their interrelations. In addition, he argued that there were correspondences or isomorphisms between systems in totally different fields. The concept of wholeness, which had been treated as some metaphysical notion, was now interpreted by concepts of hierarchic structure, stability, teleology, differentiation, steady state, and goal directedness. These properties gave rise to new disciplines for their study, such as automata theory, set theory, net theory, graph theory within mathematics, and the more technology-oriented disciplines of cybernetics, control engineering, and computers. von Bertalanffy felt that the study of these interdisciplinary isomorphisms might give rise to the ambitious aim of the unification of science.

He argued against existing mechanistic views representing the world as ''a Shakespearean tale told by an idiot'' and argued for an organismic outlook that saw the world as a great organization. He rejected the notions of logical positivism based on physicalism, atomism, and the copy theory of knowledge and emphasized the contributions of the biological sciences with their concern for properties of the whole such as interaction, transaction, and teleology. From his work, he developed a philosophy that saw man as part of a hierarchy of systems rather than a heap of physical particles. At each level of this hierarchy, truth was not represented in some objective absoluteness but was a *relationship* between the elements and the system. For man, knowledge was not an approximation of truth, but rather the expression of a relationship between knower and known.

Within psychology, the notion of system is still far from common, although we have been able to accept the concept of organization as a necessary concern. In the days when all of man's behavior was limited to what could be demonstrated by a rat, it came as a major blow that the teleology and purposefulness that some attributed to man could be demonstrated by a simple machine. I don't think the rats have ever forgiven the cyberneticists for demoting them from the center of the psychological universe; I know definitely that the rat-runners have never offered forgiveness. Instead, they reduced themselves one level in the systems hierarchy to become physiologists and from that position have reestablished themselves as the foundation for all of man's psychological behavior.

The irony in all this is that the physicists, who have traditionally held the role of the anchormen by studying the basic units of the universe, have begun to turn more and more to metaphysical speculations. The lead articles in *Science* magazine have frequently taken cosmology as their theme (Gal–Or, 1972). The physicist authors are forced to deal with the uncomfortable fact that every time they have discovered the level at which the ultimate building blocks of nature can be found, someone discovers a more fundamental level, be it electrons, hadrons, or quarks. Even more interesting is that the names they have chosen to identify these new units, such as color and charm, reflect abstract process or system properties, rather than any concrete characteristic of the particles. Moreover, these particles cannot exist in isolation but must always be part of a system.

The traditional view of the sciences has been that they represent a pyramid, with physics providing the material base and the social sciences nebulously surmounting the summit. A more recent view is still of a pyramid, but one hanging in space, where the emergence of softer areas of science at the tip is matched by the dissolution of the harder areas at the bottom as each purported ultimate particle gives way to the next newly discovered ultimate particle. But most importantly, physicists have come to see that what appears as material, in reality, represents an organization in time and space of some underlying dynamic process. Nothing has been found to exist that can be defined as a thing-in-itself. In each case, there are dynamic processes that give rise to the unit's appearance and continued existence.

The physicists are concerned with philosophy because they need it to explain their findings. Psychologists are concerned with philosophy because they study people who have philosophies. Biologists, on the other hand, represent today the stronghold of reductionism and antitheory. The biologists have no need for philosophy because they are observing the ultimate facts of life. Why worry about theories of development such as those of Waddington, a biologist adopted by psychology, when one can observe development under the microscope. Not only cells, chromosomes, and genes are revealed and manipulated, but the molecular units of which they are composed as well. Nobel prizes are given for data, not for philosophy. A systems theory is unnecessary when any given system can be analyzed concretely. Description is frequently seen as replacing rather than preceding explanation. This year's Nobel prize in economics was given to an econometricist who came up with a better math model to describe economic behavior. In any case, psychologists need not apply unless they can pass as biologists or, more recently, as an economist.

In a similar vein, some critics of theoretical systems have argued that an emphasis on theory only occurs when one doesn't know the facts. If our methodologies in the social sciences had improved to where we could be doing what the biologists are doing, then we would also give up such speculations.

von Bertalanffy spent his last efforts developing a philosophy that he called perspectivism. In his view, each epoch of history has a view of reality that is appropriate for that epoch, but also unique to that epoch. It was only by appreciating the processes of life and their organization that one could hope to approach some general theory of life.

SYSTEM PROPERTIES

The field of general systems theory is concerned with identifying the general properties that systems in different disciplines share. Because general systems theory is a discipline rather than a theory, it is natural that there are many different views as to what a general systems theory should look like.

Boulding (1979), while reflecting upon the founding of the Society for General Systems Research in 1954, pointed out that at that time a general system was defined simply as any theoretical system of interest to more than one discipline. From this view, he felt that there should be many general systems theories, not one, not so much because we couldn't produce the one, but rather because there are more than one general system in the real world. I don't know if I would agree with Boulding on that point, because I *do* believe that there is one theory that explains everything, which puts me in the school of individuals that Sheldon White (personal communication) refers to as "paranoid psychologists."

Just as in psychology, where the mechanistic and organismic metaphors have been used to differentiate theoretical perspectives, a similar division can be used to differentiate systems theories. For example, Ashby (1952), one of the early pioneers in the area, uses a cybernetic model that is merely an updated version of Descartes' machines. Although such new properties as teleology, that is, self-correcting, goal-directed behavior, have been admitted to the system, these properties are clearly rooted in such elementary units as the servomechanism. Ashby's version of systems theory detailed in his pioneering book, *Design for a Brain,* was only at Boulding's third level, the thermostat.

Of more interest are those systems theories that use the biological metaphor implicit in the organismic approach, because they cut across many more levels of the hierarchy of life, as well as clearly introducing the concept with which we are most concerned, development. In this vein, von Bertalanffy's (1968) concept of open and closed systems was a major step forward. The *open* system was defined as a structure that maintained its organization despite changes in its parts; that is, there is a throughput of material constituents, whereas the whole maintains its identity. At the most simple conceptual level, a river and a flame are given as examples of structures whose components are constantly changing, whereas the whole, the river or the flame continue. However, there is no organized differentiation within these wholes. At a more meaningful level, the living cell is an organization that maintains itself as a whole, whereas the individual molecules of which it is composed are constantly being exchanged through metabolic processes.

The *closed* system embodied in cybernetics, which could perform complex functions, did not have the additional characteristics of self-organization in the face of material change. The computer, as advanced as it has become, is still mainly limited in this ability to reconstruct itself or even build itself, which would be the key concern of a developmentalist.

From the beginnings of general systems theory with its emphasis on self-organizing properties of structures in hierarchical systems, there has been increasing formalization of various aspects of the theory. The social scientist would feel very much at sea in attempting to read either the journal or the yearbook of the Society for General Systems Theory, unless he or she were well steeped in number theory and advanced calculus. Recently, James G. Miller, a psychologist, has tried to put it all together in a book called *Living Systems* (Miller, 1978). He details a general living systems theory that is concerned with a subset of all systems, the living ones, which run through several levels from the cell to supranational systems. In a massive tome, he analyzes each of these seven levels of the hierarchy in terms of 19 subsystem processes that use concepts of thermodynamics, information theory, cybernetics, and systems engineering, as well as more classical concepts of physics. He (Miller, 1978) sees his purpose as producing: "a description of living structure and process in terms of input and output, flows through systems, steady states and feedbacks which will clarify and unify the facts of life [p. 42]." These process variables include such things as ingestors, distributors, transducers, decoders, and deciders that deal with both matter-energy and information. The time constraints of this presentation preclude any more detailed version of Miller's system, so I leave it as an extreme to which the interested student can turn.

A somewhat simpler presentation is that of Ervin Laszlo (1972), who deals with only three and a half levels and four process variables. The three levels are:

(1) physical systems; (2) biological systems; and (3) social systems. He reserves cognitive systems (the half level) for a separate presentation, because he feels that mind events are different from the physical events that characterize the natural systems. Although he maintains that he is not a dualist, the point is probably debatable. In any event, his cognitive systems follow the same processes as the other systems, so we need not be concerned with this issue here.

Laszlo defines a natural system as a joint function of four independent system properties. These are, first, the property of wholeness and order; secondly, the property of adaptive self-stabilization; thirdly, the property of adaptive self-organization; and fourthly, the property of hierarchical structuring.

The first property of *wholeness and order* is a complex version of the historic organismic notion that the whole is more than the sum of its parts, which prior to systems theory was treated as some mystical property of matter. More simply, a whole adds the property of relationship to the parts. A part taken alone cannot define a relationship. It is only in the company of other parts that the relationship can exist. The classic Gestalt examples of such patterns as melodies are appropriate here. The frequency of the notes that make up a melody can vary over a wide range as long as the relationship between the notes remains the same. At a more complex level, Simon (1973) points out that the same complex computer program can be executed by different computers using different machine languages that interface between the electronic deep structure and the logical surface structure of the program. In many systems, one has difficulty clearly defining the parts these days. At the atomic level, physicists no longer even consider the solar-system view of the atom with its electrons spinning around a nucleus core. Instead, there is the conception of a series of fields within which are embedded particle-like concentrations of energy and spin. The atom is currently conceived of as functionally interacting nuclear and electronic fields rather than the older notion of mechanically interacting parts. At the biological level, wholeness and order are found to characterize all systems. Modern definitions of any biological element or structure interpret these as only visible indices of regularities of the underlying dynamics operating in their domains (Weiss, 1969). In other words, static entities are illusions; they are all process at heart.

Laszlo's second general property of natural systems is that of *adaptive self-stabilization*. This property refers to a cybernetic stability that self-regulates the system to compensate for changing conditions in the environment, by making coordinated changes in the system's internal variables. This buffering capacity of the system reduces the effects of the environment on its constituent parts. By the use of feedback mechanisms, systems with this property become adaptive entities. If there is a larger range of effective interaction between a system and its environment, there will be a larger effect on the system of perturbations introduced from without.

A system that only responds to the temperature of the environment will need to make fewer internal adjustments than a system that is sensitive to temperature plus oxygen content, as well as visual and auditory input. The complexity is even greater when there is an interdependence between the internal subsystems, for example, when the functioning of the subsystem for maintaining visual input levels is dependent on the maintenance of an appropriate internal temperature by the thermoregulatory subsystem. What is of interest here is that as one moves up the scale of complexity, systems become more and more improbable from a thermo-dynamic perspective, and, as a consequence, they must rely to an increasing extent on precisely controlled environmental relations. What we have come to think of as unconscious processes are the reflections of the operations of the subsystems that maintain the body in a stabilized biological state such that one can engage in psychological processes. Within the psychological realm, subsystems for motivation and attention can be seen as providing the conditions in which more complex cognitive processes can occur. The maintenance of some level of homeostasis or steady state is essential to the continued identity of a system. At the biological level, this is very clear in the case of the regulation of temperature, pH levels, and oxygen saturation among many other variables. Even small changes in these parameters threaten the integrity of the system.

These self-stabilizing properties can operate in terms of a set steady state but frequently must follow a more dynamic course. Waddington (1969) had defined a developmental variation of self-stabilization in his concept of homeorhesis in contrast to Cannon's homeostasis. In homeorhetic functioning, the set point of the system's steady state changes across time. When self-stabilization occurs, it must be to the appropriate developmental set point rather than to an absolute one. When a deviation occurs during embryological development, for example, the self-righting tendencies must be directed at reaching the developmental level where the fetus should be at the current point in time, rather than the developmental level at the point in time at which the deviation occurred. A simple embryological example would be the case of identical twins, where the fertilized egg splits into two parts. The adult outcomes give no evidence that each twin started with only half the amount of biological material. One can imagine the complexity of genetic coding that is required to control the interactions of the developing infant with a temporal series of environmental conditions in order to provide an outcome with only a minimal range of variability. Considering the number of cell divisions and reorganizations that occur during the prenatal period, this feat of control is magnificent.

The third property of natural systems is that of *adaptive self-organization*. Whereas the second property of self-stabilization allows the system to resist perturbations and return to some steady-state parameters, adaptive self-organization is a reorganization of the forces and parameters within the system when subjected to the action of new constants in the environment. Laszlo (1972) defines adaptive self-organization as changes made when new external forcings act on internal constraints. The direction of change that is implied by the term adaptation is one where the existing system can best continue to function in the face of new circumstances. Piaget's concepts of assimilation and accommodation are obvious translations of these processes. To the extent that the system cannot assimilate the new environmental conditions with existing regulating subsystems, accommodation must occur in the form of new subsystems. The new regulatory functions may be fulfilled by new relationships between existing subsystems, or by the establishment of a higher order subsystem with new functions. It is important to note that adaptively reorganized systems are not necessarily more stable systems. They may deal well with forces that elicited the process of self-organization, but they may not be more resistant to all factors in the general environment. To the extent that self-organization results in a greater complexity of structure, the system becomes thermodynamically more "improbable" and potentially unstable. According to Laszlo (1972), as a consequence, the evolution of systems is: "toward increasingly adapted, yet structurally unstable states, balancing their intrinsically unstable complex structure by a wider range of self-stabilizatory functions [p. 44]." Although these higher order structures are more independent of specific environmental pressures, the price they have to pay is that they need many more internal control systems. When animals evolved from cold-blooded to warm-blooded, they increased the range of environments in which they could dwell, but the cost was the need for a variety of fine-tuned homeostatic devices to maintain the internal set-point in the face of wide fluctuations in external temperature.

Cognitive development is an example closer to home that demonstrates the same process. Piaget (1960) defined intellectual development as a movement from an intimacy of experience with the here and now to farther and farther removed levels of abstraction where there was very limited contact with the sensory world. At the sensory–motor level, children are immediately affected by each change in sensory–motor feedback, altering their view of the world as a function of which schema is operative. Object permanence permits the child to see the world in its objective reality through the development of an internal system of representation that compensates for the experiential variability of the external world. Similarly, the conservation structures of the operational child, whatever they may turn out to be, permit that child to free himself or herself from the perceptual variability of the real world. The child knows without needing to see. Internal logic replaces external perception. The consequence is that the child is able to interpret a very wide range of external input without the need to continually alter internal organization. The price he or she pays is a much more complex cognitive structure has to be maintained.

Adaptive self-organization is the most complex of the system properties and is central to our major developmental concern, the process of evolution. Whereas adaptive self-stabilization can provide the feedback requirements for maintaining a steady state in homeostasis, or even the more complex homeorhetic functions of following a developmental trajectory from the fertilized egg to the adult, it does not deal with the changes wrought when new environmental circumstances arise for which there are no existing balancing parameters. Laszlo would argue that the genotype provides for both homeostatic and homeorhetic changes, but, in the face of certain contingencies, alterations are necessary in the genotype itself, what we used to think of as mutations. These alterations are the kind of reorganizations of fundamental structures that are called evolution.

Although I might argue with Laszlo on the dividing line between self-stabilization and self-organization, I think it important for us to recognize the two types of regulations implied by these properties. The ontogeny of the individual clearly demonstrates structural changes that lead the organism from one level of complexity to another, from the single cell of the fertilized egg to the multicellular blastula through differentiations into tissues, organs, and the systems that support our adult biological functions. We can get major insights into development by studying the principles by which these processes occur. The systems perspective has placed a clear focus on the role of environment in all of these biological encounters. Without the environmental inputs at each developmental epoch, there would be no movement to the next development stage.

However, these developmental progressions, even though they incorporate a need for sensitivity to differentiated aspects of the biological environment, do not reveal for us the process of evolution, by which new adjustments might occur to the same or different environmental pressures. For this understanding, one must examine adaptive self-organization. However, this is easier said than done, because the study of evolution is for the most part a historical study, a reconstruction of past events, past environments, and past reorganizations, rather than an easily observed contemporary process.

We are frequently confronted with a picture of evolution as a tree diagram with a base of single-cell organisms subdividing to produce the many branches that represent the currently existing species on earth. What we too often forget is that there is a similar tree diagram of environments in which the primordial magma cools to evolve water and land masses, which further subdivide into areas of forest and plain containing continuously changing varieties of flora and fauna. This evolution of environments is part and parcel of the evolution of species with each in a continuous adaptive relation to the development of the other (von Foerster, 1966). Fish could not leave the water until there was land to go to, nor could apes climb into the trees until there were trees to live in.

The study of embryological development can give us some clear examples of these processes. Each alteration in the structure of the phenotype may be controlled by the genetic structure, but these alterations are in response to a specific set of parameters that are a function not only of the developmental state of the organism but also the environmental context.

Laszlo's last system property deals explicitly with the ordering of levels within a system. The property of *systemic hierarchy* is somewhat analogous to Heinz Werner's (1948) orthogenetic principle. Laszlo argues that systems that have the first three properties of wholeness and order, adaptive self-stabilization, and adaptive self-organization will develop in the direction of increasing hierarchic structuration. Simon (1973) hypothesized that complex systems will more readily evolve from simple systems, if there are stable intermediary forms. Systems that are based on hierarchies are much more stable, because failure in organization will not destroy the whole system but only decompose it to the next stable subsystem level. As a consequence, instead of starting all over again, the process of complexification can start from the stable subsystem level and reconstitute the loss in a much shorter period of time. Simon's view is that "nature loves hierarchies." Hierarchical systems were the only ones with time to evolve, which explains their prominence among natural systems. It pays for systems to cooperate in evolving more complex functions than to do the job themselves. Systems at about the same level within the same environment will tend to form suprasystems. What is most striking here is that these suprasystems incorporate both the subsystem and the subsystem's environment, which is really just another system. Observable examples can be seen in embryological ontogeny. The genetic material of the nucleus in the zygote initially is in interaction with the cytoplasmic material provided by the maternal ovum. Immediately, this small system begins reproducing itself into a small range of similar forms, which are coalesced into a new system, the blastula, which includes not only the nuclei but the cytoplasmic environments of the original cell. The bastula, a relatively homogeneous cell mass, begins to differentiate into the gastrula, an organ with specialized tissues as its subsystems. In ontogeny, this process will continue until the biological hierarchy is completed, and the child is thrust into the outside world where he or she can begin creating the psychological hierarchy.

This point is one of the most important lessons that we can take from general systems theory within this limited presentation. We too often take the perspective that we are the center of the universe independent of all we survey. We too often focus on the individual unit, be it ourselves, our children, our families, or our culture, and profess the illusion that we can follow our own destiny, independent of the fact that our destinies are inseparably intertwined with our environments. Even the most isolated recluse must be a part of an environment that provides the necessary range of temperature and foodstuffs to maintain himself or herself. One can minimize one's contact with the environment but one cannot do without. Most of us are in intimate connection with each other and our environments in a multitude of ways, and the vast majority of these connections place us in a systems context where we exhibit properties that are the concern of general systems theory.

There are no defined upper limits to the systems in which we participate. The sequence of hierarchical levels is only limited by the variety of systems available for inclusion. Each higher level in the hierarchy will have a greater diversity of functions, because it will contain a greater number of subsystems that, on the other hand, will be manifested by a smaller number of actualized systems.

Molecules are fewer in number than atoms but display a far greater array of functions and properties. Organisms are fewer in number than molecules, and societies are even fewer in number yet incorporate the widest range of functions.

An additional aspect of hierarchical organization in natural systems is that systems at each level do not have control functions over those of all lower levels. There is a dual control (Polanyi, 1968) that is limited by both the nature of the parts and the nature of the whole. The higher levels set boundary conditions for the subsystems but do not determine the activity of the subsystems. Polanyi sees these boundary conditions as extraneous to the processes they delimit. The slope of Galileo's ramp set boundary conditions for the demonstration of gravity, but it did not control the law of gravity. Boundary conditions set by higher-order systems harness the properties of the lower systems but cannot violate those properties. The DNA molecule cannot violate the laws of chemistry and physics; it can only harness those laws in the service of transmitting genetic information. Vocal language can harness but cannot violate the processes of speech production in the service of producing words.

The last point to make about hierarchical organization is that one must be very careful about the level of analysis used to interpret what one is interested in. At this stage of the game, we are all pretty sophisticated in avoiding the reductionist fallacy, but we frequently fall into the almost equally nonproductive fallacy of disregarding our roots, our subsystems. The ethologists have been the most persuasive about this issue in their attempts to reconnect psychology to our human evolutionary history (Charlesworth, 1976). Indeed, each higher level of organization, each new stage in evolution or in development brings with it new principles of organization and functioning, because it incorporates so much more than what existed before. But, at the same time, it cannot escape its connection to what came before. Our thought processes and our experiences are intrinsically connected to the biological substrate that we transcend.

A lesson of system theory is that one cannot understand a system in its own right. One must have a place to stand, a perspective. This perspective can be from above or below. We can introspect about the component parts of our thought processes or examine the social institutions to which we belong. Gödel's proof set the problem, so rather than resist the fact that a system cannot fully understand itself in isolation from its relationship to higher and lower structures, we should accept this knowledge as a key to renewed progress in our own discipline. Certainly, the work we see evolving in metacognition (Flavell, 1979) is an excellent example of systems approaches applied to psychological problems.

Bronfenbrenner (1977) has been a leader in calling us to the awareness of contexts in social development. The need for defining ecosystems at the many levels of social organization is continually reinforced by the surprises we find when we examine psychological functioning in different cultural settings, as well as within the various social strata within a single culture. The new emphasis within social psychology on the organization of social behavior within the context of scripts (Schank & Abelson, 1977) is another example of a systems approach that appears to be adding a new dimension to the social psychologists' understanding of human behavior.

Humanity may be placed in a unique position within the systems hierarchy. There is a major schizophrenia in our situation, because we are at the nexus of two hierarchical systems, a material one and an informational one. Materially, we fit in the Boulding-type hierarchy that runs from molecules to multinational political systems. Informationally, we construct another hierarchy that runs from sensory–motor coordinations to abstract logical systems. Although in an individual's development these hierarchies can be considered orthogonally, they were, most likely, intimately connected in their evolution. If we examine human cognitive development in modern societies, it would be hard to argue that one could exist without the other. The complexities of our social institutions require the complexities of our thought and vice versa. But one of the powers of thought is its ability to abstract and to isolate and even to alienate. This power has had its historic political uses in a variety of idealist or dualist philosophies that saw our thought processes as a given, either through the power of God or of our genes. General systems theory serves the valuable purpose of confronting us with our alienation and reemphasizing the need for a developmental credo that can firmly base our intellectual development within our evolutionary context.

EVOLUTION AND DIALECTICS

The preceding exposition of general systems theory was devoted to raising the issue of contexts. Every natural structure and function is embedded in a network of other structures and functions. Moreover, these networks or systems have a past and a future. The remainder of this essay is devoted to an explication of dialectical principles in an effort to explore the nature of evolution.

Dialectics has come and apparently gone in recent psychology in intimate connection with the life and death of Klaus Riegel. In his many papers in the mid 70s, he renewed a call for a genuinely "developmental" developmental psychology that was founded on the analysis of process, not of product (Riegel, 1976b, 1976c). His emphasis was on understanding the dynamic in life rather than the concrete forms that the dynamic assumed. Whether or not one agrees with the concrete form that his theory of dialectics took, one should not dismiss the core notion that all living systems are in a constant process of change.

In a recent essay, Adrienne Harris and I (Sameroff & Harris, 1979) attempted our own distillation of what was meant by a dialectical approach to development. We tried to keep it simple with less success than I hoped but were able to summarize the approach in four principles taken from Cornforth (1953) that overlapped significantly with Laszlo's four properties of natural systems. The principle with the least overlap was the one of most significance. Dialectics considers development to be motivated by *internal contradictions* inherent in all things. The notion of inherent internal contradiction makes no sense in a psychology based on stable entities. It only makes sense when the focus turns to process.

The internal contradiction in all systems is based on the fact that all entities are caught in a two-way stretch; they are at the same time parts and wholes; at once, they are part of someone else's hierarchy while containing their own. Whether the entity be man or a molecule, the issue is the same. Koestler (1967) has referred to this as the Janus principle. All elements are two-faced, one aimed outward at the wholes of which we are parts, and one aimed inward at the parts that make us whole. As humans, there are constraints on our activity placed by the properties of the various social systems in which we participate. At the same time, we are constrained by our physical, chemical, and biological constituents. The intersect between our parts and what we are part of is never complete and from a dialectical perspective never can be.

The more common expression of the dialectical process is captured by transactional approaches in which systems that function together are changed by their mutual activity (Sameroff, 1975). Homeostatic systems generally do not exhibit dialectical changes, because their components have already gone through a process of organization. In self-organization, however, there are adaptive changes in which the system is structurally altered by experience with the environment. To the extent that the environment can be identified as a system that also participates in these changes, a dialectical process can be said to be occurring. Homeorhetic processes give the impression of a dialectical process, but at higher levels of the hierarchy, the transactions between a system and its local environment have been stabilized. For example, there is little evidence of change in the structure of the genotype as the multitude of serial transactions occur that characterize embryological development, even though functioning of the genome is constantly changing as different genes are turned on and off at different stages of development. This stability of control system can occur because of the equal stability of the environment, in this case, the amniotic medium in which the fetus is growing. Evolution has insured that this medium is as stabilized as possible to insure the adequacy of the control systems. It took the miracle of modern chemistry to subvert these adapted systems with such innovations as thalidomide. If we are to be continuously exposed to such teratogens, hopefully, a new dialectic will be initiated in which our biological regulatory systems may reach some level of adaptation to the more common pollutants in our surround.

These biological examples of system functioning are important evidence of the generality of the processes of development. They lend credence to such disciplines as general systems theory, which seek some semblance of universality across the many levels of human functioning and especially human development.

As a consequence, our questions must not be addressed by explaining why something changed into something else, but rather why things appear *not* to change. It is the stabilities in life that we must question, not the processes. Our old theories of motivation presented us with passive entities that needed to be moved. This movement was identified with the extrinsic drives associated with various tissue needs or strong stimuli. Our new identification with biology through the work of Heinz Werner, Jean Piaget, and even Ludwig von Bertalanffy has removed our concern with the general issue of motivation. Activity is a given in living systems. If, indeed, we ever stopped being active, we would no longer be living systems. Because of this organismic orientation, the question is no longer to explain our activity but rather to explain the form and functions that our activity takes.

We can return for a moment to general systems theory for a possible explanation. Systems tend to maintain themselves in the face of variations in environmental perturbations. The direction of evolution has been to produce systems that are more and more capable of minimizing environmental effects through self-stabilizing processes. The evolution of DNA as a repository of genetic information was a major advance in life's self-stabilization. Despite the variation in the development of a given phenotype, the genetic material was protected in a stabilized system. Evolution did not have to reach that point again.

Of more interest to developmental psychology is what I consider to be the next major breakthrough in evolution, the establishment of the parental relationship. The newly hatched creature was no longer on its own; it was now part of a social system that endured, just as the genetic material had endured at the previous breakthrough in the ability of systems to maintain themselves. At this point, I must give a footnote to the sociobiologists who have recently documented the most cunning ways the genetic material has for maintaining itself through the generations of evolution (Wilson, 1975). However, their denial of the importance of ontogeny prevents us from fully accepting their conclusions about the essence of man (Cairns, 1979). We have yet another breakthrough to deal with and that is the cognitive breakthrough that provided us with the symbol systems of language. Language provided us with a system with which to represent reality that could be transmitted independently of that reality. Before language, parents could provide us with the information they had gleaned from their own experience but had no way of giving us the information of others, which could provide us with the ability to live in niches our parents had never considered. Our adaptational capacities had taken a great leap forward. What will be the next breakthrough in evolution? From a general systems and dialectical perspective, we need no longer be surprised by either the question or the possibility of an answer.

Life moves toward incorporating more and more of its environment into itself with the aim of reducing the effects of external perturbations. If one identifies with the process of evolution, one needs to analyze our existing systems and their environments. At that level, we will find the roots of our next developmental stage. But prediction is only a minor aspect of the greater need that I have alluded to a number of times in this presentation. It is the need to recognize that we live in an environment and that our activities are intimately connected with the characteristics of that environment. And so we come full circle. I began by bemoaning the fact that our theories of development are conditioned not only by our empirical observations but also by the social, economic, and historical conditions of the epoch in which we live. I now embrace that fact, because it is only through understanding the relationship between our theoretical speculations and the social, economic, and historical context in which they arise that we can fully understand ourselves or appreciate our place in the evolution of life.

REFERENCES

Anderson, P. M. More is different. *Science*, 1972, *177*, 393–396.

Aries, P. Centuries of childhood: *A social history of family life*. New York: Vintage, 1962.

Ashby, W. R. *Design for a brain*. London: Chapman & Hall, 1952.

Boulding, K. E. General systems theory: The skeleton of science. *Management Science*, 1956, *2*, 197–208.

Boulding, K. E. Universal physiology. *Contemporary Sociology*, 1979, *8*, 687–691.

Bronfenbrenner, U. Toward an experimental ecology of human development. *American Psychologist*, 1977, *32*, 513–531.

Buss, A. The emerging field of the sociology of psychological knowledge. *American Psychologist*, 1975, *30*, 988–1002.

Cairns, R. B. *Social development: The origins and plasticity of interchanges*. San Francisco: Freeman, 1979.

Charlesworth, W. R. Human intelligence as adaptation: An ethological approach. In L. B. Resnick (Ed.), *The nature of intelligence*. Hillsdale, N.J.: Lawrence Erlbaum Associates, 1976.

Clavell, J. *Shogun: A novel of Japan*. New York: Dell, 1975.

Cornforth, M. *Materialism and the Dialectical Method*. New York: International Publishers, 1953.

Flavell, J. H. Metacognition and cognitive monitoring: A new area of cognitive-developmental inquiry. *American Psychologist*, 1979, *34*, 906–911.

Foucault, M. *The order of things: An archaeology of the human sciences*. New York: Pantheon Books, 1970.

Gal-Or, B. The crisis about the origin of irreversibility and time anisotropy. *Science*, 1972, *176*, 11–17.

Gibson, E. J. The concept of affordances in development: The renascence of functionalism. In W. A. Collins (Ed.), *Minnesota Symposium on Child Psychology* (Vol. 15). Hillsdale, N.J.: Lawrence Erlbaum Associates, 1981.

Keniston, K. Youth: A "new" stage in life. *American Scholar*, 1970, *39*, 631–640.

Kessen, W. The American child and other cultural inventions. *American Psychologist*, 1979, *34*, 815–820.

Koestler, A. *The ghost in the machine*. New York: Macmillan, 1967.

Kuhn, T. *The structure of a scientific revolution*. Chicago: University of Chicago Press, 1962.

Laszlo, E. *Introduction to systems philosophy: Toward a new paradigm of contemporary thought*. New York: Harper & Row, 1972.

LeVine, R. A. Anthropology and child development: *New Directions for Child Development*, 1980, *8*, 70–86.

Levinson, D. J. *The seasons of a man's life*. New York: Ballantine, 1978.

Miller, J. G. *Living systems*. New York: McGraw-Hill, 1978.

Mischel, W. On the future of personality assessment. *American Psychologist*, 1977, *23*, 577–614.

Piaget, J. *Psychology of intelligence*. New York: Littlefield, Adams, 1960.

Polanyi, M. Life's irreducible structure. *Science*, 1968, *160*, 1308–1312.

Popper, K. *Objective knowledge: An evolutionary approach*. Oxford: Oxford University Press, 1973.

Reese, H., & Overton, W. Models of development and theory of development. In L. Goulet & P. Baltes (Eds.), *Life span developmental psychology: Methodological issues*. New York: Academic Press, 1970.

Riegel, K. F. *The psychology of development and history*. New York: Plenum Press, 1976. (a)

Riegel, K. F. The dialectics of human development. *American Psychologist*, 1976, *31*, (10), 689–700. (b)

Riegel, K. F. From traits and equilibrium towards developmental dialectics. In W. J. Arnold & J. K. Cole (Eds.), *Nebraska Symposium on Motivation* (Vol. 24). Lincoln: University of Nebraska Press, 1976. (c)

Sameroff, A. J. Early influences on development: Fact or fancy? *Merrill-Palmer Quarterly*, 1975, *21*, 267–294.

Sameroff, A. J., & Harris, A. Dialectical approaches to early thought and language. In M. H. Bornstein & W. Kessen (Eds.), *Psychological development from infancy*. Hillsdale, N.J.: Lawrence Erlbaum Associates, 1979.

Schank, R. C., & Abelson, R. P. *Scripts, plans, goals, and understanding*. Hillsdale, N.J.: Lawrence Erlbaum Associates, 1977.

Simon, H. A. The organization of complex systems. In H. H. Pattee (Ed.), *Hierarchy Theory: The challenge of complex systems*. New York: Braziller, 1973.

von Bertalanffy, L. *General system theory* (rev. ed.). New York: Braziller, 1968.

von Foerster, H. From stimulus to symbol: The economy of biological computation. In G. Kepes (Ed.), *Sign, image, symbol*. New York: Braziller, 1966.

Waddington, C. H. The theory of evolution today. In A. Koestler & J. R. Smythies (Eds.), *Beyond reductionism: New perspectives in the life sciences*. Boston: Beacon Press, 1969.

Weiss, P. A. The living system: Determinism stratified. In A. Koestler & J. R. Smythies (Eds.). *Beyond reductionism: New perspectives in the life sciences*. Boston: Beacon Press, 1969.

Werner, H. *Comparative psychology of mental development*. New York: International Universities Press, 1948.

Wilson, E. O. *Sociobiology: The new synthesis*. Cambridge, Mass.: Harvard University Press, 1975.

5

Epidemiological-Longitudinal Approaches to the Study of Development

Michael Rutter
Institute of Psychiatry
University of London

Other authors in this volume have dealt with contrasting theoretical perspectives on various aspects of the process of development. The task assigned to me, that of discussing epidemiological approaches, was different, in that epidemiology constitutes just one particular methodology and not a theoretical framework (apart from a firm commitment to the view that all concepts and ideas should be subjected to rigorous empirical testing). Moreover, epidemiology makes no claims to provide a comprehensive set of answers to any question. Nevertheless, as I hope to illustrate by means of some studies with which I have been involved, it *does* provide a most useful set of research tools that constitute the most powerful methodology available for *some* purposes. On the other hand, almost always the decisive test of any hypothesis must await the planned experiments and interventions that are the necessary sequelae to epidemiology. Thus, epidemiological approaches often provide an essential cog in the investigative chain, but only rarely do they constitute the complete chain.

At one time, epidemiology tended to be thought of primarily in terms of the study of the spread of infectious disease and, by extension, to the spread of noninfectious disease (with Goldberger's linkage of pellagra to dietary factors as the most famous example, Terris, 1964) and more recently to the spread of heroin abuse in a community (De Alarcón, 1969) and to hysterical epidemics (Benaim, Horder, & Anderson, 1973; McEvedy & Beard, 1970). However, nowadays epidemiology may be more often considered with respect to the determination of the prevalence of particular diseases or disorders, a datum that is crucial in the rational planning of services. This usage has been important in the field of psychiatric disorders (Cooper & Morgan, 1973; Dohrenwend, Dohrenwend, Gould, Link, Neugebauer, & Wunsch-Hitzig, 1980; Hare & Wing, 1970; Wing & Häfner, 1973).

However, neither epidemics nor prevalence constitute the subject matter of this chapter. Instead, the focus is on the role of epidemiology in understanding the course of human development. One consequence of this focus is the need to combine epidemiology with longitudinal strategies—hence the title of the chapter. Only rarely can development be studied adequately through the use of solely cross-sectional or retrospective methods. Although it is also true that many developmental questions cannot be properly answered through an exclusive reliance on longitudinal methods, they are indispensable as *part* of the set of strategies needed to answer developmental questions (Rutter, 1981a).

There is one further restriction to my discussion in that, for the most part, development is considered from the perspective of the study of the *abnormal*. As Mechanic (1970) noted, epidemiology is differentiated from many other research fields by its focus on a disease, defect, or disability as its dependent variable.

It is necessary, perhaps, to pause for a moment to consider why abnormality should be investigated in order to understand the process of development. Of course, the study of abnormal development is a legitimate interest in its own right. But also, just as knowledge of normal development carries important lessons for those wishing to unravel disease mechanisms (Rutter, 1980a), so the investigation of abnormality may shed light on the course of normal development. This is because a focus on the unusual may be crucial in "pulling apart" elements that ordinarily go together. For example, the comprehension of spoken language and the acquisition of social relationships generally develop at about the same time, and it might be thought that the former constituted a prerequisite for the latter, in that language occupies such a central place in social interchanges. But the study of dysphasic and autistic children has shown that this is not so, in that dysphasic children with a serious defect in receptive language may nevertheless develop normal social relationships (Bartak, Rutter, & Cox, 1975). Or again, sometimes it has been suggested that a child's ability to appreciate the perspectives of other people underlies social relationships and social competence. Yet, in a neat series of experiments based on Piagetian techniques, Hobson (1981) has recently shown that autistic children do *not* lack this element of social cognition (at least as measured by visual perspectives). It could still be that this ability is *necessary* for the development of social relationships, but clearly it is not *sufficient*. The same types of issue apply to attempts to understand the role of various constitutional and environmental features in shaping development, and, as I try to indicate, epidemiological methods may be invaluable in disentangling *which* features have *which* effects.

Nevertheless, although the study of the abnormal is often most illuminating regarding the processes of development, it is necessary to emphasize that extrapolations from the abnormal to the normal, or vice versa, should only be made with great caution. The factors associated with abnormality are not necessarily the same as those associated with variations within the normal range. For example, structural brain pathology of one sort or another accounts for most cases of severe mental retardation (Berg & Kirman, 1959; Crome, 1960; Rutter, Graham, & Yule, 1970), but it is most unlikely that differing degrees of brain damage explain normal variations in intellectual level. Similarly, both polygenic and environmental factors are most important with respect to mild mental retardation (and to individual differences in intelligence above the retarded level), but they are of very little importance with severe retardation (Åkesson, 1962; Reed & Reed, 1965). Or again, Patterson's (1976, 1980) data have shown that when parents of normal children punish coercive behavior, this is usually effective in *suppressing* it. In contrast, when the parents of aggressive children do the same, the likelihood is that the disruptive behavior will *increase*. The causal processes for abnormality may not always be identical with those that underlie variations within the normal range.

CHARACTERISTICS OF EPIDEMIOLOGICAL AND LONGITUDINAL APPROACHES

Before discussing possible implications for development, it is necessary to say just a few words on the characteristics of the epidemiological approach, as they are often misunderstood. The most distinctive feature of epidemiology, of course, is that it involves the study of *populations,* rather than individuals (Shepherd, 1978). In essence, the basis of the epidemiological research method lies in a study of the distribution of disorders or disabilities in a population in order to discover how the distribution varies with particular environmental or other circumstances. It is crucial to the approach that the findings apply to a defined population of known characteristics and that the results are considered in terms of population distributions. There are many advantages that flow from this crucial feature of epidemiology, but, perhaps, three require particular emphasis. Firstly, there are the implications that stem from knowledge concerning the *base rates* of the phenomena being studied (Meehl & Rosen, 1955). For example, very large verbal-performance discrepancies on the Wechsler Intelligence Scale for children have been found to occur twice as frequently in brain-damaged children as in normals (Rutter, Tizard, & Whitmore, 1970). But this does *not* mean that an individual child with a very large V–P discrepancy is likely to have suffered a brain injury. To the contrary, because normality is so very much commoner than brain damage in the general population, the odds are very high that the child does *not* have a brain injury (Yule, 1977). The same issue applies to many high risk factors in relation to psychopathology. It is possible to take the step from group differences to individual risk or prediction only if the population base rates for the independent and dependent variables are known.

Secondly, the epidemiologist is always concerned to assess the systematic biases that may arise as a result of missing data on subjects who could not be traced or who were unwilling to cooperate. Studies have consistently shown that the missing subjects tend to be systematically different from the rest of the population (Cox, Rutter, Yule & Quinton, 1977). Investigations with a high nonresponse rate or that rely on volunteers are likely to involve important distortions of findings.

Thirdly, population-based enquiries provide a necessary corrective to the biases that may result from the use of clinic samples or administratively defined categories. This is not only because such samples may be highly atypical as a result of referral or labeling biases but also because, for separate statistical reasons, the ratio of multiple problems (or diagnoses) to single problems in hospital will always be greater than in the general population (Berkson, 1946).

Nevertheless, it should be appreciated that the population studied need not necessarily be the general population in a particular community. Indeed, much of the art, as well as the science, of epidemiology lies in the choice of the most appropriate high-risk samples in order to answer particular questions or to test particular hypotheses. For this purpose, the "high risk" may be defined in terms of either the independent or the dependent variable, but that choice will have necessary implications for both data analysis and the types of conclusions that may be drawn. As Morris (1975) has made clear in this useful book on the topic, epidemiology includes a wide range of approaches that have been developed for this purpose. The popular image of psychiatric epidemiology as just a matter of sending out a mass of questionnaires to a large number of people in the hope that something useful may emerge from the mass of data accumulated could not be further from the truth.

Success in epidemiological research, as in other forms of research, relies heavily on the careful delineation of the questions to be examined; on the appropriate choice of samples, strategies, and tactics required to meet those needs; on the selection of reliable and valid standardized research instruments that are both sensitive and selective with respect to the variables under study; on systematic quality controls in the collection of data; and on the choice of penetrating and rigorous methods of analysis that are well-designed for the specific questions under study. As these issues have all been considered previously in some detail with respect to the field of child psychiatry (Rutter, 1974, 1977a, 1981b), in addition to their discussion in more general texts (Cooper & Morgan, 1973; Morris, 1975), I do not consider them further here, other than to emphasize their importance and to make a few remarks on measures, on causal questions, and on longitudinal strategies insofar as they apply to the research projects from my own group to which I make reference.

Questionnaires constitute excellent screening instruments that are readily applicable to large populations, and we have made extensive use of them for that purpose (Rutter, Tizard, & Whitmore, 1970; Rutter, Cox, Tupling, Berger, &

Yule, 1975; Rutter, Graham, Chadwick, & Yule, 1976). However, they are necessarily crude instruments, and it is only rarely that they provide an adequate tool for intensive epidemiological studies. In our research, as in many other epidemiological enquiries, we have frequently utilized a two-stage strategy that combines questionnaire coverage of very large populations (usually several thousand) with much more detailed study of selected subsamples (usually with an N of a few hundred). This combination of *ex*tensive total population coverage with the *in*tensive study of subsamples often provides a powerful investigative method. In most of the studies to which I refer, for the intensive stage, we have mainly relied on detailed interviewing conducted according to well-standardized methods.

It has proved possible to delineate many of the skills and techniques required for such interviewing (Cox, Hopkinson, & Rutter, 1981a; Cox, Rutter, & Holbrook, 1981b; Cox, Holbrook, & Rutter, 1981c; Hopkinson, Cox, & Rutter, 1981; Rutter & Cox, 1981; Rutter, Cox, Egert, Holbrook, & Everitt, 1981) and, with well-trained interviewers, the methods have proved robust, reliable, and, insofar as it could be tested, valid (Brown & Rutter, 1966; Rutter & Brown, 1966; Graham & Rutter, 1968; Quinton, Rutter, & Rowlands, 1976; Rutter, Cox, Tupling, Berger, & Yule, 1975a). However, for some of the studies, observational techniques (Rutter et al., 1979) or psychological testing (Chadwick, Rutter, Brown, Shaffer, & Traub, 1981a; Chadwick, Thompson, Shaffer, & Rutter, 1981b) or neurological examination of the child (Rutter, Graham, & Yule, 1970) have also been employed.

Another feature of the epidemiological approach is that it usually involves the testing of two (or more) competing hypotheses regarding possible mechanisms or processes. It is sometimes supposed that questions of cause cannot be tackled adequately through epidemiological techniques, because it is never legitimate to infer causation from correlation. However, this is not so. It is true that the mere presence of a correlation does not imply causation, but various means are available to test whether the causative inference is justifiable. Bradford Hill (1977) has succinctly outlined some of the requirements for a cause and effect relationship. These include the strength, consistency, and specificity of the association and, especially, the presence of a dose–response gradient. Using these and other guides, epidemiology has had some spectacular successes in finding causes— ranging from Snow's discovery of the link between cholera and the water supply in the mid-19th century to Doll and Bradford Hill's identification of the link between lung cancer and cigarette smoking a few years ago (Doll & Bradford Hill, 1964). Psychiatry includes no examples quite as dramatic and far-reaching as these, but there have been important epidemiological contributions to etiological research in psychiatry (Cooper & Morgan, 1973).

In answering causal questions, there are many advantages to the combination of epidemiological and longitudinal research strategies (Rutter, 1981b). Natural experiments of opportunity, longitudinal analyses of changes over time, and determination of the timing of associations may all serve in the more rigorous testing of causal hypotheses.

Of course, too, longitudinal data are essential for answering most developmental questions—causal or noncausal. The techniques available have been well-described by Robins (1979), who has also usefully summarized the child psychiatric knowledge that has ensued from these approaches. The importance of longitudinal studies is obvious in terms of the need to determine when particular behaviors reach their apogee and when they decline; when behaviors change and when particular associations occur; and especially in examining the sequences of development. However, longitudinal data are also invaluable for a host of other methodological and substantive issues (Robins, 1979; Rutter, 1981a). Some of these are discussed below but at this point it is necessary just to note that, unlike the total population approach of general epidemiology, longitudinal analyses require an explicit focus on the *individual*. It is not enough to know that behavior X is most prevalent at one age and Y most prevalent some years later; we also need to know whether X and Y are shown by the same or different individuals. Furthermore, it is rarely sufficient to know that a behavior at point A correlates with the same or another behavior at point Z; we also need to know what happens at the intervening points B, C, D, and so on. Moreover, often there will be an interest in the differences and similarities between those individuals who do and those who do not maintain consistency in their behavioral development.

So much for general considerations—let me now turn to the specific findings. In considering epidemiological–longitudinal approaches to the study of development, I discuss the research under five main headings: patterns of behavior, sex differences, developmental changes, syndrome definition, and causal influences.

PATTERNS OF BEHAVIOR

Perhaps the most obvious contribution of epidemiology (and certainly one of the first) was to show how many of the "symptoms" found in children seen at psychiatric clinics were also very common in children in the general population (Kanner, 1960). Thus, in the Isle of Wight study of all 10- to 12-year-old children living on the island (Rutter, Tizard, & Whitmore, 1970), confirming earlier studies, we found that over a quarter of boys and a third of girls were said by their parents to bite their nails. Nearly as many were reported as "very restless, often running about or jumping up and down, hardly ever still" and as unable to "settle to anything for more than a few moments." Of course, as worded, these items rely on the judgments of parents or teachers as to what is a "normal" level of activity or concentration. The high rates of "problem" behavior could mean no more than that many adults tend to have a rather inaccurate picture of how ordinary children behave. That could well be the case with items such as overactivity and inattention, and it is for that reason that much more detailed objective measures are now being obtained in a series of studies being undertaken by colleagues in my department. However, it is reports by parents and teachers that constitute the basis for most referrals to child psychiatric clinics. Thus, it is important that all epidemiological studies of children have agreed in finding that most symptoms are relatively common in ordinary children not attending clinics. Several implications followed from the findings: Firstly, it was clear that not too much should be read into the occurrence of these behaviors—at least, when they occur in isolation. Secondly, however, it was also evident that if the clinical significance of any of these symptoms was to be assessed, it would be necessary to obtain much more detail on the form of the behavior and on its social context, severity, frequency, and persistence (Rutter, 1975). That such detail was *actually* useful in producing a more valid assessment of abnormality is shown by our finding that, compared with questionnaire scores, the detailed interview measures were better predictors of psychiatric disorder 4 years later.

Thirdly, however, the findings raised the query as to whether some behaviors were more indicative than others of some form of overall disorder or abnormality. This question could be tackled by means of several different strategies. To begin with, it was possible to determine how far the presence of any one individual behavior, as reported on a questionnaire, was associated with more widespread behavioral deviance as reflected in a high score on the same questionnaire, in a high score on a different questionnaire referring to behavior in a different setting, or in an overall psychiatric assessment based on detailed information from parents, teachers, and the child himself. Each of these analyses is open to various biases, but the biases in each case are rather different, and there can be some confidence in findings that are similar in each of the comparisons. The results showed that nail biting and thumb sucking showed only a very weak association with overall disorder and, hence, that their inclusion in most textbook lists of ''neurotic traits of childhood'' was quite misleading in its implications. Eating and sleeping difficulties, especially when of mild degree, and somatic complaints such as headaches, stomachaches, and bilious attacks showed some association with overall disorder, indicating that occasionally they may reflect an emotional disorder, but, again, the links were weak. It appeared that, in most cases, these behaviors had no particular psychiatric significance (although obviously that does *not* mean that they were without psychological meaning).

Not surprisingly, both individual emotional items (such as fears, worries, and depression) and individual conduct items (such as stealing, truanting, and fighting) tended to be associated with all these measures of overall disturbance. This was to be anticipated if only because it is those behaviors that constitute the basis of most psychiatric judgments on disorder. However, what was perhaps less expected was that some of the strongest associations were found with poor peer relationships, poor concentration, and overactivity. Neither attention deficits nor restless, fidgety behavior played much part in psychiatric concepts at that time, but the findings certainly suggested the possibility of important links between cognitive deficits and psychiatric disturbance—links that were also suggested by the strong association found between reading difficulties and disorders of conduct.

The total population of Isle of Wight children surveyed in middle childhood were systematically re-examined at age 14 to 15 years (Graham & Rutter, 1973; Rutter et al., 1976; Rutter, 1979). This follow-up provided a different approach to the clinical significance of individual items of behavior through the examination of their importance as predictors of the subsequent course of disorders already present at age 10 to 11 years. Once again, overactivity and inattention stood out as the behaviors most strongly associated with persistence of disorder, although poor peer relationships were also linked with a poor outcome (Schachar, Rutter, & Smith, 1981). However, it was also found that the poor prognosis was most strongly associated with *pervasive* hyperkinesis—overactivity and inattention in only one setting was of less prognostic importance.

This pattern of findings has now been replicated in several independent studies with different age groups and different measures. Thus, Richman, Stevenson, & Graham (1981), in their epidemiological–longitudinal study of children living in the borough of Waltham Forest followed from age 3 years to 8 years, found that, of all individual items of behavior, overactivity was the best single predictor of continuing psychiatric disturbance. The same study also showed quite strong associations between language delay, cognitive impairment, and reading difficulties, on the one hand, and psychiatric disorder on the other. It appears that these links appear early (being evident at age 3 years) and persist throughout childhood—as shown by the Isle of Wight findings for 10- to 15-year-olds (Rutter et al., 1976; Rutter, Tizard, & Whitmore, 1970). The high consistency and persistence of this cognitive-behavioral association (Kohlberg, LaCrosse, & Ricks, 1970) indicates that it is likely to reflect rather basic developmental mechanisms or processes. However, it is much less clear quite what these might be (Rutter & Garmezy, 1981).

Poor peer relationships did not constitute a significant prognostic indicator in Richman and her colleagues' (1981) follow-up from 3 to 8 years—perhaps because the quality of a child's relationships with his peers are more difficult to evaluate in very young children. However, they have proved important prognostic indicators in other studies of older children and adolescents (Henn, Bardwell, & Jenkins, 1980; Roff, Sells, & Golden, 1972; Sundby & Kreyberg, 1968). It is not just that difficulties in interpersonal relationships tend to persist (although they do) but also that they are associated with the continuation of problems in other spheres of emotional and behavioral development. The findings point to the need for further study of the ways in which the development of social relationships may be associated with other aspects of psychological development and, in particular, of its role in the origins of personality development in early childhood. In spite of a considerable growth of knowledge about the formation of social relationships in early childhood (well-summarized by Cairns, 1979, and Maccoby, 1980, from somewhat differing perspectives), and in spite of the beginnings of an understanding regarding possible links between family attachments and peer relationships (Hartup, 1980; Sroufe, 1979), we know surprisingly little about the links between personal relationships and either emotional or behavioral development.

SEX DIFFERENCES

One specific interest within the overall topic of patterns of behavior concerns possible sex differences. Four somewhat separate issues are involved here: (1) the extent and nature of differences between boys and girls in their styles and patterns of behavior; (2) the question of whether there are sex differences in the meaning and course of development of particular behaviors; (3) the possibility that boys and girls differ in the ways in which they respond to environmental hazards and stresses; and (4) the query as to whether these various sex differences are the consequence of intrinsic biological features or, rather, differing patterns of upbringing.

A few years ago, Maccoby and Jacklin (1974) provided an excellent comprehensive review of psychological sex differences, and more recent reviews of sex differences in specific behaviors (Frodi, Macaulay, & Thome, 1977; Hoffman, 1977) have broadly confirmed their conclusions. No attempt is made here to rereview the same field, but I do wish to draw attention to a few points that have been highlighted by epidemiological studies. Firstly, there is the consistent observation that there are only minor sex differences in rates of overall emotional disturbance before puberty, but that in adult life these disturbances are very much more frequent in women (Rutter, 1979)—an issue to which I return when considering developmental trends. Secondly, not only is aggression commoner in males from early childhood onward (Frodi et al., 1977; Maccoby & Jacklin, 1974) but so also are disturbances of conduct of all kinds (Rutter & Garmezy, 1981). This has been a highly consistent finding from a wide range of studies using a variety of different methods and measures, so that there can be some confidence in its validity. On the other hand, it should be noted that less is known about sex differences in conduct disturbance during the preschool years, and, furthermore, that even in older age groups, the *extent* (although not the presence) of the sex difference has been found to vary considerably across both cultures and time. Thus, our own epidemiological studies in London have shown that there is a lesser sex difference for conduct disorders and for delinquency in youngsters from a West Indian background (Ouston, 1981; Rutter, Yule, Berger, Yule, Morton, & Bagley, 1974), but a greater sex difference for delinquency in those from a Cypriot or Asian background (Ouston, 1981). Similarly, in the United States, both self-report data (Berger & Simon, 1974; Cernkovich & Giordano, 1979) and criminal statistics (Forslund, 1970; Green, 1970) show a tendency for the sex ratio to be lower among blacks than among whites for the more serious crimes and perhaps especially for those involving personal violence. Also, in Britain, the United States, and many other countries, female crime has been rising at a faster rate than male crime with the result that the sex ratio for delinquency has been dropping (Adler, 1977; Rutter, 1979; Steffensmeier, 1978). There is still a very great male preponderance, but nevertheless the change in sex ratio has been considerable—a drop from 11.1 in 1957 to 5.1 in 1977 in the United Kingdom (Home Office, 1978). There has been a variety of suggestions regarding possible reasons for both the male preponderance and the changing sex ratio, but without any resolution of the controversies on this topic for which theoretical speculations far outstrip the empirical data (Eme, 1979).

Less is known about sex differences regarding the persistence and course of development of these (or other) behaviors. Nevertheless, there are a few pointers to the probability that such sex differences may exist. For example, Richman et al. (1981), in their London follow-up study from age 3 to 8 years, noted that disorders evident at 3 were more likely to persist to 8 in boys than in girls. Similarly, the Fels longitudinal study (Kagan & Moss, 1962) showed that aggressivity and "behavioral disorganization" (meaning destructive acts, rages, and tantrums) in the preschool years showed greater persistence into middle childhood for boys than for girls. The data are far too sparse for firm (or even tentative) conclusions, but, clearly, the possibility of sex differences in the persistence of particular behaviors needs to be systematically tested.

One of the early observations from our own epidemiological studies was the apparently greater vulnerability of boys to family stress and discord (Rutter, 1970a). It was found that whereas antisocial problems in boys were much more frequent in discordant families than in harmonious homes, this was not the case for girls except to a minor extent. The same sex difference was evident when total deviance was considered, so the finding was not an artifact of sex differences in diagnosis. Since 1970, the finding has been replicated to a greater or lesser extent in further epidemiological studies from our own research group (Wolkind & Rutter, 1973), and from others in Britain (Whitehead, 1979), as well as in several American studies using quite different sets of measures for both marital discord and conduct disturbance (Block, Block, & Morrison, 1981; Emery & O'Leary, 1981; Hetherington, Cox, & Cox, 1978; Porter & O'Leary, 1980). It appears then, that boys are more likely than girls to develop disturbances (especially of conduct) when exposed to family discord and disharmony. Whether girls are truly more resilient or whether they show their psychological scars in other ways that do not become overt until later cannot be determined from these data.

Different writers have tentatively suggested a variety of possible explanations for this interesting and provocative finding. It does not seem to be a consequence of the fact that children usually remain with the mother after divorce (so that boys, but not girls, lack a parental model of the same sex—Whitehead, 1979), because the findings apply to intact as well as to divorced families. Neither does it seem to be a function of boys and girls differing in their perceptions of parental discord (Emery & O'Leary, 1981). It could be some kind of constitutionally determined greater male susceptibility to psychological stresses—a parallel, as it were, to the well-documented greater male vulnerability to physical stresses (Rutter, 1970a). Or the answer could lie in sex-linked temperamental differences (Eme, 1979), or in sex differences with respect to the salience of the two parents, or the need to control the environment (Block et al., 1981), or in differences in the ways in which adults respond to disruptive behavior in boys and girls (Maccoby & Jacklin, 1974). It is obvious that so far we lack the evidence that might differentiate among those (and other) competing hypotheses. However, in this connection, it is relevant to note that quite apart from sex differences in children's reactions to discord, sex differences have also been noted in children's responses to a supportive parenting style (Baumrind, 1980; Claeys & De Boek, 1976), to day care (Rutter, 1981c), and to maternal intrusiveness (Martin, Maccoby, & Jacklin, 1981). Whether or not these differences reflect the same or different mechanisms is unknown. What is clear is that there are important sex differences in the styles and consequences of different types of family interaction, but we are not much nearer the answer to the riddle of what they mean (and, even less, of whether they play any role in the determination of sex differences in disturbances of conduct).

DEVELOPMENTAL CHANGES

Epidemiological data are potentially very useful (and to some extent have already been informative) in delineating the changes in patterns of behavior that take place as children grow older. Thus, it has been shown that enuresis becomes progressively less frequent with increasing age; in the Isle of Wight study, the rate for boys dropped from 1 in 5 at age 7 years to 1 in 33 at 14 years (Rutter, Yule, & Graham, 1973). However, the same studies also showed a slight *increase* in bedwetting between 5 and 7 years (Blomfield & Douglas, 1956; Macfarlane, Allen, & Honzik, 1954; Rutter et al., 1973), which indicated that something other than biological maturation was likely to be involved. This was also suggested by the finding that enuresis was consistently associated with a trebling of the risk of overall emotional and behavioral deviance in girls (and a lesser increase in risk for boys). Of course, it could be that the emotional difficulties arose as a *response* to the enuresis, which is after all a socially embarrassing and unpleasant symptom. This may well occur in some instances, but three findings suggest that this is most unlikely to constitute the whole explanation. In the first place, we found that the association was about as strong at age 5 years (when enuresis was relatively common and likely to be less subject to derogation) as it was later in childhood or adolescence. Secondly, in the subgroup of children who were dry at 5 but became wet before 7, it was found that the behavioral deviance had usually *antedated* the enruesis. Thirdly, although there was a fall in the rate of deviance following becoming dry, the rate was still more than double than that in the general population even *after* becoming dry.

The meaning of these associations can also be studied through a comparison of the background characteristics of "disturbed" and "nondisturbed" enuretic children and through a comparison of the response to treatment in these two groups. These strategies have been pursued by Rapoport, Mikkelsen and their colleagues at N.I.M.H. (Mikkelsen, Rapoport, Nee, Gruenon, Mendelsohn, & Gillin, 1981; Rapoport, Mikkelson, Zavadil, Nee, Gruenon, Mendelsohn, & Gillin, 1981). They found that psychiatrically disturbed enuretics had experienced more stresses (such as parental divorce or mental illness or prolonged hospitalization of the child) and had a slightly higher score on a neurodevelopmental examination for "soft signs"; on the other hand, the two groups did not differ in their response to tricyclic medication. Again, the findings suggested that it was *un*likely that the disturbance had arisen as a secondary response to bedwetting. However, it remains uncertain (because the study was based on a clinic sample) whether the differences in background features might have been, at least in part, a consequence of referral biases. General population data would be helpful in checking how far that was the case.

Epidemiological findings have also been helpful in identifying some of the developmental changes that take place with respect to emotional (Rutter, 1980b) and conduct phenomena (Rutter & Garmezy, 1981). However, there are difficulties in the interpretation of many of the findings, because so many of the epidemiological–longitudinal studies have relied on questionnaire reports from parents and teachers. These are prone to be influenced by people's perceptions and concepts of the behavior in question and by the implicit or explicit use of norms. For these reasons, it would be quite possible for there to be major changes in children's actual behavior without it being reflected in changes in ratings; conversely, children's behavior could remain the same, but nevertheless the ratings show a change simply because parents' and teachers' concepts of what is normal have altered with the children's increasing age (Rutter & Garmezy, 1981).

On the other hand, this is less of a problem with detailed interview data (than with questionnaires) and also less of a problem where there is information from both parents and children, combined with observations of the child—as there was in the Isle of Wight epidemiological–longitudinal studies from 10 to 15 years

(Graham & Rutter, 1973; Rutter, 1979; Rutter et al., 1976; Rutter, Tizard, & Whitmore, 1970). The findings highlight several important issues.

Adolescence

Most strikingly, adolescence is associated with a marked increase in moodiness, misery, depression, and feelings of self-depreciation. Whereas only about one in nine 10-year olds reported such feelings, nearly two-fifths of 14- to 15-year olds did so. Indeed, as many as 7 to 8% reported having had suicidal feelings. The self-rated questionnaires showed that these feelings of misery and depression were also more common in the adolescents than in their parents—suggesting that they may reach a peak sometime during adolescence. These findings refer to individual items of emotional behavior in the general population. But the same pattern is also found with clinically significant, socially handicapping psychiatric disorders. At age 10 years, there are only three cases of depressive disorder in the 2000 Isle of Wight children studied, whereas at age 14–15 years, there were nine cases, plus a further 26 with an affective disorder involving both depression and anxiety. The results are also in keeping with community-based attempted suicide rates, which are at their highest during the late teens (Kreitman, 1977). It should be noted that, compared with the young people themselves, parents and teachers in the Isle of Wight study reported far fewer depressive feelings among the adolescents (although their reports also showed an increase in this age group)—indicating that adults often remain unaware of young people's inner distress.

Although it seems well-established from epidemiological data (as well as from clinic findings—Pearce, 1978) that depression and misery increase markedly during adolescence, there are but few leads as to *why* this change occurs at this time. However, a pointer is provided by the evidence that the rise may be more strongly associated with puberty than with chronological age. The 14- to 15-year-old boys randomly selected from the general population on the Isle of Wight included both those fully mature sexually and those with as yet no signs of puberty (no analysis for girls was possible as virtually all were postpubertal). It was striking that of the 19 prepubescent boys, *scarcely any* showed depressive feelings, whereas of the 19 postpubertal boys, a *quarter to a third* did so; the findings for the 45 pubescent boys was intermediate on all measures. Of course, the findings are based on relatively small numbers and replication is required. Nevertheless, there is the suggestion that puberty rather than age may be the crucial factor—although whether this means an endocrine influence or the effects of the psychological adaptations that are consequent upon sexual maturation remain an open question.

Although depressive feelings increase in both sexes during adolescence, these years also mark a major change in the sex ratio of emotional disorders. Before puberty, such disorders are marginally more frequent in girls than in boys, but the sex ratio is fairly near unity, and, in many studies, the sex differences have fallen well short of statistical significance (Rutter, 1980b; Rutter, Tizard, & Whitmore, 1970). Then, during the course of adolescence there is a substantial alteration in sex ratio, so that by the time adulthood is reached, depressive disorders are twice as common in women as in men. This shift in sex ratio is well-documented by both epidemiological and clinic studies, and it is clear that the findings are not the result of any kind of reporting artifact (Rutter, Tizard, & Whitmore, 1970; Weissman & Klerman, 1977). Nor is it likely to be a consequence of differing life circumstances (with most men at work and many women housewives), as the sex difference in depression applies similarly to college students (Kidd & Caldbeck–Meenan, 1966). The changing sex ratio for depression is also accompanied by a similar change for neuroticism—where there is no sex difference up to age 10 years, but an increasing sex differentiation thereafter because of a rise in neuroticism in females, but not in males (Eysenck & Eysenck, 1975).

The finding of a changing sex ratio for affective disorders between childhood and adulthood is well-established. Its meaning, however, remains obscure in spite of several attempts to explore possible reasons for it (Gove & Tudor, 1973; Radloff, 1975; Rutter, 1970a, 1979; Weissman & Klerman, 1977). As with some of the other issues already discussed, epidemiological findings have been successful in delineating the questions to be tackled, but, so far, they have failed to produce very convincing answers.

Timing of Puberty

A further finding concerns the psychological implications of early or late puberty. Various American longitudinal studies have shown that early maturing boys (but not girls) tend to have a slight advantage in personality (Clausen, 1975; Graham & Rutter, 1977). In general, there has been a tendency for them to be more relaxed, more good-natured, and generally more poised. The personality tests used in these studies were not very satisfactory, and the differences found were usually quite small. However, studies of psychiatric disorder (Rutter, 1979) and of delinquency (Wadsworth, 1979) have also found that these problems are somewhat more frequent in late-maturing boys, so that the finding is not just a reflection of weak measures. But the question remains as to just what it means. In this connection, it is important to know whether the psychiatric differences arose *before* or *after* puberty. The Isle of Wight findings showed that the association (between late puberty and psychiatric disorder) mainly applied to disorders *already* present at age 10 years (at an age when none of the boys had reached puberty), rather than to psychiatric conditions arising *de novo* during adolescence. It is clear that the association could not reflect any psychological response to late puberty. Rather, the association is likely to reflect the lower intelligence, less-muscular physique, or larger families found with late-maturing boys (Clausen, 1975; Wadsworth, 1979).

Age of Onset of Disorders

Most studies of psychiatric disorder among adolescents have been based on *all* disorders present in some sample of that age group. However, such disorders will include both conditions that have arisen during the teenage years (and hence might properly be regarded as adolescent disorders) and also those with an onset in early or middle childhood that have persisted into adolescence. The two types of disorder might be thought to carry rather different developmental implications. The findings from the Isle of Wight study (Rutter et al., 1976) suggest that indeed they do. Because the young people studied at age 14-15 years had also been studied at age 10-11 years, it was possible, within the group all of whom had psychiatric conditions at 14-15, to differentiate between those that had already been present at age 10-11 and those that arose at some point after that age. Major differences were found between these two groups defined in terms of age of onset. The disorders beginning earlier in childhood mainly occurred in boys (sex ratio of 2.3 to 1), whereas those arising in adolescence had a sex ratio nearer unity (1.3 to 1). Also, whereas the disorders arising early were strongly associated with indicators of family problems (such as breakup of the parents' marriage, the child going into care, marital discord, parental irritability to the child, and mental disorder in the mother), this was substantially less so with disorders arising during adolescence. This difference appeared to be mainly a function of chronicity, as family pathology was also not very strongly associated with disorders arising before 10 but remitting before 14. However, the greatest difference between the two groups was the finding that, whereas disorders persisting from earlier childhood were *strongly* associated with reading retardation, those arising during adolescence showed *no* such association. This was not a function of chronicity, because educational difficulties were as strongly associated with nonpersistent disorders arising before 10 as with those lasting into adolescence. The association with reading retardation, then, is a characteristic of an early age of onset. Very few other studies have made comparisons according to age of onset, but, insofar as they have done so, the results have been generally similar (Robins & Hill, 1966; Werner & Smith, 1977).

Of course, that rather leaves open the question of just what *are* the causes of psychiatric disorder beginning during adolescence, if they are not particularly associated with either family adversity or educational retardation. The "popular" answer might be that parent-child alienation provides the explanation. It is supposed to be characteristic of adolescence that the young people withdraw from their families, rebel against their parents, and cease to communicate with them. However, not only did we *not* find this to be so, but also, when it was present, it was not particularly associated with disorders arising during adolescence (indeed, it was actually slightly more frequent in the case of disorders with an earlier onset). Of course, that is not to say that parent–child relationships do not change during adolescence (obviously they do), nor is it to say that parent–child alienation does not occur (Rutter, 1979). Clearly, it does with some young people but the findings are clear-cut in showing that it is not the *usual* pattern and moreover that it is not a particular feature of disorders arising during adolescence.

Behavioral Continuities and Discontinuities

The last feature to mention with respect to developmental change concerns the matter of continuities and discontinuities in behavioral development. The concepts and the empirical questions are both complex and multiple (Emmerich, 1968; Kagan, 1980; McCall, 1977; Moss & Susman, 1980). Much heat has been generated over the years by controversies over the supposed long-term effects of experiences in infancy (Rutter, 1980c) and by the supposed predictive power of behavioral measures in infancy (Rutter, 1970b). In both cases, the evidence has been generally negative in that it has suggested considerable plasticity in development and also the major impact on development of experiences later in childhood and adolescence, or even adult life. However, it is also apparent that the questions are bedevilled by methodological difficulties and that much of the crucial evidence is still lacking. But my concern here is with the rather different issue of continuities and discontinuities in behavioral and emotional expression during the years *after* infancy. Epidemiological data have been useful in highlighting two rather separate issues. Firstly, it is clear that the picture on continuity differs according to the method of analysis chosen (Rutter, 1977b). For example, in our 4-year longitudinal study of London schoolchildren, the correlation between data collected 4 years apart for the teacher questionnaire measure of behavioral deviance was only 0.25—a highly significant correlation, but one that accounted for only 6% of the variance. On the other hand, the children who were deviant initially showed a rate of deviance 4 years later that was 1½ times that for the children initially nondeviant. This *sounds* a better level of prediction, although the data giving rise to the statistics are precisely the same in the two cases.

The British National Child Development Study (Ghodsian, Fogelman, Lambert, & Tibbenham, 1980) makes the point even more dramatically in terms of behavioral measures at 7 years and 16 years—a 9-year time span. The correlation between the 7 and 16-year measures for the school questionnaire was 0.31, a significant but quite modest correlation. However, of the children deviant at age 16 years (defined in terms of a score in the top 13%), 30% had also been deviant at age 7—a 2½-fold increase over the base rate. The attenuating effect of imperfect reliability combined with the rather arbitrary nature of cutoff points is shown by the results of a broader-based comparison asking what proportion of the children deviant at 16 years had been in the top 50% of the distribution for deviance at age 7 years. The answer found was 92%! In other words, of the young people who would show deviance 9 years later, the vast majority were already in the deviant half of the distribution at age 7 years.

Of course, in a way this is just a matter of whether you prefer to say the glass is half full rather than half empty. But also, it is more than that. Correlations tend to give a misleading picture of discontinuity just because they test whether there is absolute consistency in behavior. Clearly there is not; children change as they grow older, but also our measures have too low a level of validity for such precise quantitative measures to have much meaning. On the other hand, if, instead, one asks how likely is it that a child who is in the bottom half of the distribution for deviance at 7 years will show persisting deviance at 11 and 16 years, the answer is that it is very *un*likely; or, how likely it is that a child who is deviant at 7 and 11 years will be in the bottom half of the distribution for deviance at 16; again, the answer is very *un*likely. Considered in broad terms then, there is a substantial degree of continuity in behavioral expression over the school-age years.

But, these same findings bring out another difference—that between *persisting* deviance and *transient* deviance. This was examined in our own 4-year longitudinal study (Rutter, 1977b) by defining persistence as deviance that had been present on *at least* three out of the five assessment occasions over the 4 years. This applied to 14.7% of the total population. Of the 338 children who were initially nondeviant, only 5.3% later showed persisting deviance. In sharp contrast, persisting deviance was present in 51.7% of those deviant on the first occasion—a 10-fold difference. The implication is that quite a high proportion of children show behavioral deviance at some stage in their development, but that in most cases this proves to be a transient problem. On the other hand, there is a smaller group of children with persisting difficulties. At any one assessment occasion, this latter group constitutes about half, but, over multiple occasions, they are greatly outnumbered by the former group of children with transient problems (who also constitute about half on any one occasion, but, of course, each time *different* children make up that half—hence, the rather modest correlations).

The point of the analysis is not to produce any quantitative estimate of the frequency of persisting deviance, as obviously this must vary according to the method of assessment, the definition of persistence, the type of deviance considered, and the duration of time in question. Rather, there are implications for two rather different conceptual issues. Firstly, not only are *single* measures of any kind subject to the problems of imperfect reliability, but also they are open to the influence of important situational and interactional effects. Both contribute to the rather low correlations usually found when dealing with single measures at two points in time (or in space, for that matter). However, much greater behavioral stability is evident when the behavior in question is averaged over a sufficient number of occurrences (see Epstein, 1979, for a good discussion of these issues). From moment to moment and situation to situation, there is great variability in how any one person behaves (Mischel, 1979), but this is no way incompatible with the fact that there is also substantial consistency over time (Eysenck & Eysenck, 1980; Olweus, 1979, 1980).

Secondly, however, it may not be appropriate to consider the children with transient deviance and those with persisting deviance as sharing similar characteristics. Of course, they may constitute different ends of the same continuum, but equally they have rather different origins and involve different mechanisms. Thus, self-report studies show that the great majority of boys commit minor delinquent acts at some time (Belsen, 1975; Gold, 1970; Shapland, 1978). These boys do not differ from the bulk of the general population, because they *are* the bulk of that population. On the other hand, not only do persistent delinquents differ markedly from other children in both their family background and life-style characteristics (West & Farrington, 1977), but also many severely antisocial children maintain such behavioral differences well into adult life (Robins, 1978). Rather than attempt to obtain some overall general figure for consistency in behavioral development, it may be more useful both to ask what is different about those individuals showing particularly high consistency and also to consider consistency at the extremes.

The limited available evidence suggests that persistence may be greater in the case of clinically significant psychiatric disorder. For example, in our follow-up from age 10–11 to 14–15 years on the Isle of Wight (Graham & Rutter, 1973), of the children with disorder at 10, three-fifths still showed a socially handicapping disorder 4 years later (on an assessment that was "blind" to the children's state at age 10). Similarly, in their follow-up from 3 to 8 years, Richman et al. (1981) found that 62% of those with a disorder at 3 still showed a disorder at 8. It is important that two-fifths of the disorders remitted, but it is equally important that three-fifths did not, even after a period of 4 or 5 years that took the child from infancy to school age or from middle childhood to adolescence.

Several different features have been shown to differentiate those with persistent disorders from those with transient problems. Firstly, both community-based and clinic studies of all age groups have been consistent in showing that emotional disorders are much less likely to persist than are conduct disorders (Robins, 1979). For example, in the Isle of Wight follow-up into adolescence, 54% of emotional disorders cleared up by age 14–15 years, but only 25% of conduct disorders did so (Graham & Rutter, 1973). Similarly, in the 4-year London follow-up, based on questionnaire measures, two-thirds of emotional disorders remitted but only one-third of conduct disorders did so (Rutter, 1977b). Secondly, disorders that are pervasive over situations are more likely to be persistent over time. Thus, Campbell, Endman, & Bernfeld (1977) and Schachar et al. (1981) showed this with hyperactivity and Robins (1966, 1978), in several longitudinal studies, has shown that the prognosis for antisocial behavior is worse either when it includes many different antisocial symptoms or when it is shown in many different settings. As already noted, disorders are also more likely to persist when they involve poor relationships with peers. Thirdly, as shown by the Isle of Wight follow-up (Rutter et al., 1976b), the London longitudinal study (Rutter, 1977), the Buckinghamshire study (Shepherd, Oppenheim, & Mitchell, 1971), and the Cambridge Study of Delinquent Development (West & Farrington, 1973, 1977), to mention but a few examples, persistence is more likely when there is parental mental illness, family discord, or disturbed parent–child relationships.

Syndrome Definition

Epidemiological approaches may also be utilized to facilitate the process of syndrome definition. Perhaps the most basic issue here is whether it is appropriate or helpful to consider syndromes at all. Certainly, some psychologists have argued that the very notion of diagnosis and classification has no place in psychiatry; rather, behavior, both normal and abnormal, is better considered in terms of personality dimensions that are measured on a continuum rather than in categorical terms (Eysenck, 1960). There are many reasons for doubting the applicability of a dimensional approach to certain severe and rare syndromes such as infantile autism (Rutter & Schopler, 1978) which, even in its milder forms, does not appear to shade off into normality. It is also dubious whether the problem is most usefully considered in "personality" terms so far as children's disorders are concerned (and certainly the proposed personality dimensions of "neuroticism" and "extraversion" seems to have very little explanatory power—see Farrington, Biron, & LeBlanc, 1980; Powell, 1977; Macmillan, Kolvin, Garside, Nicol, & Leitch, 1980). On the other hand, with the broader range of emotional and conduct disorders of childhood, both psychologists (Quay, 1979) and psychiatrists (Graham, 1979) have argued that problems are most appropriately thought of in dimensional terms. The point is that, for the most part, these disorders seem to represent quantitative, and not qualitative, departures from normality (Rutter, 1975), and hence the decision as to how "abnormal" a pattern of behavior must be for it to be considered a disorder is somewhat arbitrary. On the other hand, it must be said that the issue is far from resolved—particularly with the more severe and handicapping conditions seen in hospital practice. As with adults, there is continuing dispute on whether the more "common or garden" varieties of problems seen in community surveys are milder varieties of the same disorders seen in hospitals, or, rather, whether they constitute different conditions with overlapping phenomenology but with a different meaning and with different origins (see Brown & Harris, 1978; Dohrenwend et al., 1980; Tennant & Bebbington, 1978, for discussion of the parallel issues in the case of depression in adults).

Emotional and Conduct Disorders

However, the further issue of how disorders (or behavioral dimensions) should be categorized or divided does not depend on the resolution of that matter in that the answers seem to be much the same either way. Much the best supported differentiation is that between disturbances of emotions and disorders of conduct (Rutter, 1978). Numerous factor analytic and cluster studies (Achenbach & Edelbrock, 1978; Quay, 1979) have shown that these two sets of behavior tend to fall into separate groups. Moreover, when children are followed over several years (see Robins, 1979, for a review of the findings) or are recontacted in adulthood (Robins, 1966, 1979; Zeitlin, 1971, 1981), it has been found that the symptoms, when they continue, tend to remain of the same type. The two groups differ in sex ratio, with conduct disturbances much commoner in boys and emotional disorders marginally more frequent in girls (see earlier). As just discussed, the short-term and long-term prognosis are different for the two types of disorder. Conduct disorders are often associated with reading difficulties, whereas this is much less often the case with emotional disorders (Clark, 1970; Rutter, Tizard, & Whitmore, 1970). Also, family discord and disharmony are quite strongly linked with conduct disturbances, but the link with emotional difficulties is much weaker (Emery & O'Leary, 1981; Rutter, 1971). Epidemiological and longitudinal data, then, provide pretty clear-cut evidence for the differentiation of emotional and conduct disturbances.

On the other hand, the same studies also showed quite substantial overlap between the two types of disturbance, and the question remains as to how to classify these "mixed" disorders. Although no firm conclusions on that issue are yet possible, epidemiological–longitudinal data are helpful in indicating some of the considerations to be taken into account. To begin with, the overlap does not apply equally to all types of emotional disturbance. Children with conduct disorders fairly frequently show mood disturbances, but they are substantially less likely to exhibit anxiety, fears, or obsessions (Rutter, Tizard, & Whitmore, 1970). On follow-up into adult life, the same pattern is evident in that antisocial children not infrequently develop depressive conditions (often in association with a personality disorder), but they are much less likely to develop anxiety states, obsessional disorders, or other so-called "neurotic" conditions (Zeitlin, 1981). This finding, like the results of symptom clustering (Pearce, 1978), suggests that depression may constitute a rather different set of problems from other types of emotional disturbance. Also, when considered longitudinally, the overlap acts more in one direction than the other. Whereas it is decidedly unusual for a child with a purely emotional disturbance to develop a conduct disorder during the course of follow-up to adolescence (Graham & Rutter, 1973) or adult life (Robins, 1978; Zeitlin, 1981), the converse is not the case. A substantial minority of children with conduct problems later exhibit emotional difficulties. On the whole, the epidemiological features of "mixed" disorders are closer to those of conduct disorders than to emotional disorders (Rutter, Tizard, & Whitmore, 1970), although in outcome they are intermediate (Graham & Rutter, 1973). The question of the meaning of "mixed" disorders and the implications for classification of the overlap in phenomenology have not been adequately explored in any of the studies so far, and there is a great need for systematic multivariate analyses that take account of the severity, as well as the presence, of both types of symptomatology.

Hyperactivity

The other big overlap issue is that between hyperactivity and conduct problems. All major systems of classification have quite separate categories for these two patterns of behavior, but studies of general population samples (Sandberg, 1981; Sandberg, Wieselberg, & Shaffer, 1980) as well as clinic investigations (Sandberg, Rutter, & Taylor, 1978) have all shown that a very high proportion of children with one set of behaviors also show the other. The question arises, therefore, as to whether there is any reason to differentiate between them. We have approached this issue in several different ways. Sandberg and her colleagues' (1980) study of London primary-school schildren showed that both dimensions of behavior had very similar familial and neurodevelopmental correlates. Her clinic study divided psychiatric patients in the same age group into those with and those without hyperactivity as measured on Conner's parent or teacher scale (Sandberg et al., 1978). Again, no differences could be found, and it seemed that the presence of hyperactivity was of no differentiating value. But this conclusion was based on *single* measures of hyperactivity. There were only seven children with *pervasive* hyperactivity at home, at school, and as shown by systematic observations during the psychological examination. These seven *did* differ significantly from matched controls in terms of an onset during the pre-school years, more errors on the Matching Familiar Figures Test, and more abnormalities on a neurodevelopmental examination. It seemed that the presence of *pervasive* hyperkinesis (a much rarer phenomenon) might be of some importance, but the numbers were too small for firm conclusions.

Schachar et al. (1981) pursued this possibility further through a reanalysis of data from the Isle of Wight studies. The total population of children studied at both age 10 and age 14 were subdivided into the 2% with "pervasive" hyperactivity (as shown by deviant scores on the hyperactivity factor of *both* the parent and teacher questionnaires), the 14% with "situational" hyperactivity (i.e., a deviant score on one or other but not both questionnaires), and the remainder who were without hyperactivity as measured. Situational hyperactivity proved to have little differentiating value, but pervasive hyperactivity stood out as different in terms of a relatively strong association with cognitive impairment, a strong association with general disorder or deviance, and, within those with a general disorder, a significant association with a worse prognosis. A comparison with pervasive and situational ''unsociability'' (a measure of poor peer relationships) showed that the findings were specific to pervasive hyperactivity. The inference from this part-series of studies is that pervasive hyperactivity may constitute a meaningfully separate behavioral category or dimension, but situational hyperactivity probably does not do so.

Clearly the process of empirically based syndrome definition is still very much in the early stages of development (Rutter, 1978) and equally clearly ''official'' systems of classification include many subcategorizations for which there is no supporting evidence (Rutter & Shaffer, 1980). Epidemiological-longitudinal approaches cannot solve these problems; but, as shown already, they can clear the way in showing which leads are likely to be worth following.

CAUSAL FACTORS

The last topic to consider is the study of causal influences. This field includes several examples where epidemiological–longitudinal approaches have been successful in carrying the etiological search quite a long way. The process of enquiry may be illustrated by taking three contrasting examples from the series of studies undertaken by colleagues and myself.

Brain Damage

The first example is provided by the question of the behavioral consequences of brain damage in childhood (Rutter, 1980a). Clinicians from Still (1902) onward had noted that many children with cerebral palsy, epilepsy, encephalitis, or other brain conditions showed some form of emotional or behavioral disturbance, and causal inferences had been made. However, before even considering causation, it was necessary to check whether such disturbances were actually more frequent than those found in children with physical handicaps *not* involving brain damage or disease. The Isle of Wight epidemiological study (Rutter, Graham, & Yule, 1970) provided data of this kind with systematic standardized psychiatric assessments for all groups by the same team of investigators using the same measures. The results showed that the rate of psychiatric disorder was indeed considerably raised in the children with some form of brain damage, even after equating the groups for IQ and other possibly relevant factors. The finding was unlikely to be an artifact of the means of assessment in that the differences were closely similar whether based on information from parents, from teachers, or from the child himself/herself. However, it was possible (although the pattern of findings suggested otherwise) that the difference might be a consequence of the presence of physical crippling in the brain damage group as against its infrequency in the other physical handicap group (many of whom had conditions such as asthma, diabetes, or heart disease, which were unassociated with the obvious visible disabilities found with cerebral palsy).

This possibility was tested by means of a study of children in North London, all of whom were of normal intelligence, but all of whom had some form of visible crippling (Seidel, Chadwick, & Rutter, 1975). Children whose crippling was due to some form of brain disease or damage were compared with those whose handicaps were due to some other cause (paralyses following spinal poliomyelitis constituted the commonest of those). Again, psychiatric problems were significantly more frequent in the brain damage groups, strengthening the causal inference.

But, the limitation of this epidemiological strategy is that it is heavily dependent on having controlled for all the relevant variables—an almost impossible task. This difficulty may be overcome, however, by examining the behavioral *changes* that follow brain damage when it occurs at some point during childhood. Severe head injury provided the obvious example of such an occurrence. Children with head injuries resulting in a posttraumatic amnesia of at least 1 week were individually matched with children suffering orthopedic injuries (Brown, Chadwick, Shaffer, Rutter, & Traub, 1981; Rutter, Chadwick, Shaffer, & Brown, 1980). Whereas, obviously, it was not possible to obtain behavioral measures before the accident, it was possible to obtain measures of the child's preaccident behavior through interviews and questionnaires given very soon after the accident and before it could be known if the child was going to have any behavioral sequelae. These showed the two groups were closely comparable in their preaccident behavior (as well as in their family characteristics). Further behavioral assessments were then made 4 months, 1 year, and 2¼ years after the injury. These showed (when "blindly" rated from protocols with all identifying information excluded) a very marked increase in psychiatric disturbance following the accident in the children suffering severe head injuries, but not in the orthopedic controls. The rate of disorder in the head injury group remained double that in the controls for the whole of the 2¼ year follow-up period. The *change* in behavior following brain injury in this study strongly suggested that the injury (or something closely associated with it) *caused* the increase in emotional/behavioral disturbance.

However, the causal inference can be tested more rigorously by determining whether there is a systematic "dose-response" relationship—in other words, does the psychiatric risk increase progressively in direct relationship to the severity of the brain injury? Both the Isle of Wight study (Rutter, Graham, & Yule, 1970) and the head injury study (Brown et al., 1981) provided evidence of some connection of this kind (in the former by the greater psychiatric risk from bilateral brain disorders and in the latter by the association with duration of posttraumatic amnesia and the presence of abnormalities on a neurological examination). But the associations were neither very strong nor very consistent. The findings provided some support for the causal inference, but their relative weakness also suggested that the behavioral consequences of brain damage were unlikely to represent a very *direct* effect of brain pathology.

This could be further tested by determining whether the behavioral sequelae were further associated with any specific type of neurological deficit (on the grounds, outlined by Bradford Hill, 1977, that the more specific the association, the stronger the likelihood of direct causation). Once more, the results were somewhat equivocal in that there were *some* associations, but none was very strong. Thus, in the Isle of Wight study (Rutter, Graham, & Yule, 1970), disorder was more frequent when the brain disorder resulted in epileptic fits (suggesting that active physiological disturbance might be more disruptive than loss of function), and when the fits were psychomotor in type (suggesting that temporal lobe pathology might be most likely to cause behavioral sequelae). On the other hand, in a separate follow-up study of children with localized penetrating head injuries (Shaffer, Chadwick, & Rutter, 1975; Shaffer, Bijur, Chadwick, & Rutter, 1981), no associations between psychiatric disturbance and locus of injury were found (however, these included very few cases of temporal lobe damage, because this part of the brain is relatively well protected by its location, against direct external injury).

Specific associations could also be examined the other way round by asking if either generalized brain injury or particular types of brain injury resulted in specific types of emotional or behavioral disturbance. This possibility was examined in all the studies with largely negative results (as also in Shaffer, McNamara, & Pincus, 1974, study utilizing detailed quantitative behavioral measures). However, social disinhibition was found to be particularly linked with brain injury (Brown et al., 1981), and there was some tentative suggestion of a possible link between right frontal damage and affective disturbance (Shaffer et al., 1981).

Finally, the causal inference could be further explored by determining whether other non-neurological features were also associated with psychiatric disorder in brain-injured children, and whether the presence of brain injury in any way altered the usual pattern of epidemiological associations. The only alteration in pattern found was a marked reduction in (or sometimes obliteration of) the usual male preponderance (Brown et al., 1981; Rutter, Graham, & Yule, 1970). The reason for this effect remains as obscure as the reason for the generally increased male vulnerability in children (relative to the female); nevertheless, the alteration in sex ratio tends to support the suggestion that brain damage does have a causal impact. On the other hand, the findings within the group of children, all of whom had severe head injuries, that both preinjury behavior and psychosocial adversity were associated with the development of psychiatric disorder, clearly indicated that brain damage did *not* swamp the effects of other variables. Together with the findings on specificity already discussed, it also suggests that in large part the behavioral effects of brain damage are indirect rather than direct.

This conclusion, incidentally, differs from that with respect to cognitive sequelae where the strong and consistent dose-response relationship does suggest a greater direct effect (Chadwick et al., 1981a).

It is also noteworthy that the cognitive findings suggest that, to some extent, the effects of brain damage in childhood may differ somewhat from those in adult life. The localized head injury study (Chadwick et al., 1981b) failed to show the specific patterns of cognitive deficit usually associated with right- and left-sided damage in adults. Queries remain as to whether this negative finding indicates greater plasticity of brain functioning in childhood, or whether it means that the effects of injury on *developing* cognitive skills are different from those on already *established* skills, or whether indeed the apparent age difference is an artifact of the different types of brain lesions incurred in childhood compared to those that arise in adults. Either way, however, it is evident that important developmental issues remain to be resolved; their resolution could also have implications for the behavioral sequelae of brain injury. Nevertheless, in the meanwhile, we may conclude that epidemiological-longitudinal approaches have gone a long way toward proving the causal inference with respect to the effects of brain injury on behavioral disturbance, whereas, at the same time, casting doubt on the suggestion that the effects are direct.

Broken Homes and Separation Experiences

The second causal question involves a slightly different problem—namely, the identification of the relevant causal feature in an established statistical association involving a broad variable of little meaning in its own right, that of "broken homes." My interest in the matter came from a linking of the large literature that showed that broken homes were associated with an increased risk of delinquency (Wootton, 1959), with Bowlby's early claim (1946) that: "prolonged separation of a child from his mother (or mother substitute) during the first five years of his life stands foremost among the causes of delinquent character formation and persistent misbehaviour [p. 41]." The initial research question posed was whether separation from parents constituted the key mediating variable in the association between broken homes and delinquency. The most obvious alternative explanation was that family discord, rather than separation, was the crucial feature (as parental separation or divorce constituted the most frequent cause of a "broken home").

These two alternatives could be directly contrasted by comparing the effects of homes broken by death (where relationships are likely to have been fairly normal prior to the break) and homes broken by divorce or separation (where the break is likely to have been preceded by discord and quarrelling, or at least by a lack of warmth and affection). At the time I first became interested in the matter (Rutter, 1971), there were three separate studies that provided data on this comparison (Douglas, Ross, Hammond, & Mulligan, 1966; Douglas, Ross, &

Simpson, 1968; Gibson, 1969; Gregory, 1965). All agreed in showing that the delinquency rates were nearly double for boys whose parents had divorced or separated, but only slightly (and nonsignificantly) raised for those who had lost a parent by death. The implication was that it was the discord and disharmony associated with the break, rather than the breaking of the family as such, that had led to antisocial behavior.

In passing, I may note that it is in this situation that the test of nonreplication becomes applicable. There is an unfortunate tendency in the social sciences to pay too little attention to nonreplications, on the totally wrong-headed notion that if positive results outweigh negative ones, then, on the football-score criterion, the hypothesis wins! Of course, there may be a host of methodological reasons why any one particular study fails to produce the same results as those from other investigations. However, if the discrepant result stems from a good quality study using a research strategy that was appropriate for the purpose, it is always necessary to seek to determine *why* the results were different.

An example was provided by our own epidemiological studies in London and the Isle of Wight using the same research strategy and the same measures employed by the same team of investigators (Rutter et al., 1975a). In spite of the close comparability of the studies in the two areas, in one (London), "broken homes" was associated with behavioral deviance, whereas in the other it was not. The problem was explored by examining the circumstances of the children subject to family breakup, in order to determine if "broken homes" represented the same experience in the two populations (Rutter, 1974). It did not, and therein lay both the reason for the apparent nonreplication and also a finding that further supported the hypothesis that discord rather than separation constituted the key variable. Three features differentiated broken homes in London and the Isle of Wight. Firstly, the reasons for the breakup differed, in that on the Isle of Wight a higher proportion were due to parental death or adoption rather than divorce or separation. Secondly, in London, the parents were less likely to remarry so that more children were living with unsupported mothers. Thirdly, among those in London who did remarry, the second marriage was more likely to result in discord and disharmony than was the case on the Isle of Wight. It seemed that the circumstances leading to the separation, present during the separation and operating after the separation, were most important.

In order to take the matter further, it was necessary to turn to a different set of comparisons. If discord rather than separation was crucial, discord ought to be associated with conduct disturbances in *un*broken homes. We were able to test that suggestion in our community-based longitudinal study of children of parents with a psychiatric disorder (Rutter, 1971). None of the boys living in a harmonious home showed antisocial disorder, but the rate rose to 22% in homes where the parental marriage received an intermediate rating, and 39% in those with a severely discordant parental marriage. The highly significant linear trend confirmed that parental discord *was* associated with antisocial disorder in *un*-

broken homes. That finding was based on a sample in which discord was also associated with parental mental disorder, and it was necessary to go on to check whether the association still held in the general population. Our epidemiological studies in both London and the Isle of Wight (Rutter, Yule, Quinton, Rowlands, Yule, & Berger, 1975b) showed that it did (although the relationships were not as strong as in the patient sample).

Similarly, of course, it should also follow that within groups of children, all of whom have experienced family breakup, the psychiatric risk should be related to the extent to which divorce or separation is accompanied by continuing tensions or increasing harmony. That is not a research strategy that we ourselves have followed but the results of studies undertaken by Hetherington (Hetherington et al., 1978, 1979), Wallerstein (Wallerstein & Kelly, 1980), Hess (Hess & Camara, 1979), and their associates; all have shown that continuing discord between the divorced parents is associated with child disorder even within a group all of whose parents have divorced.

Those results applied to permanent separations, but the same strategy could also be applied to temporary separations by asking if it mattered whether or not the separation was associated with discord. In our longitudinal study of the families of parents with a psychiatric disorder, we compared separations due to family discord (usually temporary breakups resulting from parental quarrels) with those *not* associated with discord (mostly admissions to hospital for a physical illness or a prolonged, usually convalescent, holiday). The results showed that the former type of discordant separation was strongly associated with antisocial disorder in the children, whereas the latter showed no such association.

The evidence all pointed to the importance of discord rather than separations per se. However, the hypothesis needed further testing through other strategies. Two were immediately possible within the data already collected in the studies to which I have referred (Rutter, 1971). Firstly, it was possible to determine if *changes* in the quality of family relationships were accompanied by parallel changes in the psychiatric risk for the children. This was tested by taking the subgroup of children (from the longitudinal study of patients' families), all of whom had been separated from their parents in early childhood as a result of family discord and disharmony. This subgroup was then subdivided into those living in homes that were *still* discordant and quarrelsome, and those currently in families where relationships were relatively harmonious or at least not openly conflicting. Both sets of children showed rates of antisocial disorder that were well above population norms, but those whose homes had become more harmonious showed a rate of disorder *half* that shown by those living in persistently discordant families.

The finding that *improvements* in family relationships were accompanied by a reduction in the risk to the children strengthened the hypothesis that discord constituted the mediating causal variable. The other test was whether the association between parental discord and child deviance would be modified if the child had a good relationship with at least one of the parents. The argument was that if the quality of relationships was crucial, the effects on the child of discord *between* the parents should be reduced if the child was still able to maintain one good relationship with a parent in spite of the discord. The results showed that this was the case (although the effects of discord were only reduced and not removed).

The pattern of epidemiological findings constituted quite a strong case in favour of the proposition that discord rather than separation was likely to be the crucial causal factor in the statistical association between broken homes and conduct disturbances in the children. However, numerous questions and problems still remain. Most obvious of all is the fact that discord remains almost as general a variable as broken homes, and it is by no means self-evident what psychological mechanism might be involved (Rutter & Garmezy, 1981). One of the major problems is that when there is family discord, there tends also to be a complex set of other family adversities, including parental depression, difficulties with discipline and supervision of the children, parental criminality, and various other psychosocial hazards. So far, it has not proved possible satisfactorily to disentangle this web of intermeshed family variables in order to determine which are the most important operative factors. That remains a major research task for the future.

However, there are at least two other research issues that stem from the questions on separation with which we started. As already noted, we found no *long-term* adverse effects from children being admitted to hospital (although short-term effects have been well-documented by others). But, in our initial analyses, we did not differentiate between single and multiple admissions. When this was done, first by Douglas (1975) and then by ourselves (Quinton & Rutter, 1976), it was found that there *were* adverse long-term sequelae following *multiple* admissions, although there were not any after single admissions. This did not appear to be just the additive effect of several minor acute stresses in that *no* long-term effects could be detected following single admissions. Part of the explanation lay in the observation that children experiencing multiple hospital admissions were also more likely to have experienced chronic family adversities of other kinds (so that the association with admissions was really a function of the chronic adversities rather than the admissions as such). But this did not seem to be the whole explanation and the matter requires further study—probably by means of a longitudinal study focussing on the changes in children's behavior and in family patterns that are associated with repeated admissions. Again, the mechanisms involved have not yet been identified.

The other research issue comes back to Bowlby's (1946) initial observations regarding early separation experiences. His study was based on a highly selected clinic sample open to a host of biases, so that great caution is needed in interpreting any of the findings. Nevertheless, study of his case histories suggested two possibilities: firstly, that the key factor may have been a lack of opportunity to develop initial bonds and attachments in infancy (rather than separations); and, secondly, that the relevant dependent variable may have been impaired personal relationships rather than delinquency. Studies of institutional children (Wolkind, 1974) lent support to the plausibility of that suggestion and research on the development of attachments (Bowlby, 1969; Rutter, 1981d) also indicated that this was something worth exploring.

In order to investigate that possibility, it was necessary to choose a sample of children brought up in a *non*discordant home but also brought up in conditions that were likely to impair the development of initial bonds. An institutional upbringing from infancy seemed the nearest approach to those conditions in that modern residential nurseries provide generally good conditions for children, except for the very striking failure to provide any kind of continuity in parenting. Thus, Barbara Tizard's studies (Tizard, 1977; Tizard & Hodges, 1978; Tizard & Tizard, 1971) showed that children frequently experienced over 50 different caretakers during the preschool years with the consequence of considerable discontinuity in parenting, although in most cases each caretaker provided a quite reasonable upbringing in other respects. Her follow-up of institutional children to age 8 years showed that, when young, they tended to lack close attachments and that, when older, they appeared attention-seeking, restless, disobedient, and unpopular at school. These findings were certainly consonant with the suggestion that a lack of opportunity for bonding in infancy predisposed to later problems in social relationships. However, to test that hypothesis adequately, further steps were needed. In order to check whether it was truly the infancy experiences that were crucial, it was necessary to identify a subgroup of children whose experiences *after* infancy appeared satisfactory—late-adopted children constituted just such a group. It was striking that, in Tizard's studies, their behavior at school (although not at home) was very similar to that of the children who remained in institutions. The implication is that the infancy experiences (or lack of experiences) constituted the relevant factor in terms of the later social deficits.

Dixon's (1981) study takes the matter somewhat further in three respects. Firstly, her study of 5-to 8-year-old children brought up in institutions from infancy included the same measures as those used by Tizard. Her findings were closely similar, so providing a replication in an independent sample. Secondly, Tizard's behavioral measures all relied on interviews or questionnaires that could have given rise to findings that were biased by people's preconceptions of how institutional children "should" behave. Dixon's direct observations in the classrooms ruled out that possibility in that the observational data produced much the same pattern of findings. Thirdly, she was able to provide a more direct focus on the effects of an institutional upbringing by comparing children reared in residential nurseries with children reared by foster parents in a personal family setting. The two groups were similar in family backgrounds (in both, the parents were markedly deviant in numerous respects), but the foster group had experienced continuous personal parenting from one set of parents only, whereas the institutional group had experienced a group upbringing with many changes of house parents. Both groups differed from normal controls, but the institution-reared children were substantially more deviant than the fostered children. The results suggested that, although it was not the only relevant factor, an institutional upbringing did constitute the main predisposing influence.

Both Tizard's and Dixon's studies were based on rather small numbers, and there are many other possible explanations for the findings that require testing. Obviously, the matter remains open and in need of further investigation. Nevertheless, it does appear that a failure to develop bonds in infancy may have important sequelae and that the possibility warrants further exploration.

School Influences

The third, and last, set of possible causal factors to be considered, namely school influences, are different in at least one crucial respect and therefore required a rather different set of research strategies. Both brain damage and family discord are most conveniently thought of in terms of variables that might influence *individual* predispositions to deviant behavior. Accordingly, the appropriate unit of analysis was the child. Schooling was conceptualized rather differently in terms of a set of variables that are best considered in terms of an influence on *group* or *ecological* predispositions (see Rutter, 1979, for a discussion of concepts of causative influences). The hypothesis tested was that differences in the quality of schooling might have an effect in raising (or lowering) overall levels of pupil behavior and attainment. This meant that, for most purposes, the *school* had to be the unit of analysis (i.e., the question was whether *schools* differed in the levels of outcome achieved by their pupils). This is not the same question as that asked by Jencks, Smith, Acland, Bane, Cohen, Gintis, Heyns, & Michelson (1972) with respect to whether raising the standard of schooling would reduce inequalities of attainment; nor is it the same as asking whether schools account for a high proportion of population variance in children's behavior and attainments (i.e., account for individual differences).[1]

The research problem started with the observation that schools differed markedly in their levels of disruptive behavior and of reading difficulties (Rutter et al., 1975b, 1979). The first issue was whether these differences were the consequences of differing patterns of intake (i.e., that some schools admitted higher proportions of children already showing behavioral or educational problems) and

---

[1]Our evidence on both questions is in keeping with that of others; that is, there is no indication that variations in the quality of schooling substantially influence the *spread* of individual scores on tests of scholastic attainment; and although school influences do contribute significantly to individual differences in attainment, their effect is much less than either individual intelligence or family variables (Rutter et al., 1979; Maughan et al., 1980).

hence nothing to do with any influence of the school at all. Or, rather, whether the differences in pupil outcome reflected an *effect* of the school on the children, such that a child in one school would have a different outcome from a similar child attending another school, in spite of both children having shown similar characteristics at the time of admission to the school. The only satisfactory way to tackle that question was to systematically assess all children in a particular geographical area just *before* they transferred to secondary schools (i.e., schools taking children from 11 or 12 years onward) and then to follow their progress right through secondary schooling with a further reassessment at the time of school-leaving.[2] In essence, that is what we did with respect to children attending primary (i.e. elementary) schools in one inner London borough (Rutter et al., 1979). The results showed that there were differences between schools in intake characteristics, but that even after partialling out the effects of intake differences, large and highly significant school differences remained with respect to pupil attendance, behavior, delinquency, and scholastic attainment. Thus, in the top ability band, pupils at the most successful school had *four* times as many national examination passes as those in the least successful school. Similarly, the delinquency rate for boys of broadly similar background at one end of the school range was three times that for the school at the other extreme of the range.

Of course, these findings do not prove that there was a school effect. All that they show is that the differences were *not* due to the intake variables that were assessed. Inevitably, only a limited range of measures could be obtained at intake, and there will always be the possibility that the differences were the result of some other variable that was not measured. Nevertheless, that does not seem likely in that we had data on the children's sex, socioeconomic background, home neighborhood, primary school attended, ethnicity, nonverbal intelligence, reading, verbal reasoning, and behavior in primary school.

However, the matter should not be resolved by adding yet further intake measures in the hope of increasing the list of factors that do *not* account for school differences. Rather, the next step needed to be the direct determination of whether school variables *did* account for the differences. For this purpose, over the course of 3 years, we made a very detailed study of the 12 secondary schools that took the bulk of the children from the area—interviewing over 200 teachers, obtaining questionnaires from nearly 3000 pupils, undertaking systematic minute by minute observations in some 500 lessons, and making a variety of other observations about the schools. These data, together with information from official records, were used to derive a series of measures of different aspects of school life and functioning. These school measures were then related to the pupil outcome measures, after having taken into account the already noted intake

---

[2]The children were also followed up 1 year after leaving school in order to investigate outcome in terms of employment (Gray, Smith, & Rutter, 1980).

characteristics of the pupils at each school. The results showed quite strong associations between pupil outcomes and such school characteristics as degree of academic emphasis, styles and skills of classroom management, models of teacher behavior, the availability of incentives and rewards, good conditions for pupils, and opportunities for them to take responsibilities.

The finding of a significant correlation between school characteristics and pupil outcomes is consistent with the hypothesis of a school *effect* on children's behavior and attainments. However, before accepting that hypothesis, it was necessary to ask whether the pupil characteristics had influenced the school functioning, or whether it was the other way round. Of course, in reality, it is bound to be a two-way interaction (actually, multiple ways, in that there are also many external forces that impinge on schools and their pupils). Nevertheless, it is both legitimate and necessary to ask which effect predominated with respect to the particular variables studied. This issue was tackled by determining whether the pupil characteristics *at intake* correlated as strongly with the school measures as did the pupil characteristics at the time of leaving the school. It was found that the intake measures had only weak (and generally statistically nonsignificant) associations with the school variables—indicating that it was *un*likely that the school functioning and the teacher performance had been shaped in a major way by the characteristics of the pupils admitted to the school. Thus, the school "process" score correlated 0.39 with children's behavior at intake, but 0.92 with their behavior later in their secondary schooling; and 0.44 with academic attainment at intake, but 0.76 with academic attainment at the end of their high-school career.[3] This increase in correlation suggests that the main effect was of school factors on pupil behavior, rather than the other way round (although the inference is somewhat weakened by the fact that inevitably the measures at the beginning and end of schooling could not be identical).

Taken as a whole, the results constitute a strong circumstantial argument for a causal influence of schooling on children's behavior and attainments—an argument that is strengthened by the fact that, insofar as they are comparable, other studies have produced a generally similar pattern of findings. That is about as far as epidemiological approaches can take the causal issue (although they could do much more to aid understanding of the processes involved). As with most other causal questions, the final step must be the evaluation of some form of planned change or intervention, in short, the educational experiment.

CONCLUSIONS

In this chapter, my aim has been to illustrate some of the ways in which epidemiological-longitudinal approaches can contribute to an understanding of

---

[3]These correlations all refer to correlations between schools, with respect to the overall school "score" on the variables mentioned, rather than to correlations between individual children.

children's development, by taking examples from some of the research undertaken by my colleagues and myself. In all the examples used, the investigative story has been incomplete—both because these approaches have not yet accomplished all that they could, and, more especially, because in no case could epidemiology produce the answers on its own. It does provide a most useful and versatile set of research strategies and tactics that are not sufficiently understood and utilized. Nevertheless, when all is said and done, it remains just one methodology that must always be combined with other approaches. As a result, this chapter has necessarily resulted in a rather awkward unfinished patchwork quilt of ideas and findings. I hope, however, that it has shown something of the payoff possible from employing epidemiological-longitudinal approaches to the study of patterns of behavior in childhood, of developmental trends and changes, of sex differences, of syndrome definition, and of questions of causation.

ACKNOWLEDGMENTS

This chapter is based on several, interlinked research programs, and I am deeply indebted for both ideas and empirical findings to the many colleagues who were jointly responsible for the studies on which I mainly draw. I owe the greatest debt to the late Sir Aubrey Lewis, who led me into this area of research, to the late Jack Tizard, who taught me most of what I know about epidemiology, and to the late Herbert Birch, who helped me see how these methods could and should be applied to developmental problems. I am also especially grateful to Kingsley Whitmore, Philip Graham, and Bill Yule, who (with Jack Tizard) were jointly concerned with the Isle of Wight studies; to David Quinton and Bridget Yule with the several family studies; to David Shaffer, Oliver Chadwick, and Gill Brown with the head-injury studies; and to Barbara Maughan, Peter Mortimore, Janet Ouston, and Bridget Yule with the school studies.

REFERENCES

Achenbach, T. M., & Edelbrock, C. S. The classification of child psychopathology: A review and analysis of empirical efforts. *Psychological Bulletin,* 1978, *85,* 1275-1301.

Adler, F. The interaction between women's emancipation and female criminality: A cross-cultural perspective. *International Journal of Criminology and Penology,* 1977, *5,* 101-112.

Åkesson, H. O. Empirical risk figures in mental deficiency. *Acta Genetic et Statistica Medica,* 1962, *12,* 28-32.

Bartak, L., Rutter, M., & Cox, A. A comparative study of infantile autism and specific developmental receptive language disorder. I. The children. *British Journal of Psychiatry,* 1975, *126,* 127-145.

Baumrind, D. *Gender-differences and sex-related socialization effects.* Submitted for publication, 1980.

Belson, W. A. *Juvenile theft: The causal factors.* London: Harper & Row, 1975.

Benaim, S., Horder, J., & Anderson, J. Hysterical epidemic in a classroom. *Psychological Medicine,* 1973, *3,* 366-373.

Berg, J. M., & Kirman, B. H. Some aetiological problems in mental deficiency. *British Medical Journal,* 1959, *2,* 848-852.

Berger, A. S., & Simon, W. Black families and the Moynihan report: A research evaluation. *Social Problems*, 1974, *22*, 145-161.

Berkson, J. Limitations of the application of four-fold table analysis to hospital data. *Biometrics*, 1946, *2*, 247-253.

Block, J. H., Block, J., & Morrison, A. Parental agreement-disagreement on childrearing orientations and gender-related personality correlates in children. *Child Development*, in press, 1981.

Blomfield, J. M., & Douglas, J. W. B. Bedwetting prevalence among children aged 4-7 years. *Lancet*, 1956, *1*, 850-852.

Bowlby, J. *Forty-four juvenile thieves: Their characters and home-life*. London: Baillère, Tindall, & Cox, 1946.

Bowlby, J. *Attachment and loss. 1. Attachment*. London: Hogarth Press, 1969.

Bradford Hill, A. *A short textbook of medical statistics*. London: Hodder & Stoughton, 1977.

Brown, George W., & Harris, T. *Social origins of depression*. London: Tavistock, 1978.

Brown, George W., & Rutter, M. The measurement of family activities and relationships: A methodological study. *Human relations*, 1966, *19*, 241-263.

Brown, Gillian, Chadwick, O., Shaffer, D., Rutter, M., & Traub, M. A prospective study of children with head injuries III. Psychiatric sequelae. *Psychological Medicine*, 1981, *11*, 63-78.

Cairns, R. B. *Social development: The origin and plasticity of interchanges*. San Francisco: W. H. Freeman, 1979.

Campbell, S. B., Endman, M. W., & Bernfeld, G. A three-year follow-up of hyperactive preschoolers, into elementary school. *Journal of Child Psychology and Psychiatry*, 1977, *18*, 239-249.

Cernkovich, S. A., & Giordano, P. C. A comparative analysis of male and female delinquency. *Sociological Quarterly*, 1979, *20*, 131-145.

Chadwick, O., Rutter, M., Brown, G., Shaffer, D., & Traub, M. A prospective study of children with head injuries II. Cognitive sequelae. *Psychological Medicine*, 1981, *11*, 49-61. (a)

Chadwick, O., Rutter, M., Thompson, J., & Shaffer, D. Intellectual performance and reading skills after localized head injury in childhood. *Journal of Child Psychology & Psychiatry*, 1981, *22*, 117-139. (b)

Claeys, W., & DeBoek, P. The influence of some parental characteristics on children's primary abilities and field independence: A study of adopted children. *Child Development*, 1976, *47*, 842-845.

Clark, M. M. *Reading difficulties in schools*. Harmondsworth: Penguin, 1970.

Clausen, J. A. The social meaning of differential physical and sexual maturation. In S. E. Dragastin & G. H. Elder (Eds.), *Adolescence in the life cycle: Psychological change and social context*. London: Halsted Press, 1975.

Cooper, B., & Morgan, H. G. *Epidemiological psychiatry*. Springfield, Ill.: Charles C Thomas, 1973.

Cox, A., Holbrook, D., & Rutter, M. Psychiatric interviewing techniques VI. Experimental study: Eliciting feelings. *British Journal of Psychiatry*, in press, 1981c.

Cox, A., Hopkinson, K., & Rutter, M. Psychiatric interviewing techniques II. Naturalistic study: Eliciting factual information. *British Journal of Psychiatry*, 1981a, *138*, 283-291.

Cox, A., Rutter, M., & Holbrook, D. Psychiatric interviewing techniques V. Experimental study: Eliciting factual information. *British Journal of Psychiatry*, 1981b, *139*, 29-37.

Cox, A., Rutter, M., Yule, B., & Quinton, D. Bias resulting from missing information: Some epidemiological findings. *British Journal of Preventive and Social Medicine*, 1977, *31*, 131-136.

Crome, L. The brain and mental retardation. *British Medical Journal*, 1960, *1*, 879-904.

De Alarcón, R. The spread of heroin abuse in a community. *Bulletin of Narcotics*, 1969, *21*, 17-22.

Dixon, P. Paper in preparation, 1981.

Dohrenwend, B. P., Dohrenwend, B. S., Gould, M., Link, B., Neugebauer, R., & Wunsch-Hitzig, R. *Mental illness in the United States: Epidemiological estimates*. New York: Praeger, 1980.

Doll, R., & Bradford Hill, A. Mortality in relation to smoking: Ten years' observations of British doctors. *British Medical Journal*, 1964, *1*, 1399–1410, 1460–1467.

Douglas, J. W. B. Early hospital admissions and later disturbances of behaviour and learning. *Developmental Medicine and Child Neurology*, 1975, *17*, 456–480.

Douglas, J. W. B., Ross, J. M., Hammond, W. A., & Mulligan, D. G. Delinquency and social class. *British Journal of Criminology*, 1966, *6*, 294–302.

Douglas, J. W. B., Ross, J. M., & Simpson, H. R. *All our future: A longitudinal study of secondary education*. London: Peter Davies, 1968.

Eme, R. F. Sex differences in childhood psychopathology: A review. *Psychological Bulletin*, 1979, *86*, 574–595.

Emery, R. E., & O'Leary, K. D. Children's perceptions of marital discord as related to behavior problems of boys and girls. *Journal of Abnormal Child Psychology*, in press, 1981.

Emmerich, W. Personality development and concepts of structure. *Child Development*, 1968, *39*, 671–690.

Epstein, S. The stability of behavior I. On predicting most of the people much of the time. *Journal of Personality and Social Psychology*, 1979, *37*, 1097–1126.

Eysenck, H. J. Classification and the problem of diagnosis. In H. J. Eysenck (Ed.), *Handbook of abnormal psychology: An experimental approach*. New York: Basic Books, 1960. Pp. 1–31.

Eysenck, H. J., & Eysenck, S. B. G. *Manual of the Eysenck Personality Questionnaire (Junior and Adult)*. London: Hodder & Stoughton, 1975.

Eysenck, M. W., & Eysenck, H. J. Mischel and the concept of personality. *British Journal of Psychology*, 1980, *71*, 191–204.

Farrington, D. P., Biron, L., & LeBlanc, M. Personality and delinquency in London and Montreal. In J. C. Gunn & D. P. Farrington (eds.), *Advances in forensic psychiatry and psychology*. Chichester: Wiley, 1980.

Forslund, M. A. A comparison of negro and white crime rates. *Journal of Criminal Law, Criminology, & Police Science*, 1970, *61*, 214–217.

Frodi, A., Macaulay, J., & Thome, P. R. Are women always less aggressive than men? A review of the experimental literature. *Psychological Bulletin*, 1977, *84*, 634–660.

Ghodsian, M., Fogelman, K., Lambert, L., & Tibbenham, A. Changes in behaviour ratings of a national sample of children. *British Journal of Social & Clinical Psychology*, 1980, *19*, 247–256.

Gibson, H. B. Early delinquency in relation to broken homes. *Journal of Child Psychology & Psychiatry*, 1969, *10*, 195–204.

Gold, M. *Delinquent behavior in an American city*. Monterey, Calif.: Brooks/Cole, 1970.

Gove, W. R., & Tudor, J. F. Adult sex roles and mental illness. *American Journal of Sociology*, 1973, *78*, 812–835.

Graham, P. J. Epidemiological studies. In H. C. Quay & J. S. Werry (Eds.), *Psychopathological disorders of childhood*. New York: Wiley, 1979. Pp. 185–209.

Graham, P., & Rutter, M. The reliability and validity of the psychiatric assessment of the child II. Interview with the parent. *British Journal of Psychiatry*, 1968, *114*, 581–592.

Graham, P., & Rutter, M. Psychiatric disorder in the young adolescent: A follow-up study. *Proceedings of the Royal Society of Medicine*, 1973, *66*, 1226–1229.

Graham, P., & Rutter, M. Adolescent disorders. In M. Rutter & L. Hersov (Eds.), *Child psychiatry: Modern approaches*. Oxford: Blackwell Scientific, 1977. Pp. 407–427.

Gray, G., Smith, A., & Rutter, M. School attendance and the first year of employment. In L. Hersov & I. Berg (Eds.), *Out of school: Modern perspectives in truancy and school refusal*. Chichester: Wiley, 1980.

Green, E. Race, social status, and criminal arrest. *American Sociological Review*, 1970, *35*, 476–490.

Gregory, I. Anterospective data following childhood loss of a parent. *Archives of General Psychiatry*, 1965, *13*, 110–120.

Hare, E. H., & Wing, J. K. (eds.). *Psychiatric epidemiology*. London: Oxford University Press, 1970.

Hartup, W. W. Peer relations and family relations: Two social worlds. In M. Rutter (Ed.), *Scientific foundations of developmental psychiatry*. London: Heinemann Medical, 1980. Pp. 280–292.

Henn, F. A., Bardwell, R., & Jenkins, R. L. Juvenile delinquents revisited: Adult criminal activity. *Archives of General Psychiatry*, 1980, *37*, 1160–1163.

Hess, R. D., & Camera, K. A. Postdivorce family relationships as mediating factors in the consequences of divorce for children. *Journal of Social Issues*, 1979, *35*, 79–96.

Hetherington, E. M., Cox, M., & Cox, R. The aftermath of divorce. In J. H. Stevens & M. Matthews (Eds.), *Mother–Child, Father–Child Relations*. Washington, D.C.: National Association for the Education of Young Children, 1978.

Hetherington, E. M., Cox, M., & Cox, R. Play and social interaction in children following divorce. *Journal of Social Issues*, 1979, *35*, 26–49.

Hobson, R. P. Early childhood autism and the question of egocentrism. Submitted for publication, 1981.

Hoffman, M. L. Sex differences in empathy and related behaviors. *Psychological Bulletin*, 1977, *84*, 712–722.

Home Office. *Criminal Statistics England and Wales, 1977*. London: Her Majesty's Stationery Office, 1978.

Hopkinson, K., Cox, A., & Rutter, M. Psychiatric interviewing techniques III. Naturalistic study: Eliciting feelings. *British Journal of Psychiatry*, 1981, *138*, 406–415.

Jencks, C., Smith, M., Acland, H., Bane, M. J., Cohen, D., Gintis, H., Heyns, B., & Michelson, S. *Inequality: A reassessment of the effect of family and schooling in America*. New York: Basic Books, 1972.

Kagan, J. Perspectives on continuity. In O. G. Brim & J. Kagan (Eds.), *Constancy and change in human development*. Cambridge, Mass.: Harvard University Press, 1980.

Kagan, J., & Moss, H. A. *Birth to maturity*. New York: Wiley, 1962.

Kanner, L. Do behavioural symptoms always indicate psychopathology? *Journal of Child Psychology & Psychiatry*, 1960, *1*, 17–25.

Kidd, C. B., & Caldbeck-Meenan, J. A comparative study of psychiatric morbidity among students at two different universities. *British Journal of Psychiatry*, 1966, *112*, 57–64.

Kohlberg, L., LaCrosse, J., & Ricks, D. The predictability of adult mental health from childhood behavior. In B. Wolman (Ed.), *Handbook of child psychopathology*. New York: McGraw-Hill, 1970.

Kreitman, N. (Ed.). *Parasuicide*. London: Wiley, 1977.

Maccoby, E. E. *Social development: Psychological growth and the parent–child relationship*. New York: Harcourt Brace Jovanovich, 1980.

Maccoby, E. E., & Jacklin, C. N. *Psychology of sex differences*. Stanford, Calif.: Stanford University Press, 1974.

Macfarlane, J. W., Allen, L., & Honzik, M. P. *A developmental study of the behavior problems of normal children between 21 months and 14 years*. Berkeley: University of California Press, 1954.

Macmillan, A., Kolvin, I., Garside, R., Nicol, A. R., & Leitch, I. M. A multiple criterion screen for identifying secondary school children with psychiatric disorder: Characteristics and efficiency of screen. *Psychological Medicine*, 1980, *10*, 265–276.

Martin, J. A., Maccoby, E. E., & Jacklin, C. N. Consequences of mothers' responsiveness to interactive bidding and nonbidding in boys and girls. *Child Development*, in press, 1981.

Maughan, B., Ouston, J., Rutter, M., & Mortimore, P. Fifteen thousand hours: A reply to Heath and Clifford. *Oxford Review of Education*, 1980, *6*, 289–303.

McCall, R. B. Challenges to a science of developmental psychology. *Child Development*, 1977, *48*, 333–344.

McEvedy, C. P., & Beard, A. W. Royal Free epidemic of 1955: A reconsideration. *British Medical Journal*, 1970, *1*, 7–11.

Mechanic, D. Problems and prospects in psychiatric epidemiology. In E. H. Hare & J. K. Wing (Eds.), *Psychiatric Epidemiology*, London: Oxford University Press, 1970. Pp. 3–22.

Meehl, P. E., & Rosen, A. Antecedent probability of the efficiency of psychometric signs, patterns, or cutting scores. *Psychological Bulletin*, 1955, *52*, 194–216.

Mikkelson, E. J., Rapoport, J. L., Nee, C., Gruenan, C., Mendelsohn, W., & Gillin, J. C. Childhood enuresis I. Sleep patterns and psychopathology. *Archives of General Psychiatry*, in press, 1981.

Mischel, W. On the interface of cognition and personality: Beyond the person–situation debate. *American Psychologist*, 1979, *34*, 740–754.

Morris, J. N. *Uses of epidemiology (3rd ed.)*. London: Longman, 1975.

Moss, H. A., & Sussman, E. J. Longitudinal study of personality development. In O. G. Brim & J. Kagan (Eds.), *Constancy and change in human development*. Cambridge, Mass.: Harvard University Press, 1980.

Olweus, D. Stability of aggressive reaction patterns in males: A review. *Psychological Bulletin*, 1979, *86*, 852–875.

Olweus, D. The consistency issue in personality psychology revisited—with special reference to aggression. *British Journal of Social & Clinical Psychology*, 1980, *19*, 377–390.

Ouston, J. E. *A comparison between delinquents and nondelinquents attending 12 London secondary schools*. In preparation, 1981.

Patterson, G. R. The aggressive child: Victim and architect of a coercive system. In E. J. Mash, L. A. Hamerlynck, & L. C. Handy (Eds.), *Behavior modification and families*. New York: Brunner/Mazel, 1976.

Patterson, G. R. Mothers: The unacknowledged victims. *Monographs, Society for Reserach in Child Development*, 1980, *45*, No. 5, 1–63.

Pearce, J. B. The recognition of depressive disorder in children. *Journal of the Royal Society of Medicine*, 1978, *71*, 494–500.

Porter, B., & O'Leary, K. Marital discord and childhood behavior problems. *Journal of Abnormal Child Psychology*, 1980, *8*, 287–296.

Powell, G. E. Psychoticism and social deviancy in children. *Advances in Behavior Research & Therapy*, 1977, *1*, 27–56.

Quay, H. C. Classification. In H. C. Quay & J. S. Werry (Eds.), *Psychopathological disorders of childhood*. New York: Wiley, 1979. Pp. 1–42.

Quinton, D., & Rutter, M. Early hospital admissions and later disturbances of behaviour: An attempted replication of Douglas' findings. *Developmental Medicine and Child Neurology*, 1976, *18*, 447–459.

Quinton, D., Rutter, M., & Rowlands, O. An evaluation of an interview assessment of marriage. *Psychological Medicine*, 1976, *6*, 577–586.

Radloff, L. Sex differences in depression: The effects of occupation and marital status. *Sex Roles*, 1975, *1*, 249–267.

Rapoport, J. L., Mikkelson, E. J., Zavadil, A., Nee, L., Gruenon, C., Mendelsohn, W., & Gillin, J. C. Childhood enuresis II. Psychopathology, plasma tricyclic concentration and antienuretic effect. *Archives of General Psychiatry*, in press, 1981.

Reed, E. W., & Reed, S. C. *Mental retardation: A family study*. Philadelphia: W. B. Saunders, 1965.

Richman, N., Stevenson, J. E., & Graham, P. J. *Upset and upsetting: A longitudinal study of preschool children*. Submitted for publication, 1981.

Robins, L. *Deviant children grown up*. Baltimore: Williams & Wilkins, 1966.

Robins, L. Sturdy childhood predictors of adult antisocial behaviour: Replications from longitudinal studies. *Psychological Medicine*, 1978, *8*, 611-622.

Robins, L. Longitudinal methods in the study of normal and pathological development. In K. P. Kisker, J. E. Meyer, C. Müller, & E. Stromgren (Eds.), *Psychiatrie der Gegenwart. Band 1. 'Grundlagen und Methoden der Psychiatrie'*, 2 Auflage. Heidelberg: Springer-Verlag, 1979.

Robins, L., & Hill, S. Y. Assessing the contributions of family structure, class, and peer groups to juvenile delinquency. *Journal of Criminal Law, Criminology & Police Science*, 1966, *57*, 325-334.

Roff, M., Sells, S. B., & Golden, M. M. *Social adjustment and personality development in children*. Minneapolis: University of Minnesota Press, 1972.

Rutter, M. Sex differences in children's responses to family stress. In E. J. Anthony & C. Koupernik (Eds.), *The child in his family*. New York: Wiley, 1970. a

Rutter, M. Psychological development: Predictions from infancy. *Journal of Child Psychology & Psychiatry*, 1970, *11*, 49-62. b

Rutter, M. Parent-child separation: Psychological effects on the children. *Journal of Child Psychology & Psychiatry*, 1971, *12*, 233-260.

Rutter, M. Epidemiological strategies and psychiatric concepts in research on the vulnerable child. In E. J. Anthony & C. Koupernik (Eds.), *The child in his family: Children at psychiatric risk* (Vol. 3). New York: Wiley, 1974.

Rutter, M. *Helping troubled children*. Harmondsworth: Penguin, 1975.

Rutter, M. Surveys to answer questions: Some methodological considerations. In P. J. Graham (Ed.), *Epidemiological approaches in child psychiatry*. London: Academic Press, 1977. a

Rutter, M. Prospective studies to investigate behavioral change. In J. S. Strauss, H. M. Babigian, & M. Roff (Eds.), *The origins and course of psychopathology*. New York: Plenum, 1977. b

Rutter, M. Diagnostic validity in child psychiatry. *Advances in Biological Psychiatry*, 1978, *2*, 2-22.

Rutter, M. *Changing youth in a changing society*. London: Nuffield Provincial Hospitals Trust, 1979 (Cambridge, Mass.: Harvard University Press, 1980).

Rutter, M. Introduction. In M. Rutter (Ed.), *Scientific foundations of developmental psychiatry*. London: Heinemann Medical, 1980. a

Rutter, M. Emotional development. In M. Rutter (Ed.), *Scientific foundations of developmental psychiatry*. London: Heinemann Medical, 1980. b

Rutter, M. The long-term effects of early experience. *Developmental Medicine and Child Neurology*, 1980, *22*, 800-815. c

Rutter, M. Longitudinal studies: psychiatric perspective. In S. A. Mednick & A. E. Baert (Eds.), *Prospective longitudinal research: An empirical basis for primary prevention of psychosocial disorders*. Oxford: Oxford University Press, 1981. a

Rutter, M. Epidemiological/longitudinal strategies and causal research in child psychiatry. *Journal of the American Academy of Child Psychiatry*, in press, 1981. b

Rutter, M. Social/emotional consequences of day care for preschool children. *American Journal of Orthopsychiatry*, 1981, *51*, 4-28. c

Rutter, M. *Maternal Deprivation Reassessed (2nd ed.)*. Harmondsworth: Penguin, 1981. d

Rutter, M., & Brown, G. W. The reliability and validity of measures of family life and relationships in families containing a psychiatric patient. *Social Psychiatry*, 1966, *1*, 38-53.

Rutter, M., Chadwick, O., Shaffer, D., & Brown, G. A prospective study of children with head injuries I. Design and methods. *Psychological Medicine*, 1980, *10*, 633-645.

Rutter, M., & Cox, A. Psychiatric Interviewing Techniques. I. Methods and measures. *British Journal of Psychiatry*, 1981, *138*, 273-282.

Rutter, M., Cox, A., Egert, S., Holbrook, D., & Everitt, B. Psychiatric interviewing techniques IV. Experimental study: Four contrasting styles. *British Journal of Psychiatry*, 1981, *138*, 273-282.

Rutter, M., Cox, A., Tupling, C., Berger, M., & Yule, W. Attainment and adjustment in two geographical areas I. The prevalence of psychiatric disorder. *British Journal of Psychiatry,* 1975, *126,* 493–509. a

Rutter, M. & Garmezy, N. Atypical social and personality development. In M. Hetherington (Ed.), *Carmichael's manual of child psychology: Social and personality development.* New York: Wiley, in press, 1981.

Rutter, M., Graham, P., Chadwick, O. F. D., & Yule, W. Adolescent turmoil: fact or fiction? *Journal of Child Psychology & Psychiatry,* 1976, *17,* 35–56.

Rutter, M., Graham, P., & Yule, W. *A neuropsychiatric study in childhood.* Clinics in developmental medicine 35/36. London: Heinemann/SIMP, 1970.

Rutter, M., Maughan, B., Mortimore, P., Ouston, J., & Smith, A. *Fifteen thousand hours: Secondary schools and their effects on children.* London: Open Books; Cambridge, Mass.: Harvard University Press, 1979.

Rutter, M., & Schopler, E. (Eds.), *Autism: A reappraisal of concepts and treatment.* New York: Plenum, 1978.

Rutter, M., & Shaffer, D. DSM-III: A step forward or back in terms of the classification of child psychiatric disorders? *Journal of the American Academy of Child Psychiatry,* 1980, *19,* 371–394.

Rutter, M., Tizard, J., & Whitmore, K. (Eds.), *Education, Health, and Behaviour.* London: Longmans, 1970.

Rutter, M., Yule, B., Quinton, D., Rowlands, O., Yule, W., & Berger, M. Attainment and adjustment in two geographical areas III. Some factors accounting for area differences. *British Journal of Psychiatry,* 1975, *126,* 520–533. b

Rutter, M., Yule, W., Berger, M., Yule, B., Morton, J., & Bagley, C. Children of West Indian immigrants I. Rates of behavioural deviance and of psychiatric disorder. *Journal of Child Psychology and Psychiatry,* 1974, *15,* 241–262.

Rutter, M., Yule, W., & Graham, P. Enuresis and behavioural deviance: Some epidemiological considerations. In I. Kolvin, R. MacKeith, & S. R. Meadow (Eds.), *Bladder control and enuresis.* Clinics in Developmental Medicine, 48/49. London: Heinemann/SIMP, 1973.

Sandberg, S. T. On the overinclusiveness of the diagnosis of hyperkinetic syndrome. In M. Gittelman (Ed.), *Intervention Strategies with Hyperactive Children.* New York: Sharpe, in press, 1981.

Sandberg, S. T., Rutter, M., & Taylor, E. Hyperkinetic disorder in psychiatric clinic attenders. *Developmental Medicine and Child Neurology,* 1978, *20,* 279–299.

Sandberg, S. T., Wieselberg, M., & Shaffer, D. Hyperkinetic and conduct problem children in a primary school population: Some epidemiological considerations. *Journal of Child Psychology & Psychiatry,* 1980, *21,* 293–311.

Schachar, R., Rutter, M., & Smith, A. The characteristics of situationally and pervasively hyperactive children: Implications for syndrome definition. *Journal of Child Psychology & Psychiatry,* in press, 1981.

Seidel, U. P., Chadwick, O. F. D., & Rutter, M. Psychological disorders in crippled children: A comparative study of children with and without brain damage. *Developmental Medicine and Child Neurology,* 1975, *17,* 563–573.

Shaffer, D., Bijur, P., Chadwick, O., & Rutter, M. *Localized cortical injury and psychiatric symptoms in childhood.* In preparation, 1981.

Shaffer, D., Chadwick, O., & Rutter, M. Psychiatric outcome of localized head injury in children. In R. Porter & D. FitzSimons (Eds.), *Outcome of Severe Damage to the Central Nervous System,* Ciba Foundation Symposium 34 (new series). Amsterdam: Elsevier; Excerpta Medica-North Holland, 1975.

Shaffer, D., McNamara, N., & Pincus, J. H. Controlled observations on patterns of activity, attention, and impulsivity in brain-damaged and psychiatrically disturbed boys. *Journal of Psychological Medicine,* 1974, *4,* 4–18.

Shapland, J. M. Self-reported delinquency in boys aged 11 to 14. *British Journal of Criminology,* 1978, *18,* 255-266.

Shepherd, M. Epidemiology and clinical psychiatry. *British Journal of Psychiatry,* 1978, *133,* 289-298.

Shepherd, M., Oppenheim, B., & Mitchell, S. (Eds.). *Childhood behaviour and mental health.* London: University of London Press, 1971.

Sroufe, L. A. The coherence of individual development: Early care, attachment, and subsequent developmental issues. *American Psychologist,* 1979, *34,* 834-841.

Steffensmeier, D. J. Crime and the contemporary woman: An analysis of changing levels of female property crime, 1960-75. *Social Forces,* 1978, *57,* 566-584.

Still, G. F. Some abnormal physical conditions in children. *Lancet,* 1902, *1,* 1008-1012, 1077-1082, 1163-1168.

Sundby, H. S., & Kreyberg, P. C. *Prognosis in child psychiatry.* Baltimore: Williams & Wilkins, 1968.

Tennant, C., & Bebbington, P. The social causation of depression: A critique of the work of Brown and his colleagues. *Psychological Medicine,* 1978, *8,* 565-576.

Terris, M. (Ed.), *Goldberger on Pellagra.* Baton Rouge: Louisiana State University Press, 1964.

Tizard, B. *Adoption: A second chance.* London: Open Books, 1977.

Tizard, B., & Hodges, J. The effect of early institutional rearing on the development of 8-year-old children. *Journal of Child Psychology & Psychiatry,* 1978, *19,* 99-118.

Tizard, J., & Tizard, B. The social development of 2-year-old children in residential nurseries. In H. R. Schaffer (Ed.), *The origins of human social relations.* London: Academic Press, 1971.

Wadsworth, M. *Roots of delinquency: Infancy, adolescence, and crime.* Oxford: Martin Robertson, 1979.

Wallerstein, J., & Kelly, J. B. *Surviving the breakup: How children and parents cope with divorce.* New York: Basic Books, 1980.

Weissman, M. M., & Klerman, G. L. Sex differences and the epidemiology of depression. *Archives of General Psychiatry,* 1977, *34,* 98-111.

Werner, E. E., & Smith, R. S. *Kauai's children come of age.* Honolulu: University Press of Hawaii, 1977.

West, D. J., & Farrington, D. P. *Who becomes deliquent?* London: Heinemann Educational, 1973.

West, D. J., & Farrington, D. P. *The delinquent way of life.* London: Heinemann, 1977.

Whitehead, L. Sex differences in children's responses to family stress: A re-evaluation. *Journal of Child Psychology & Psychiatry,* 1979, *20,* 247-254.

Wing, J. K., & Häfner, H. *Roots of evaluation: The epidemiological basis for planning psychiatric services.* London: Oxford University Press, 1973.

Wolkind, S. N. The components of "affectionless psychopathy" in institutionalized children. *Journal of Child Psychology & Psychiatry,* 1974, *15,* 215-220.

Wolkind, S., & Rutter, M. Children who have been "In Care"—an epidemiological study. *Journal of Child Psychology & Psychiatry,* 1973, *14,* 97-105.

Wootton, B. *Social science and social pathology.* London: Allen & Unwin, 1959.

Yule, W. Diagnosis: Developmental psychological assessment. *Advances in Biological Psychiatry,* 1977, *1,* 35-54.

Zeitlin, H. *A study of patients who attended the children's department and later the adults' department of the same psychiatric hospital.* M. Phil. Thesis, University of London, 1971.

Zeitlin, H. The natural history of psychiatric disorder in children. In preparation, 1981.

6

COMMENTARY

Rochel Gelman
University of Pennsylvania

Eleanor Maccoby
Stanford University

Robert LeVine
Harvard University

COMPLEXITY IN DEVELOPMENT AND
DEVELOPMENTAL STUDIES

As I listened to the various papers and thought back over 20 years, I concluded that we have come a long way. I well remember the then dominant position of Behaviorism and its implications for what we studied and how we studied it. As a metaphysical doctrine, Behaviorism ruled out the study of nonvisible matters such as mentation; prescribed a set of experimental procedures; held that we could study the laws of association and end up with an account of behavior; and assumed that the laws of behavior would be free of age and species constraints. There were debates as to whether all learning was based on the classical conditioning of new stimuli to available reflexes on whether there weren't two learning paradigms—classical and instrumental learning. There were debates as to whether learning could take place without reinforcement and or the organism responding to stimuli (see Schwartz, 1978, for an excellent review). Despite the differences, there was nevertheless considerable agreement on the fundamentals: If we studied the laws of associative learning, we would come to know how organisms represented and acted on their environment—children included.

It was about 20 years ago that discordant voices in the background moved into the foreground. There was Chomsky's (1959) review of Skinner's *Verbal Behavior,* which made it very clear that, among other things, we had to recognize that different species responded differently to the same stimuli. There was Simon telling us that it was permissible to use verbal reports from subjects as data.

145

There was Piaget telling us that we had to interview children if we really wanted to probe their minds. There was Garcia (Garcia & Koeling, 1966) telling us certain learnings were biologically prepared in animals and that the nature of these varied as a function of the beast and its' particular ecological niche. There were ethologists and developmentalists like Piaget who insisted that the age or developmental level of an organism could dramatically alter the ability to learn about at least some things. In short, there were rumblings from divergent sources that the doctrine of Behaviorism vis-à-vis methodology and what to study had to give. And it eventually did, not without struggle to be sure, but it did give in very important ways.

The study of perception and cognition are now more than legitimate topics of study. A diverse set of methodologies are used. And as Flavell noted, a structuralist view has come to dominate the fields of experimental psychology—including developmental psychobiology, human development, and cognitive psychology. It is not simply because the attitudes, assumptions, and methods of our discipline have changed that make me say we've made progress. Rather, it is what we've heard here about what has been accomplished in the current intellectual environment that makes me say it is so.

Consider the impact of Piagetian theory. When skeptics tried to show that it would be trivial to train preoperational children to conserve, classify, and seriate, they initially found that this wasn't so. There then came an acceptance of the stage theory that was subjected to rigorous experimental efforts. And, in the end, the idea that there are grand stages of development has not stood the test of time. This is mainly because we now have much more information and not because the field is, in principle, loathe to accept stage descriptions of development. It's the research findings that are driving the theorizing and not a particular dogma.

As Flavell notes, there are many lines of evidence against the Piagetian stage theory. The kinds of predicted correlations between task performances do not obtain. The model, as inclusive as it is, fails to account for and deal with a range of important phenomena. And the characterizations of a child at a certain stage of development do not hold in many cases. Preschoolers are more competent than expected. Indeed, as Eleanor Gibson and her students have shown, babies *do* coordinate and use information about objects from different modalities. In general, the findings show abilities at earlier and earlier ages than expected within a Piagetian framework. As such, they call into question two related Piagetian views: (1) that structures are in no sense innate; and (2) that there are successive stages of development that bring with them the *creation* of new structures that are different from and more complex and powerful than the preceeding structures.[1]

---

[1]My presentation of Piagetian theory is based on the published version of the Piaget–Chomsky debate, edited by Piattelli–Palmarini (1980).

First, the evidence with regard to the issue of truly novel capacities: It used to be commonplace to point to the failure of preschoolers to conserve, seriate, and classify. And the explanation offered was that the young child's structures were not operational. Most people took this to mean that the young child had yet to develop the capacity to form classifications; impose systematic orderings on objects of different dimensions; keep straight whether a particular transformation was quantity relevant or not, and so on. As such, the young child's knowledge was not operative. From this view, the idea that preschoolers think differently about cause and effect, are unable to coordinate two perspectives at once, or center their own perspective followed quite easily. For there was the overall impression of a novel qualitative change in cognitive capacity.

However, we now know that preschoolers can use a hierarchical classification scheme, have a concept of number, and can order relative lengths. I focus on these domains because they have figured so centrally in the account of concrete operations. Gelman and Baillargeon (1981) review the evidence on these capacities and so here I cover but a few illustrative finds. Consider the use of hierarchical classification schemes. Chi (1980) has looked into the interests of preschoolers—especially 4-year-old boys—in dinosaurs. There are, as it happens, 4-year olds running around this country who are experts on dinosaurs. When asked to tell what dinosaurs they know and what they know about them, they come back with a list that is hierarchically organized by some of the most abstract criteria I can think of, including land-living or not, meat-eaters or not, and so on. They could not do this if they lacked the ability to work with hierarchical classification schemes. Likewise, preschoolers couldn't solve transitive inference problems (Trabasso, 1975) if they couldn't impose an ordering relation on stimuli. Nor could they keep separate number-irrelevant and number-relevant transformations if they could not organize addition and subtraction operations in a separate category from displacement, rearrangement, and item substitution ones (Gelman & Gallistel, 1978).

Findings like these shed doubt on the particular concrete versus preoperational structural account that Piaget gave us. For preschoolers can be shown to solve tasks that require some of these abilities. Hence, at the very least, the descriptive adequacy of the Piagetian stage theory is called into question. But perhaps there are other domains that do dictate a theory that states that there are structural abilities that are absent or different in young children than there are in older children? I'm beginning to have serious doubts. Merry Bullock, Renée Baillargeon, and I conclude that the principles of causal reasoning about physical events used by young children are much like those used by older children and adults (Bullock, Gelman, & Baillargeon, 1981). Flavell and his collaborators have shown that young children can and do take more than one perspective into account (Lempers, Flavell, & Flavell, 1977); and that they know others have minds (Wellman, in press). Sue Carey (1980) shows that young children do not endow inanimates with animistic characteristics—a fact confirmed by Keil's (1979) work on ontological categories of knowledge as well as research that Elizabeth Spelke, Betty Meck, and I are doing. And so on, the story goes.

In brief, Flavell is quite right—the evidence to date for grand qualitative stage changes is weak. I put it somewhat differently: The evidence that young children have different cognitive structures or, more accurately, parts thereof than older children is not there. Instead, it looks like there is much in common. Although I and disinclined to accept the idea that we need to develop a theory that has the young child using different structural units than an older child, I do not want to say that there is no development of interest. I return to this issue at the end of my comments.

I have often been asked, if preschoolers have so many abilities, where did *these* come from. I've been wary of answering this question but think I should now. It's not just that preschoolers are more competent than we thought; so are babies. Eleanor Gibson went over some of the research. By 3 months of age, babies will not reach for an object that is too far away for them to grasp. And even in the beginning attempts to reach for moving objects, they put their hands where the object *will* be rather than where it is. They pick up visual information that allows them to determine whether an object is rigid or not. They can coordinate visual and auditory information and hence assign the mood of a speaker to that speaker's face. And so on (see Spelke, 1980 for further evidence of early perceptual competence).

In addition to having remarkable perceptual abilities at rather early ages, babies can classify common basic objects (Cohen & Caputo, 1978); and they can abstract the numerical values of small sets of objects and events (Starkey & Cooper, 1980; Starkey, Spelke, & Gelman, 1980; Strauss & Curtis, 1980). Thus, they will habituate to the class of three heterogeneous items in a visual display and then show renewed interest in changes in number. They will also match the number of sounds they hear from a centrally placed loudspeaker to the one of two pictures that show the same number of heterogeneous items (Starkey, Spelke, & Gelman, 1981). Two related conclusions are inescapable: There probably are innate constraints on knowledge acquisition; and the perceptual world of a young baby is far more veridical than the Piaget constructionist account would have it.

So part of my answer to the question of whence the preschooler's ability is that humans come to the world with *pieces* of innate knowledge that serve to guide knowledge acquisition. I say "pieces of innate knowledge" intentionally. I see no reason to adopt the old and extreme nativist position that gave the environment nothing more than a triggering role. Despite demonstrations of early capacities that we did not know about 20 years ago, these capacities are far from full blown: They do develop as the child grows and interacts with his/her environment. Further, the lessons from developmental psychobiologists make it clear to me that it is possible to have an account that acknowledges that there are innate constraints on the course of development and yet requires a great deal of learning for development to proceed. Consider Marler's (1970) work on the acquisition of bird song.

The adult white-crown sparrow has a characteristic song. By varying the kind of environment available to the young, Marler has been able to show that experience plays a central role in the development of that song, which is characteristic of the region the bird lives in. For, if a baby sparrow is raised in isolation, it will sing a distinctly odd song as an adult. Experts agree that this odd song is the basic form of the adult song. It is odd because it is never heard in nature and lacks those characteristics that give it the status of one dialect or another. If the young bird is exposed to the adult song during its first 10–15 days of life but never again, the young bird will grow up to sing the characteristic adult song. This is true even if it is deafened after the exposure. Marler argues from such findings (and other related ones) that the white-crown sparrow is born with a template for the basic song. Experience serves to tune the template so as to allow the young bird to learn its particular dialect. The bird brings to the interaction with the environment a structural advantage that helps him focus attention on, or in Piagetian terms, to assimilate one set of songs as opposed to others. In interacting with the environment, he develops the particular song of his locale (i.e., he accommodates the template).

The idea is *not* that development is a bit of innate structure and a bit of experience; it is a function of a particular organism's interaction with its environment. The genotype sets the range of stimuli that will influence development; nevertheless, the interaction with the environment *must* take place for development to proceed. Put differently, there is a great deal of learning involved in development, but the learning is helped or guided by the innate constraints particular organisms bring to their environments. Psychobiologists and learning theorists alike have shown us that different species, and even the same species in different environments, are often prepared to learn what it is they will learn during development (see Seligman & Haeger, 1972, for an excellent selection of relevant papers). I believe that a similar view is required for accounts of early perceptual and cognitive development.

In some ways, the view I come to today is like Piaget's; I think of development involving an active organism, which seeks out (assimilates) a supporting environment, and which comes away from an interaction with the environment with a changed (accommodated) capacity. The major difference is that I believe these processes are initially guided by some innate constraints on the knowledge that an organism can and will development.

There is a major research agenda for those who agree with my conclusions regarding the interpretation of findings of richer capacities than anticipated even 10 years ago. The basic task is to describe in precise detail what these constraints are; how the constraints guide development as a child interacts with his/her environments; what kinds of environments do or do not affect particular developmental courses, and how best to characterize the capacities at different points in development. It won't do for us to say to Eleanor Gibson that her recent research leads to the conclusion that babies must have some representation of objects in the world. I'm inclined to this view, but I agree that we shouldn't put pictures of objects in a baby's head. What's needed is a precise description of the nature of the stimuli "out there" that are responded to, as well as a precise account of what it is about the baby's perceptual–cognitive capacities that allows him/her to respond to those stimuli as he/she does. I am comfortable with the idea that in at least some cases there is a representation that guides the baby's ability to respond veridically to a variety of objects and events. Others are not, and I understand—this because we haven't spelled out what we mean. We must do so now.

The idea that there are constraints on the course of human development is more than in the air. Ann Brown (in press) has made related comments. Newport (in press) is trying to work out the nature of learning in language acquisition. Mandler (1980) outlines some structural invariants. Keil (in press) has pulled together the data that we now have on what might be some of the constraints on cognitive development. Spelke (1980) has provided an argument regarding the kinds of perceptual principles that are innate in infants and how these allow for rapid learning. And Wexler and Culicover (1980) have provided one formal account of the constraints on the learnability of a language.

I should point out that the view that there are some innate constraints guiding development is consistent with Flavell's optimism about the payoff that will follow from detailed studies of sequences in development. Further, it avoids the logical problem entailed by Piaget's rejection of the idea that *some* structures or pieces of structures are available for cognitive development to proceed along the very uniform path it does. (I've often wondered how it was possible that normal children all over the world share pretty much the same cognitive structures up to and through the concrete operational period.) Yet, it avoids Piaget's criticism of the form of nativism that treats the environment as nothing but a trigger. Indeed, it calls out for a need to use Piagetian notions like assimilation and accommodation (Gelman & Baillargeon, 1981). But it tempers the extent to which knowledge is constructed, allowing that at least some perceptions are veridical.

Developmental psychobiologists provide many valuable lessons as to how we proceed. Levine makes the point that a multilevel analysis of development is required. Consider the idea that the nature of the organism constrains its behaviors, perceptions, and cognitions. The constraints need not be at just the cognitive level. To mention just a couple of other levels: First, the size of an organism influences the definition of the affordable environment. A twig in a tree affords sitting-on for small birds and bugs, but a twig does not afford sitting for large mammals. Likewise, a lake affords underwater living for fish but not men. These constraints are at the level of analysis that is congruent with the laws of physics. Second, structural features of a given organism's perceptual apparatus constrain the definition for that organism of certain perceptual experiences; thus, for an eye to pick up color, it must contain cones. Because Sameroff deals at length with the complexity of the levels of analysis involved in the ultimate account of many developmental phenomena, I leave off here on this matter.

The work by development psychobiologists makes yet another methodological point. This is that much can be learned about the normal course of development, and what environmental influences are or are not causal from studies of abnormality. Of course, researchers who study children cannot deafen them or produce any other abnormalities. But there are children who have suffered the burden of nature's damage, the cruel treatments of caretaker's, etc. Having heard the many elegant uses of the comparison between normal and abnormal children made by Rutter, I doubt that I need dwell on this message. And again, it is in the air, especially by those who study language acquisition (Feldman, Goldin-Meadow, & Gleitman, 1978; Lenneberg & Lenneberg, 1976 a,b).

Arguments about innate constraints are often supported with evidence about universality, the clear case being the ability to acquire language. It was not just that I found preschoolers could count or that babies can abstract the number of objects an event presented them that pushed me to the preceding view. There was evidence from cross-cultural work that converged on the idea that the ability to count and invent counting algorithms are natural cognitive abilities (see Gelman, in press, for a review). One way to test a hypothesis regarding a natural ability is to go cross cultural and thereby bring another level—the comparative one—on the issue of analysis to bear.

Having talked about the brilliance of the infant and preschooler, I now turn to a puzzle. Despite the many competences of the young, they nevertheless fail or err on a wide range of tasks that do not seem to be *that* difficult. The fact remains that young children fail the many concrete-operational, Piagetian tasks. If they have the competence as reflected on many new tasks, why not on the seemingly similar Piagetian tasks? If they are so much like older children, how can they yet be so different? Obviously, something or some things are developing, but what?

Brown (in press) points to one major development. Whereas preschoolers can apply their ability to only very special tasks, older children can apply the ability more broadly. Development involves, in part, the ability to transfer or generalize a capacity. The work by Flavell and others on metacognition points to yet another major developmental course. Children come to be able to reflect on their abilities to use language and remember things. I agree with Brown that metacognitive skills contribute to the ability to generalize their implicit abilities. And related to these arguments are notions about development making explicit the implicit knowledge a child has at an earlier point (Greeno, 1976). Although I grant preschoolers an implicit set of counting principles, I do not believe they have explicit, stateable knowledge of these principles.

With development also comes the ability to access the structures underlying early cognitive and perceptual abilities and to them combine those to produce novel abilities (Fodor, 1972; Rozin, 1976). To my knowledge, no one believes that the ability to read is itself coded in genes. However, as Rozin points out, in some cases at least, related abilities are. I believe that an important aspect of learning to read is learning to compute a phonetic representation of written material and recognize the lawful relationship between spelling and pronunciation. But it is known that young children have trouble accessing the speech stream for purposes of obtaining a phonetic representation (Liberman, Shankweiler, Liberman, Fowler, & Fischer, 1977; Rozin & Gleitman, 1977). Eventually they do, and as Rozin and Gleitman argue, take a major step toward developing the ability to read.

Following up on Rozin's ideas, I see that development involves yet another trend. The young child, to be sure, has many pieces of competence. However, they are exceedingly fragile (Gelman, 1979). The older child can show that competence across a wide range of tasks. Hence, the idea is that development involves going from the fragile (and probably rigid) application of capacity to a widely based use of these. Indeed, for those who want to study the why and wherefore of transfer and generalization, I submit that the preschool to elementary-school period is a remarkable target for finding out how this happens, because it clearly does.

Sue Carey (1980) and others suggest that development involves the filling in of incomplete theories about the world and the substitution of more correct theories for incorrect ones. As an example of what kind of substitution might be required, I draw attention to work by Green, McCloskey & Caramazza (1980) and others who are finding that college students use an Aristotelian theory of physics. Obviously, a theory change is required. This position is congruent with those that argue that an increasing amount of knowledge is part of the developmental story. But, it goes beyond that. The idea is not just that children need to acquire a list of facts. They may have to reorganize those facts to accommodate yet further facts. Or, as we (Bullock, Baillargeon, & Gelman, in press) suggest, they may have to acquire an understanding of the nature of a good explanation.

Flavell drew attention to yet another trend in development, this being one of going from novice to expert. Experts do things quite differently, and, in general, young children are universal novices. And I agree that this is one theme in development. However, I don't think that all development can be characterized as nothing but a move from novice to expert. In the case of language acquisition, it is quite clear that it is the young who are more expert at learning a second language than are the old.

Actually, I've come to doubt that there will be one grand account of how development will proceed. The facts dictate that many things are happening, and as I look at it today, I wonder why I didn't see the hand writing on the wall at any earlier point. So much develops that it has to be a complex tale we will tell. Again, we've been forced to accept the complexity because of the amount of progress we have already made. Yes, we have a long way to go. But I submit that the papers presented at this symposium provide many insights as to what does or does not develop, what our research programs will look like, and how to best get the data.

ACKNOWLEDGMENT

Preparation of this manuscript was partially supported by NSF Grant BNS-8004881.

Rochel Gelman
University of Pennsylvania

REFERENCES

Brown, A. L. Learning and development: The problem of compatibility and development. *Human Development,* in press.

Bullock, M., Gelman, R., & Baillargeon, R. The development of the understanding of physical causality. In W. Friedman (Ed.), *Development of time concepts.* Academic Press, projected for in press.

Carey, S. *Are children fundamentally different kinds of thinkers and learners than adults?* Paper presented at the NIE-LRDC Conference on Thinking and Learning, University of Pittsburgh, 1980.

Chi, M. T. H. *Interactive roles of knowledge and strategies in development.* Paper presented at the NIE-LRDC Conference on Thinking and Learning, University of Pittsburgh, 1980.

Chomsky, N. Review of B. F. Skinner. *Verbal Behavior: Language,* 1959, *35,* 26–58.

Cohen, L. B., & Caputo, N. F. *Instructing infants to perceptual categories.* Paper presented at the Midwestern Psychological Association, Chicago, 1978.

Feldman, H., Goldin-Meadow, S., & Gleitman, L. Beyond Herodotus: The creation of language by linguistically deprived deaf children. In A. Lock (Ed.), *Action, gesture, and symbol: The emergence of language.* New York: Academic Press, 1978.

Fodor, J. A. Some reflections on L. S. Vygotsky's, *Thought and Language. Cognition,* 1972, *1.* 83–95.

Garcia, J., & Koelling, R. Relation of cue to consequence in avoidance learning. *Psychonomic Science,* 1966, *4,* 123–124.

Gelman, R. Preschool thought. *American Psychologist,* 1979, *34,* 900–905.

Gelman, R. Basic numerical abilities. In R. Sternberg (Ed.), *Advances in Human Intelligence* Vol. 1. Hillsdale, N.J.: Lawrence Erlbaum Associates, in press.

Gelman, R., & Baillargeon, R. A review of Piagetian concepts. In J. H. Flavell & E. M. Markman (Eds.), *Cognitive Development* (Vol. 3), of P. Mussen (Ed.), *Manual of child psychology.* New York: Wiley, Projected for 1981.

Gelman, R., & Gallistel, C. R. *The child's understanding of number.* Cambridge, Mass.: Harvard University Press, 1978.

Gibson, E. J. *Development about intermodal unity: Two views.* Paper presented at the Jean Piaget Society, Philadelphia, 1980.

Green, G. F., McCloskey, M., & Caramazza, A. *The relation of knowledge to problem solving with examples from kinematics.* Paper presented at the NIE-LRDC Conference on Thinking and Learning, University of Pittsburgh, 1980.

Greeno, J. G. Cognitive objectives of instruction: Theory of knowledge for solving problems and answering questions. In D. Klahr (Ed.), *Cognition and instruction.* Hillsdale, N.J.: Lawrence Erlbaum Associates, 1976.

Keil, F. *Semantic and conceptual development.* Cambridge, Mass.: Harvard University Press, 1979.

Keil, K. C. Constraints on knowledge and cognitive development. *Psychological Review,* in press.

Lempers, J. D., Flavell, E. R., & Flavell, J. H. The development in very young children of tacit knowledge concerning visual perception. *Genetic Psychology Monographs,* 1977, *95,* 3–53.

Lenneberg, E. H., & Lenneberg, E. *Foundations of language development: A multidisciplinary approach.* Vol. 1.: New York, Academic Press, 1976a.

Lenneberg, E. H., & Lenneberg, E. *Foundations of language development: A multidisciplinary approach.* Vol. 2.: New York, Academic Press, 1976b.

Liberman, I. Y., Shankweiler, D., Liberman, A. M., Fowler, C., & Fischer, F. W. Phonetic segmentation and recoding in the beginning reader. In A. S. Reber & D. L. Scarborough (Eds.), *The proceedings of the CUNY Conference.* Hillsdale, N.J.: Lawrence Erlbaum Associates, 1977.

Mandler, J. *Structural invariants in development.* Paper presented at the Jean Piaget Society, Philadelphia, 1980.

Marler, P. A comparative approach to vocal learning: Some development in white-crowned sparrows. *Journal of Comparative and Physiological Psychology,* 1970, 1–25.

Newport, E. L. Constraints on structure: Evidence from American sign language and language learning. In A. Collins (Ed.), *Minnesota Symposium on Child Psychology* (Vol. 14). Hillsdale, N.J.: Lawrence Erlbaum Associates, in press.

Piatelli-Palmarini, M. (Ed.). *Language and learning: The debate between Jean Piaget and Noam Chomsky.* Cambridge, Mass.: Harvard University Press, 1980.

Rozin, P. The evolution of intelligence and access to the cognitive unconscious. In J. M. Sprague & A. D. Epstein (Eds.), *Progress in psychobiology and physiological psychology* (Vol. 6). New York: Academic Press, 1976.

Rozin, P., & Gleitman, L. R. The structure of acquisition of reading II. The reading process and the acquisition of the alphabetic principle. In A. S. Reber & D. S. Scarborough (Eds.), *Toward a psychology of reading: The proceedings of the CUNY Conference.* Hillsdale, N.J.: Lawrence Erlbaum Associates, 1977.

Schwartz, B. *Psychology of learning and behavior.* New York: Norton, 1978.

Seligman, M. E. P., & Hager, J. (Eds.). *Biological boundaries of learning.* New York: Appleton-Century-Crofts, 1972.

Spelke, E. S. *Perceptual knowledge of objects in infancy.* Unpublished manuscript, University of Pennsylvania, 1980.

Starkey, P., & Cooper, R. G. Numerosity perception in human infants. *Science,* 1980, *210,* 1033–1035.

Starkey, P., Spelke, E., & Gelman, R. Number competence in infants: Sensitivity to numeric invariance and numeric change. *Paper presented at the meeting of the International Conference on Infant Studies,* New Haven, Conn., April, 1980.

Starkey, P., Spelke, E., & Gelman, R. *Infant abstraction of number across item and sense modality.* Unpublished manuscript, University of Pennsylvania, 1981.

Strauss, M. S., & Curtis, L. E. Infant perception of numerosity. *Paper presented at the meeting of the International Conference on Infant Studies,* New Haven, Conn., 1980.

Trabasso, T. R. Representation, memory, and reasoning: How do we make transitive inferences. In A. D. Pick (Ed.), *Minnesota Symposium on Child Psychology* (Vol. 9). Minneapolis: University of Minnesota Press, 1975.

Wellman, H. M. A child's theory of mind: The development of conceptions of cognition. In S. R. Yussen (Ed.), *The growth of reflection.* New York: Academic Press, in press.

Wexler, K. P., & Culicover, P. W. *Formal principles of language acquisition.* Cambridge, Mass.: MIT Press, 1980.

ORGANIZATION AND RELATIONSHIPS IN DEVELOPMENT

The chapters in this volume provide rich intellectual fare. It is an imposing task to attempt to identify some themes that bind them together, and some issues that distinguish them.

Perhaps a good place to begin is to consider how the several papers make use of the concept of *organization*. For Sameroff, it is axiomatic that one cannot understand human behavior by attending to it in bits and pieces. Drawing upon general systems theory, he asks us to consider a set of levels where it is the systemic or organizational properties of the system that become the focus of concern, rather than the elements of which the system is composed. The ever-compelling example of the river, which constantly changes its constituent elements while retaining its whole properties, is offered to remind us of characteristics of systems that do not derive from the characteristics of the components (although they cannot violate the limits imposed by these characteristics). We see that a system maintains its organization despite changes in its parts and can stabilize itself in the face of changing external conditions. Certain more advanced systems can reconstruct or change themselves according to internal programs that are not fully at the command of external events, although the changes may be coordinated with, or integrated with, external changes. Thus, general systems theory seems to yield a description that most of us recognize as a pretty good approximation to the developing child.

Sameroff adds the interesting idea (from Laszlo) that adaptive self-stabilization in the face of environmental change calls for increases in complexity of organization and that such complexity carries a price: the more complex the adaptive process, the less stable the system. This is an element in the theory that I find counter-intuitive (that's professional-courtesy language for saying: "I don't believe it!"). Although clearly during development, gains are made in adaptive self-stabilization, it seems unlikely that the human person is an organized system that becomes less stable with development. Such a consequence of our adaptive capacity might be inevitable were it not for the ability that individuals develop to choose an environment which is compatible with their own system characteristics; thus, environments can contribute to the stabilization of the system, rather than necessarily calling for adaptations that destabilize it. I cannot tell whether Sameroff agrees with Laszlo or not, for he does point out that an advantage of hierarchical systems (and highly complex systems are claimed to be hierarchical, almost of necessity) is that they are more stable than systems not hierarchically organized. Clarification is needed concerning what kind of instability is meant to be inherent in the developmental progression toward system complexity, and what the implications of such instability might be.

Sameroff and Gibson agree in their emphasis on the close interrelationships between the complexity of the organism's environment and the complexity of the organisms's level of functioning. Gibson, true to the great Gestalt tradition in writings about perception, leaves the reader in no doubt that perceptions are organized rather than atomistic. Like Sameroff, she urges that this organization is a product of the interflow between the individual and the external environment. However, Gibson goes farther than Sameroff would in arguing that the systems properties lie primarily (only?) in the external world, not in the perceiving organism. The Gibsons' opposition to prototypes, schemata, cognitive structures, and the like—in short, to structured processes within the perceiver—undoubtedly reflects their concern that such conceptions may render the perceiver as too autistic a creature—too prone to construct a largely fictitious external world and operate in an imaginary arena. They have insisted—and convinced most of us—that perception is highly realistic and adaptive. Their recent concept of affordances stresses the intimate relationship between the properties of the environment and the utilization of the properties by the behaving organism according to its requirements for life-sustaining activity. If a bird needs unobstructed spaces to fly through, it is quick to detect whether the environment affords such spaces. A gopher would be detecting different properties of the "same" environment. Is the property of "fly-throughableness" in the environment or in the bird? Surely, this is a question that has no answer, and one that we ought not even to ask. Fly-throughableness must be a property of the relationship between the bird and its habitat. Sameroff makes the same point when he says "The complexities of our social institutions require the complexities of our thought and vice versa." I believe that Gibson is right in insisting that our perceptions are not pure constructions (in the sense of unconstrained inventions)—that perceptions are and must be intimately adapted to the realities of our environment. But I also believe that the structuralists are right in insisting that the individual constructs internal systems that serve to support interaction with the environment.

Flavell's paper reminds us of the long, painstaking effort to find structural, system-like properties in cognitive development. He tells us that the effort has been successful with respect to the vertical organization of thought, but not with respect to horizontal organization. He pictures a number of developmental miniladders, each coherent in its own right, but with a child's rates of ascent up the various ladders being uncoordinated with one another. His prototype is that of the precocious young computer scientist, whose thinking is highly advanced in one area and relatively immature in other respects. In the extreme cases, we would seem to have a kind of intellectual Jekyll and Hyde—two or more unconnected intellectual "persons" within the same skull, operating at different and unconnected levels, with the child switching from one to the other under partially specifiable circumstances. Such a conception flies in the face of much that we know. Whereas two domains of thought may differ in the sophistication of the vocabulary of concepts they draw upon and in the complexity of the mental operations brought to bear upon them, they do surely share a large repertoire of both memory contents and mental subroutines. Such sharing is attested to by the substantial "g" factor documented by the mental testers and the positive correlations among distinguishable mental abilities.

As I see it, the picture Flavell presents—which is not the picture he would *prefer* to find, but the one that he believes the data support—is not truly compatible with at least one tenet of systems theory. To quote Sameroff: "Systems within the same environment will tend to form suprasystems." If we count systems that are inside the same head as being in the same environment, then there ought to be some form of horizontal organization. In the case of the young computer scientist, there ought to be some form of linkage between his thinking in his advanced area and his thinking (and action) in his less mature areas. Either systems theory is simply wrong, and it is indeed possible for us to operate with tightly separated systems which are quite insulated from each other; or there are forms of horizontal linkage which we haven't yet uncovered. Flavell seems to opt for the former as the likelier truth. He refers to the human tendency to try to find more rationality, more order, in the behavior of persons that is actually there. He cites the Mischelian view that behavior is highly situationally specific and asks whether there is reason to believe that our intellectual life has any greater degree of consistency, organization, or integration than has been found in the study of personality.

I think we should not yet dismiss the system theory claim, nor the possibility of considerable horizontal organization, even though I recognize the abundance of negative evidence. For one thing, horizontal system properties in the cognitive domain have been looked for primarily in the form of a search for *same-level* operation; that is, we have asked whether a child who is functioning at a given level of maturity in one domain operates at a similar level of maturity in another domain. It is reasonable that we should investigate this issue, considering that it is the major one Piaget proposed and defended. For this form of horizontal organization, it has been difficult to know what ought to be considered the "same" level from one domain to another (and difficult to keep measurement comparable).

We need to ask: Are other forms of horizontal organization possible, other than the "same-level" form? Perhaps we can get some clues by pursuing further the analogy to personality theory. It is true that until quite recently the dominant view has been that personality is fractionated. But, as I see it, we have begun to emerge from the long period of dominance of this view into something more sophisticated. No one denies that an individual's behavior varies greatly with context; what is now clear is that it is possible for such variability to coexist with a substantial degree of individual consistency across time and situations. The recent papers by Seymour Epstein (1977, 1980), make the point neatly: The amount of coherence that one discovers depends on the variety of situations, times, and measures that are employed in assessment. Few consistencies are found if one observes children briefly in one situation and correlates the scores with those obtained in a single other briefly observed situation. If one aggregates over a sufficient body of instances, however, impressive degrees of individual consistency may be found. It is a matter of one's personal research agenda whether one chooses to study situational variability or individual consistency—both are real. Even if one focuses on the search for integration and consistency, the search is not always successful. Sometimes, of course, this simply means it isn't there. But we should be aware of how much skill it takes to identify a productive level of aggregation. I am overcome with admiration—and no little envy!—when I contemplate Michael Rutter's work and note his spectacular success in showing continuities using global distinctions (such as that between emotional disorders and behavior disorders), which most of us psychologists would have considered far too broad to be meaningful. A similar showing of individual consistency emerges from the work of Lee Robins (1966) on childhood deviance and its sequelae. Closer to home, Sroufe and his colleagues (following Ainsworth) have found a level of analysis in the realm of attachment behavior that yields impressive individual consistency where little was found with more atomistic approaches. No doubt, I (and others who point to the emerging evidence for individual consistency) will be accused of reintroducing a long-banished "trait" psychology. If it were so, 'twould be a grievous fault; and I have no doubt that we will have to answer for it grievously. I do not know whether the recent shift toward a less atomistic view of personality development offers any clues for ways in which we might attack the problem of lack of conceptual horizontal structure that Flavell so clearly presented to us. I leave the issue as food for thought.

Sameroff reminds us that individuals—who each constitute discrete systems—are also elements in a larger system: the family. And that families are elements in still larger social systems. He warns us that in this sort of hierarchical set of systems, systems at each level do not necessarily have control over those at lower levels. And that each level must be understood in terms of its own principles of organization. Nevertheless, the levels do intersect. The family is normally a force for bringing about some degree of intergenerational continuity, and for equipping children for participation in a larger social system with a set of preestablished roles. Yet, in certain social situations, the family may not serve this function, with fascinating results.

We are powerfully reminded of the impact of social-system phenomena on families and individual children by a recent account of a brief historical period in Australia (Burns & Goodnow, 1979). The situation that Burns and Goodnow describe arose during a brief period in the late 1700s and early 1800s. At this time, England began sending large numbers of criminal and indigent persons to Australia. The ratio of men to women was about five to one. There was no prior social organization among the people arriving in the new land. There was a high incidence of prostitution, drunkenness, gambling, and brawling. Children were born into this disorganized social setting. Many were seriously neglected—some abandoned, others growing up with parents who provided very little nurturance, teaching, or regulation. A group of social reformers undertook the task of rescuing this generation of children through education, and established free public schools for them, incorporating strong elements of religious education. The children grew up, by and large, to be sober and industrious; they mainly rejected their dissolute and illiterate parents; they took their first jobs by about the age of 12, and (perhaps largely because they were among the few literate persons in the society) moved up rapidly to become the financial and social leaders of the new white society of Australia. Of course, the next generation of ''undesirables'' being sent out from England also produced children, but these children had an entirely different fate. The social system was no longer open for them, and they were sent to schools where they were taught to be the servants of the new ruling class. Thus, there was only a brief window of time during which the society was sufficiently destabilized so that a child's family origins did not function as an instrument for continuity in the way they normally do. This story reminds us that the family, in its functioning as a socializing entity, depends on certain characteristics of the larger society of which we may not be at all aware until extraordinary circumstances disrupt them. (Perhaps the converse is also true!) There are a few among us (e.g., Bronfenbrenner) who continue to bring these connections to our attention; most of us, however, will do well if we simply manage to remind ourselves occasionally of the existence of the connections, while we focus our attention on lower levels of the hierarchy.

I would argue that we need to pay much more attention to the interface between the next two lower levels, namely, the individual child and the family as a social system. Our current work on socialization is forcing us to come to grips with this relationship in ways that we did not anticipate. Let me give an example of the ways in which this has happened. In our work on parent–child interaction at Stanford, we have been attempting to understand the role of parental responsiveness and child compliance in the development of the parent–child relationship. We started out with the assumption that parental responsiveness is a dimension that describes a characteristic of *parents,* one that is reasonably independent of the children's characteristics. There is some evidence that the better defined a child's bids for attention become, the more responsive the parent is. Thus, if a young child makes specific demands rather than simply making a distressed sound whose meaning is difficult to read, the parent is more likely to respond. The reverse relationship is seen in work by Schaffer and Crooke (1980): *Children* are more responsive (i.e., more compliant to a parental demand) if the demand is geared to the momentary attentional state of the child. Thus, if a child is not attending, the parent is more effective in guiding the child's behavior by first issuing a demand for orientation (e.g., ''Look here!'') before specifying a desired action. A child's compliance, then, is as much a function of the parent's skill in timing demands appropriately and adapting them to the child's state as it is of any disposition on the part of the child to comply. In these instances, what appeared to be a score characterizing an individual child or individual parent may be seen to be in fact a *pair* score[1]—one that describes a characteristic of an interacting pair. Even the analysis of sequential probabilities, it turns out, usually does not succeed in identifying the contribution of individual persons to an interaction. (See Martin, Maccoby, Baran, and Jacklin, 1981) for further explication of this problem.

In short, devising ways of assessing the characteristics of individuals while they are engaged in interaction with others is more difficult than we have thought. It seems wise for us to acknowledge this fact and adapt to it. One way to adapt, of course, is to use more sophisticated means for partialling out partner effects in studying subject behaviors. But another approach is to make a virtue out of necessity and frankly switch to scores that describe the interacting system rather than the behavior of individuals taken one at a time. Pair scores, or group scores, can then be used as either predictive or outcome measures in relation to individual characteristics measured outside the context of the dyad. Thus, we could assess the characteristics of a parent–child dyad (e.g., amount of cooperation or length of mutually coercive chains) and relate these to the child's social behavior in nursery school or to the child's scholastic achievement.

As we begin to develop means of assessing the characteristics of pairs or groups, we can ask some interesting developmental questions. To take a phrase from Flavell, there must be some "developables" here. Clearly, a parent–child pair cannot interact in the same way when the child is 2 as they can when the child is 10. We know something from the work of Selman (1976), Damon (1977), and others concerning the developmental changes that occur in some aspects of children's social cognition—changes that ought to have an impact on the way they react, for example, to guidance efforts emanating from their parents. What has not been studied is the way in which parents adapt to the changing capacities of their children for social understanding. One of the things that surely must change is the pair's ability to construct joint social scripts. Among mature adults, of course, the construction of such scripts takes time, and interaction is very different among persons in long-term, stable relationships than it is among new acquaintances. In family relationships, a different element is added to the normal familiarization and mutual adaptation process that occur between adults who are becoming intimate, namely, the deeper developmental changes occurring in the child, which force a greater degree of change in the patterns of interaction than would otherwise occur. We are only beginning to understand what such developmental change in a family's interaction may look like. For the present, the point I would like to stress is that development is something that can

---

[1]Note that "pair" is used here to refer to an interaction system made up of more than one person. The points being made are meant to apply to three-person and larger family systems.

characterize the interaction systems in which children are involved, in addition to characterizing the individual children themselves.

Eleanor E. Maccoby
Stanford University

REFERENCES

Burns, A., & Goodnow, J. *Children and families in Australia.* George Allen & Unwin, No. Sydney, Australia, 1979.

Damon, W. *The social world of the child.* San Francisco, Calif.: Jossey-Bass, 1977.

Epstein, S. The stability of behavior: II Implications for psychological research. *American Psychologist,* 1980, *35,* 790-806.

Epstein, S. Traits are alive and well. In D. Magnusson & N. S. Endler (Eds.), *Personality at the crossroads.* Hillsdale, N.J.: Lawrence Erlbaum Associates, 1977.

Martin, J. A., Maccoby, E. E., Baran, K. E., & Jacklin, C. N. The sequential analysis of mother-child interaction at 18 months: A comparison of several microanalytic methods. *Developmental Psychology, 17,* 146-157.

Robins, L. N. *Deviant children grown up.* Huntington, N.Y.: Krieger, 1966.

Schaffer, H. R., & Crook, C. K. Child compliance and maternal control techniques. *Developmental Psychology,* 1980, *16,* 54-61.

Selman, R. Social-cognitive understanding: A guide to educational and clinical practice. In T. Lickona (Ed.), *Moral development and behavior.* New York: Holt, Rinehart, & Winston, 1976.

CULTURE, CONTEXT, AND THE CONCEPT OF DEVELOPMENT

As the only anthropologist on the program of this symposium, I am obliged to point out once again the discrepancy between the claims of human universality made in developmental formulations, including those presented here, and the narrow range of human populations on which serious developmental research has been conducted. Having fulfilled that obligation, I turn to other thoughts stimulated by the papers.

First, there is the importance of biology as a source of theory and a model for research. We've heard much of organization, adaptation, ecology, and other biological concepts from all the papers, and although this was also true of earlier generations of developmental psychologists, the use of evolutionary biology is more selective and sophisticated now than 25 years ago, reflecting advances in that field broadly defined and also in its application to problems in human development. The biological framework is appropriate not only for developmental research but also for integrating developmental psychology with anthropology and the other social sciences.

One aspect of biology I find particularly important as a model for research on child development is the complementarity of several methodologies mentioned by Michael Rutter in reviewing epidemiological and longitudinal studies, and also by Seymour Levine in referring to naturalistic studies of monkeys that are in the background to his own experimental work. In biological and medical research, there is a recognition that each methodological approach—laboratory, clinical, and field studies—generates questions that must be answered by the others and that a general strategy for scientific progress requires all three. This recognition and this general strategy is to a large extent lacking in developmental psychology, where it is often assumed that good research follows one model rather than striving for multiple sources of data, each with its own angle of vision. In my chapter on cross-cultural study in child psychology in *Carmichael's Manual* (LeVine, 1970), I argued that cross-cultural studies could serve child psychology as epidemiology does medical research, in the ways Rutter has outlined in his paper, but with respect to more diverse human populations. I proposed cross-cultural study as a research strategy parallel to the study of psychopathology (examining abnormal development) and comparative psychology (examining development in nonhuman species). These research strategies are available to child psychology to obtain types of data inaccessible in the laboratory or in studies of normal development within the range of variation in our own society. Implementing this proposal has not proved so simple as we might have hoped, and I say a few things about why that is in the context of the various papers in the symposium.

This symposium has helped me to see that we need a selective principle for the relevance of data on other human populations to different developmental domains and to different developmental formulations. We lack such a principle at present: I cannot tell you for which particular theory or which particular set of problems in development you must have cross-cultural evidence of one sort or another, and for which it would be useful but not essential, and for which it might be simply supportive or peripheral. There are several reasons for this. One is that anthropologists have not adequately communicated to developmental psychologists what we mean by culture, the various things we mean by culture. In other words, the question of what culture is and what variation in it consists of is not at all clear. I am pleased to announce that the Committee on Social and Affective Development during Childhood of the Social Science Research Council has recognized this problem and is sponsoring a conference in May, 1981, on culture and its acquisition. Its goal is to bring anthropologists, psychologists, and linguists together to hammer out some statements comprehensible to developmentalists and to represent some new formulations from the anthropologists about what culture is, what cultural variation consists of, and how we might develop models for the acquisition of culture, as language acquisition research has done for language.

Another reason we lack clear selective criteria for the use of cross-cultural data in developmental work has to do with the diverse ways in which cross-cultural research currently relates to developmental studies. When I think of how my own cross-cultural work bears on the papers of this symposium, for example, I find that the bearing varies in its *type* of relevance (conceptual, methodological, empirical, theoretical) from one paper to another. My colleagues, P. Herbert Leiderman, T. Berry Brazelton, and I have been studying attachment and separation in African and American samples, with attention to some of the group context variables mentioned by Seymour Levine in his paper, but with no data on the physiological reactions he is able to monitor in laboratory research on squirrel monkeys. Here we do not differ in our basic concepts, and we have taken parallel tracks, straddling the attachment research of Mary Ainsworth, Alan Sroufe, and other child psychologists, which does not directly study variations in social interaction as wide-ranging as in our cross-cultural research or the physiological responses accessible in animal experiments. These three tracks will eventually contribute complementary and equally systematic information to a general understanding of attachment and separation.

Sometimes, however, observational facts incidentally collected in anthropological field work can contribute to a line of developmental research. In thinking about the concept of affordance as presented in Eleanor Gibson's paper from a cross-cultural viewpoint, I came up with the observations from New Guinea, Sorenson, 1977) and Africa (in my own experience) that where toddlers are not prevented from handling sharp knives and machetes, they routinely use them as playthings—without hurting themselves. This seems to indicate that the range of physical objects affording safe exploration and playful handling by a child in the second year of life is relative to a capacity for avoiding injury (based on an ability to perceive the consequences of a sharp blade?) that has not been detected in the West because we do not permit the situation that elicits it (that we define as inherently dangerous) to occur. Knowledge of these incidental New Guinea and African observations, at the very least, poses new questions for research and may shed light on some otherwise dark corner of the topic.

In other cases, cross-cultural research raises thorny problems of method that it may not be able to solve. Our attempt to replicate in an African community some of the Western studies in psychiatric epidemiology reviewed in the paper by Michael Rutter illustrates this point. In our intensive observations of preschool children in that community, we found them strikingly less active physically and verbally in home settings than their Western counterparts; only a few came close to what we take for granted as an average amount of moving and talking for a child of that age. Thus, when we surveyed the mothers concerning hyperactive children (as translated into their language), they reported a certain number of them—more than we would have expected, if we assumed they were using the same criteria we might have used. As Rutter points out, however, you have to know the standards of normal activity being applied by parents classifying children as hyperactive before you can accurately interpret and compare their responses to a survey question. There is every reason to suspect that a mother from our African community would classify an average American child as extremely hyperactive (i.e., she would be using a standard derived from her own experience with children). If these standards can vary as widely across cultures as I am suggesting, then the epidemiological survey can provide only limited information without an associated program of observational research and a recalibration of the survey measure in each cultural setting. This real problem is essential to confront but discouraging in the short run to cross-cultural comparison in the epidemiology of children's behavior disorders.

A final example deals not with the data or methods of cross-cultural research but with the perspectives of culture theory and developmental theory. John Flavell mentioned in his paper that once a child has become literate in numbers or reading, decoding is automatic and involuntary: A number or word "jumps out" at him. Without denying the importance of this phenomenon, the anthropologist cannot ignore that such literacy is code-specific: Numbers and words written in Japanese and Urdu are as unintelligible to me as to a baby. If your focus is on the acquisition of the cognitive capacity underlying literacy in whatever medium, then the code-specificity may seem a detail. If your focus is on the attainment of communicative competence, then both the social limits of that competence and the particularities of the subjective world to which it gives one access are of paramount importance. It is possible to believe in universal sequences of cognitive development, varying only in timing and in whether terminal points are ever reached, without denying the importance of cultural differences in thinking. As I read the cross-cultural evidence on cognition, there are few demonstrable differences among human populations in the information-processing abilities in which psychologists have been most interested. There seem to be substantial cultural differences, however, in the purposes to which these discrete abilities are put, in the way they are assembled for task performance, and in the tasks of greatest salience and frequency. In order to describe and analyze differences at this level, a psychology that is functional in its orientation is likely to be more appropriate than a structuralist one. A functionalist human psychology requires a notion of culture in order to conceptualize the purposes of individual task performance and the relevant standards of competence.

Culture in this context can be thought of as a collective schema that serves as an organizer of goals, purposes, and intentions for individuals. It has the effect in development of selectively focusing attention on some environmental domains rather than others, forcing the overlearning of some skills and leaving others unlearned. A cultural schema involves the relations of affects such as pride and shame to what is learned, and individuals who acquire the schema acquire also a culturally distinctive set of relationships between affects and skills and a corresponding set of personal saliencies and priorities that affect task performance. The acquisition of culture in these terms is relatively unexplored in child development research, but it seems to me the most promising arena for cross-cultural investigations of cognitive development.

In the foregoing comments, I have attempted to illustrate the diversity of relationships between cross-cultural research and child psychology. Although a selective principle relating the two is needed so that child psychologists can accord a high enough priority to data from other cultures, it would not be fruitful to confine the flow within the terms of any methodological mandate. Implicit in my comments is the notion that cross-cultural research experience and exposure to anthropological perspectives are valuable for child development specialists in more ways than can be anticipated by any abstract formulation.

A functional perspective on the individual, explicitly proposed in Eleanor Gibson's paper, is also essential to the systems approach discussed by Arnold Sameroff. It is ironic that systems models, so effectively used in biology and so popular in economics, sociology, anthropology, political science, and psychiatry, have been so little used in developmental psychology. Academic psychologists of the last 30 years have focused attention on specific psychological functions and processes that lend themselves to empirical research without building models of the systems in which these specific components might be embedded. The lack of conceptualization at a more molar level poses a particular problem for developmentalists who, like their forebears in embryology, are supposed to be investigating the growth of organization. But what is the psychological organization of the individual, and how does it operate? What are the mature forms of psychological organization that represent developmental targets for the immature humans studied by child psychologists? Having set aside such questions in order to concentrate on empirical research, child psychologists have been more vulnerable than they should have been to the structuralism of Piaget, which at least provided a general conception of intellectual organization and development, though without attending to functional relationships between cognition and affect and between the individual and culture. As the Piagetian conception declines in the face of the findings reviewed by Flavell, the need for theoretical models at the molar level of analysis becomes evident once more.

Sameroff describes the theoretical resources of the general systems approach and illustrates some of the ways they could be used in developmental research. His concept of a developmental agenda is one I find particularly promising, because it captures the fact that caregivers have goals, strategies, and timetables that affect their interaction with the child and that also (I would add) represent a significant dimension of variation between cultures. Systems theory, by sensitizing the investigator to goal orientations in behavior and the ways in which response patterns become organized by internal and external goals, can generate the models needed to transcend existing boundaries among empirical research traditions in child psychology.

Robert LeVine
Harvard University

REFERENCES

LeVine, R. A. Cross-cultural study in child psychology. In P. Mussen (Ed.), *Carmichael's Manual of Child Psychology,* 3rd ed. New York: Wiley, 1970.

Sorenson, Richard, *The Edge of the Forest.* Washington, D.C.: Smithsonian Institute Press, 1976.

List of Contributors

John H. Flavell is professor of psychology at Stanford University. He received his doctorate from Clark University in 1955, and held faculty posts at the University of Rochester and at the Institute of Child Development at Minnesota.

Rochel Gelman is professor of psychology at the University of Pennsylvania, she holds a doctorate from the University of California in Los Angeles.

Eleanor J. Gibson is Susan Linn Sage Professor of Psychology, Emeritus, at Cornell University. Her doctorate was earned at Yale. She is a member of the National Academy of Sciences.

Robert A. LeVine is professor in the Graduate School of Education at Harvard. An anthropologist, he has written widely on the topic of cross-cultural research on child development.

Seymour Levine, who holds a doctorate from New York University, is professor in the Department of Psychiatry and Behavioral Sciences at Stanford University Medical School. He is also director of the Stanford Outdoor Primate Facility.

Eleanor E. Maccoby is Richard Starr Jordan Professor of Social Sciences at Stanford, where she has been a professor of psychology since 1959. She formerly taught at Harvard's Laboratory of Human Development.

Michael Rutter is professor of child psychiatry in the Institute of Psychiatry, University of London. He did his medical training at the University of Birmingham Medical School.

Arnold Sameroff is professor of psychology at the University of Illinois at Chicago Circle and director of research at the Illinois Institute for Developmental Disabilities. He holds a doctorate from Yale.

Author Index

Numbers in *italics* denote pages with complete bibliographic information.

Subject Index